Sport, Revolution
and the Beijing Olympics

Sport, Revolution and the Beijing Olympics

GRANT JARVIE, DONG-JHY HWANG AND MEL BRENNAN

Oxford • New York

English edition
First published in 2008 by
Berg
Editorial offices:
First Floor, Angel Court, 81 St Clements Street, Oxford OX4 1AW, UK
175 Fifth Avenue, New York, NY 10010, USA

Berg is the imprint of Oxford International Publishers Ltd.

Library of Congress Cataloging-in-Publication Data
Jarvie, Grant, 1955-
 Sport, revolution and the Beijing Olympics / Grant Jarvie, Dong-Jhy Hwang
and Mel Brennan. — English ed.
  p. cm.
 Includes bibliographical references and index.
 ISBN-13: 978-1-84520-100-5 (cloth)
 ISBN-10: 1-84520-100-0 (cloth)
 ISBN-13: 978-1-84520-101-2 (pbk.)
 ISBN-10: 1-84520-101-9 (pbk.)
 1. Olympic Games (29th : 2008 : Beijing, China) 2. Olympics—Political
aspects—China. 3. Human rights—China. 4. Civil rights—China. I. Hwang,
Dong-Jhy. II. Brennan, Mel. III. Title.

GV7222008 .J37 2008
796.48—dc22   2008004822

British Library Cataloguing-in-Publication Data
A catalogue record for this book is available from the British Library.

ISBN 978 1 84520 100 5 (Cloth)
      978 1 84520 101 2 (Paper)

Typeset by Avocet Typeset, Chilton, Aylesbury, Bucks
Printed in the United Kingdom by Biddles Ltd, King's Lynn

www.bergpublishers.com

Contents

Acknowledgements

This book has been researched during periods of sabbatical research leave granted by the University of Stirling, for which I am grateful. Like many books *Sport, Revolution and the Beijing Olympics* owes its existence to many people. Berg publishers and, in particular, Hannah and Kathryn have been extremely patient as this book progressed from initial idea to draft to completion – thank you. The advice given by two anonymous reviewers helped to sharpen up our thinking on some aspects of this study. This study is meant to complement and add to previous research into sport in China and therefore it would be remiss of us not to mention the contribution made by Susan Brownell, Dong Jinxia and Fan Hong to name but a few. Henning Eichberg and Jim Riordan have commented upon earlier drafts of this manuscript.

Abbreviations

AAA	All-China (Amateur) Athletic Federation
ACSF	All-China Sports Federation
BOBICO	Beijing 2008 Olympic Games Bidding Committee
BOCOG	Beijing Organizing Committee for the Olympic Games
CCP	Chinese Communist Party
CNAAF	China's National Amateur Athletics Federation
COC	Chinese (National) Olympic Committee
CTOC	Chinese Taipei Olympic Committee
FIFA	Fédération Internationale de Football Association
IOC	International Olympic Committee
KMT	Kuomintang (Chinese Nationalist Party)
NATO	North Atlantic Treaty Organization
NBA	National Basketball Association (USA)
NPC	National People's Congress (of China)
PLA	People's Liberation Army
PRC	People's Republic of China
ROC	Republic of China (Taiwan)
TOP	Olympic Partnership Programme
UN	United Nations
USA	United States of America
USSR	Union of Soviet Socialist Republics
WHO	World Health Organization
WTO	World Trade Organization
YCL	Young Communist League
YMCA	Young Men's Christian Association
YWCA	Young Women's Christian Association

CHAPTER 1

Sport, Revolution and the Beijing Olympics:
An Introduction

The rise of China has been hailed as one of the most important trends in the world for the next century, and with good reason. Deng Xiaoping's market reforms, subsequently developed by Prime Minister Wen Jianbo and President Hu Jintao, have turned China into one of the fastest-growing economies in the world. Since 1978 China's economy has grown by an average of more than 9 per cent per year, and since 1991 by more than 11 per cent. Even if China's growth rate slows it is likely that it will in the early part of the twenty-first century march past that of the United States of America (USA) and others, and after a five-hundred year hiatus reclaim its place at the centre of the world economy. Since Deng Xiaoping marginalized Maoism in the 1980s, he has urged the Chinese to strive for the American way of life – a lifestyle based upon above all insatiable consumption. In the current climate of free-market popularity, enthusiasm for China's market reforms extends even to the left with born-again post-Maoist scholars embracing entrepreneurship, market efficiency and rationality. As Paul Bowles and Xiao-yuan Dong assert, China is not simply a case of a successful state-led development – it is an example of a successful socialist-state-led development (Smith, 1997: 2).

The origin of modern sport in China according to the Chinese Olympic Committee is complicated in that there were no words in the Chinese vocabulary which corresponded to the Western terms of 'sport' and 'physical education', It was not until the nineteenth century that sport in the modern sense of the word found its way into China, first in the form of military drills and then as part of the curriculum of Western-type schools (Blanchard, 1995; Brownell, 1995; Close et al., 2007). Sport was first translated as 'ticao', or physical training. Indeed one of the indications of both the construction of modern sport and a process of modernization in China is the social construction of sport itself as a modern phenomenon. The Qing government by 1911 had certainly engaged Western instructors to teach foreign drills and physical training including athletics, boxing, fencing, football, gymnastics and swimming. The introduction of modern sport was facilitated by the emergence of influential military schools and colleges and YMCA and YWCA institutions founded by American, British and other nations who had a vested interest in the spread of Christianity.

The study of sport and physical culture in China has been taken forward as the result of a number of groundbreaking and valuable contributions which have primarily been anthropological or historical. The study of sport in China has not dominated the anthropological study of sport but it is necessary to mention the work of Susan Brownell (1995; 1998; 2001; 2004; 2005) not simply because of its originality and impact, but also because of the place and space carved out for the study of sport in China as a result of the author's significant and sustained contribution. More recently further work on gender, media and nationalism has appeared but much of this has grown out of her groundbreaking 1995 work *Training the Body for China: Sports in the Moral Order of the People's Republic*. This analysis of sport in China uses the culture of the body as a focal point to explore the tensions between local and global organizations, the traditional and the modern and men and women. In particular the author's intimate knowledge of social and cultural life in China help her to explore in a unique way how gender, the body and nation are core stepping stones for telling various stories about Chinese culture, the Olympics and the body that is perhaps lacking within the more conventional empirical work on women in sport in China.

Brownell focuses on sports as daily practice and as cultural performance (Brownell, 1995: 15). She argues that the concept of body culture can be used to analyse any level of difference – ethnic, national, class, gender – because it draws our attention to the practical differences that really matter. Bodies are immensely important to the people to whom they belong. Pain, hunger, fatigue, sexual desire and so on are central to the people who are experiencing such phenomena. An ethnographic account that overlooks the body may, it might be argued, omit the centre of human experience. Brownell thinks that the human body's feeling is important as daily practice and cultural performance. Nonetheless, it is also important to rethink the precise relationship between imperialism and the colonized human body's feeling. For example, Fanon constantly exposes the interplay of psychological and political factors showing that colonialism affects individuals as well as societies. Fanon's work (1956; 1967; 1986; 1990) forces us to take psychoanalysis seriously and to attend to the pervasive influence of empire in fantasy, fiction, ideology and sport.

Brownell's synthesis provides a valuable contribution in terms of empirical references, observations on Chinese sport and body culture, and the relatively theoretical informed text which relies in part upon a Western academic grounding – the influence of Eichberg is evident. It is the contention of this study that the research perhaps undervalues the notion of imperialism, postcolonialism and other political themes as a basis for interrogating the development of sport in China and between the two Chinas. *Training the Body for China: Sports in the Moral Order of the People's Republic* might have considered the relationship between native or indigenous cultural identity and 'otherness'. This is especially the case given the Chinese resistance and opposition to contemporary Western forms of political thought. The crucial paradox at the heart of the challenge of China, as Brownell correctly asserts, is that China seeks to 'break out of

Asia and advance into the world' with a strong political purpose (Brownell, 1995: 33). It might not be unreasonable to envisage a hybridized ambivalence to sport in China. While Chinese leaders intend to appropriate Western sports as a tool to promote Chinese nationalism, at the same time they resist Western culture as a means of enlightenment in terms of democracy. This then is one of the challenges of China – how to advance out of China into a world of global capitalism without necessarily conceding to the pressures to adopt Western style forms of democracy.

The story of sport in China has also been influenced by the work of feminist historical writers such as Dong Jinxia (2001, 2005) and Fan Hong (1997, 2005). With the exception of Brownell's contribution, the promise of the study of women in sport in society in China to some extent remains under-theorized in comparison to the extensive contribution to the study of sport, culture and society made by feminist writers in the West. The work tends to remain valuable in the sense that it tells untold stories. Elite sports programmes for women according to Dong Jinxia (2001: 27) have developed rapidly since about 1949. The author's work, based upon three case studies of Beijing, Guangdong and Sichuan, illustrates that women post 1956 took part in both national and international sports competitions in increasing numbers. Add to this the work of Fan Hong (1997) and the study of women in sport in China is beginning to be provided for with a significant empirical base. Fan Hong (2001: 162) asserts in her critical essay on the two roads to China that much of the output of Western interpretations of Chinese sport allegedly lacks evidence, and yet it is important to understand that empirical accounts of sport without any epistemological grounding are just as unsatisfactory as unsubstantiated accounts of sport or imperialist or colonialist accounts of sports history.

Published in 1997, Fan Hong's *Footbinding, Feminism and Freedom: The Liberation of Women's Bodies in Modern China* provides a deeply textual and well-documented account of the struggle and contribution made by women's physical culture in Modern China. The author's central thesis is that the emancipation of women cannot be understood adequately without recognizing their struggle for physical freedom (Hong, 1997: 78). The study contributes not only to our knowledge about sport and physical culture in Modern China, but also to a growing body of feminist literature on sport which marks as its point of departure the emancipation of women through sport and exercise. Her research acknowledges, perhaps belatedly, the place of theory in that the historical story draws upon dense historical archival documentation with theory lurking in the background without it being up front as the front-seat driver. Fan Hong's research acknowledges that exercise is an important cultural practice in the construction of male supremacy, patriarchy and social control in China.

The strengths of Fan Hong's research are many, with the following being some of key contributions, that (i) the study exposes a conservative/traditional Chinese culture which had contributed to the control of women in modern China; (ii) it highlights empirically the struggle for emancipation within the women's movement in China; (iii) it provides an evolutionary study of women's exercise and its relationship to their emancipation within modern Chinese society; and (iv) it acknowledges that modern Chinese women's participation in physical activity has not only challenged traditional patriarchy and its definition of women, but has also helped to contribute to a vision of freedom for some Chinese women. However, it has been argued that perhaps the author buys into the colonialist perspective that Western men were responsible for liberating Chinese women from Chinese men, thus removing Chinese women from the making of their own history.

Issues of freedom and the promise and possibilities for change in sport have also been part of an extensive discussion about the political economy of sport (Close et al., 2007; Jarvie, 2006; Gruneau, 1999; Kidd, 1996). Classical Marxist and liberal theories of political economy have tended to provide a basis for a socio-economic analysis of sport. In short, what is the politics that arises out of an analysis of sporting economics? Liberal political economy as opposed to Marxist political economy also developed around several themes more closely associated with the discipline of economics or more precisely the interrelationship between economic theory and political action. It encompassed several broad themes, such as an economic theory of historical progress; a theory of accumulation and economic growth through the division of labour; a redefinition of wealth as comprised of commerce and not just treasure; a theory of individual behaviour which reconciled the pursuit of self interest with the collective good; and a labour theory of value which argued for labour as a measure and sometimes a source of value.

In *The Beijing Olympiad: The Political Economy of a Sporting Mega-Event* (Close et al., 2007) the authors take on balance an optimistic, pragmatic approach to questioning the significance of the Beijing Olympic Games to the people of China. The optimism lies in the possibilities of renegotiating the relationship of the PRC with the rest of the world and the Chinese people. The authors argue that the Games provide good grounds for acknowledging the impact of China not just in the overall balancing act of globalization but an acknowledged accountability for sharing the problems and issues posed by capitalism, the imbalance between the West and the rest and the North and the South. Gruneau (1999: 125) has argued that where there is no truth, only power, and where power is said to circulate everywhere, politics can only be understood as an ongoing localized tactical project. In this sense one form of domination or subordination is as relevant as any other, so political struggles through sport could easily be seen as little more than an arena of choice closely associated with one's self-identity. Without any normative standards for evaluating the politics of sport within China or between that of China and those of other society's, or when some forms of power are more prevalent than others at any point in time, or for evaluating the conditions by which different political Olympic agendas come into conflict with one another, social criticism loses its potential.

Close et al. (2007) are careful not to predict the outcome of the 2008 Beijing Olympiad in terms of utopian, futuristic almost universalistic thinking, and they do chart a valuable history of the Olympics as an event. They provide one of the few contributions which acknowledge that China in economic, social and political terms has undergone an impressive process of rapid development between the start of Deng-Xiaoping's market-oriented reforms in 1978 and the present. In September 2004, the Central Committee of the Chinese Communist Party endorsed the concept of a 'harmonious society' signalling an increasing concern that the CCP should be seen to be addressing the evident imbalances between social goals and economic growth. There is little doubt that the awarding of the 2008 Olympic Games to Beijing has had an impact, but there remain questions over a range of potential implications in relation to its legacy and China's part in future international relations.

While – in adopting a cautious approach to the promise and possibilities of what the Olympic Games might do for China – there is an almost tacit underlying uncritical acceptance of the notion of globalization, little is said about sport as a facet of anti-globalization or indeed internationalism. While sport at times reproduces the politics of contested national and other identities, it should not be at the expense of an acceptance of the possibility of internationality or focus upon common humanity. Living sporting identities are in constant flux, producing an ever-changing international balance of similarities and differences that may contribute to what it is that makes life worth living, and what connects us with the rest of the changing world. If we are to come to terms with the contemporary crisis of sporting identities, then Close et al. (2007) and others need to transcend the nationalist or global-local simplicities and celebrate difference without demonizing it. Increasing similarity of sporting tastes, choices and aspirations can exist without implying homogeneity. As such, the notion of international sport and new forms of internationality must remain part of the social vocabulary of global and regional sporting debates, not just because it is a more reality-congruent way of explaining the governance of sport today, but because it tempers the all-consuming notion of globalization and provides grounds for explaining the 'other' worlds of sport outside the transnational corporation.

In *China Can Say No* (Chiou et al., 1996), the authors argue that what is required is no more than a reproduction of an exhausted form of 'Third-World' nationalism, itself a vengeful echo of 'First-World' imperialism. What is disturbing about this claim, however, is much less its apparent extremism than the fact that the West, in particular the United States, remains its implied addressee and thus a preferred 'Other'. Contemporary Chinese centrism, in other words, relies for its own anchoring precisely on a perpetuated reactive relation to the West. In this view, any discussion of China could be inadequate without some attempt to address the issues of China's relation with those deemed internally to be politically and culturally subordinate. It is important not to forget China's internal relationship with Tibet and Taiwan, not to mention its relationship with other places and social formations – such as Africa – whose cultures and histories are often denied identity and validity in the eyes of the People's Republic. These other 'Chinese' cultures, insofar as they constitute China's repressed, are and should be a vital part of any consideration to explain the development of sport in and between China and other places. For Chinese intellectuals to confront the realities of these other spaces would mean that they would need to abandon the obligatory reactive position vis-à-vis the West that has habitually been occupied. There are two important points of departure. First, domestically, it points to the undermining of the so called 'Chinese narrative' of official ideology; and second, internationally, it speaks to the deconstruction of Western imperialism's alleged dominance over world culture and discourse.

Sport, Revolution and the Beijing Olympics attempts to critically analyse, describe and explain sport today as a social, historical, cultural and political phenomenon in China. It attempts to complement and add to previous studies of sport in China rather than dissecting them on epistemological grounds, although it is necessary to take a progressive approach to the subject matter. The position taken throughout this book is that, while it is important to explain and understand sport in society, the more important intellectual and practical questions emanate from questions relating to historical and social change.

A genuine social understanding of sport in non-Western societies remains crucial to providing a more holistic understanding of the sporting world in which we live. Sport needs to be critically contextualized and evaluated from other points of view in order to fully explain why sport is the way it is today. Only at that point can we fully claim to have a more international (although not global) understanding of sport involving other parts of the world. The premise that differentiates this study from many conventional explanations of sport in society is that the approach adopted here is not one of attempting to just understand the relationship between sport and a particular non-Western society but to examine the role of sport, exercise and physical culture during periods of revolution, evolution, socialism and communism, culminating in a successful bid to host one of the most commercially driven international sporting events – the 2008 Olympic Games. Why would the hosting of the Olympic Games be important to the People's Republic of China?

More than twenty years ago critical commentators on sport were asking, 'What is the transformative value of sport? Can sport truly make a difference to people's lives?' These questions are as important for students, teachers and researchers of sport, culture and society today as they were more than twenty years ago. The Palestinian activist and intellectual Edward Said (2001b) was openly explicit about the public role of the intellectual as being 'to uncover the contest, to challenge and defeat both an imposed silence and the normalised quiet of unseen power wherever and whenever possible'. The role of the public intellectual in the field of sport, culture and society is desperately needed as a partial safeguard against a one-dimensional world-view of sport in which that which is not said tells you perhaps more than what is actually said. Popular knowledge and discussion of sport in China is being opened up slowly. Yet within Western cultures suspicion, mythology and rational debate about sport in China is missing. Sport in China tends to be either glorified or despised. There is certainly on balance a greater circulation of ideas, interpretations and myths about sport in the Western world than there is about sport in places such as China, India and Africa – not to mention specifically Taiwan, Pakistan, Tibet and Libya.

The core questions at the heart of this book are as follows:

- What empirical evidence can we draw upon to substantiate aspects of sport, physical culture and society in China?
- What theories and concepts can we draw upon to explain and analyse sport and society in China?
- What capacity does sport have to transform or intervene to produce social change in China?
- How should we evaluate and think about the hosting of the Olympic Games in China?
- Why is it important to think about and research other sporting communities?
- How should we make sense of the politics of sport in the case of the two Chinas?
- What is the contemporary role of the student, intellectual or researcher in the public arena?

One of the objectives of the book is to encourage students, teachers and researchers to reflect upon sport, culture and society in China, drawing upon specific concepts, theories and themes but also on a body of substantive research from different sports, societies and communities. The constant interplay between theory, explanation, evidence and intervention is one of the hallmarks of the approach adopted. The advocate, researcher or critical interpreter of sport in society should be continually faced with three interrelated challenges. These are, what evidence do you have, how are you going to make sense of it and what recommendations are you going to make as a result of the first two parts of this exercise (although the production of knowledge and policy rarely comes in such a neat package or process)?

In order to tackle the issues and challenges outlined above, the text is divided into six key chapters and a critical conclusion. Chapter 2 charts the early introduction of sport and physical culture through Western agents and agencies, while chapter 3 reflects upon the role of sport within early nationalist and communist thinking prior to 1949. Very little has been written about the place of sport within China's Cultural Revolution or the period of the great leap forward between 1957 and 1967. Chapter 4, drawing upon original research material, charts the contribution made by sport and physical activity to socialism and the cultural revolution prior to about 1978, while chapter 5 brings sport in China during the last quarter of the twentieth century to a close by examining the issues of sport and national identity, the quest for Olympic recognition and the opening up of sport in China to the outside world. It provides a basis for making sense of sport in China today. Chapter 6 is more futuristic in that it examines China's successful bid to host the 2008 Beijing Olympic Games and reflects upon the relationship between a number of social and economic factors affecting the bidding process for any Olympic Games, not just in China. The book concludes by drawing together the main themes touched upon in this study and championing the role of student, researcher and teacher as public intellectuals in the field of sport. The book is supported by additional sources of information provided at the end of each chapter. These include a short list of key readings, key journal articles, and other key readings.

The informed student of sport who can develop the skills of presenting complex issues in a communicative way, participate in public debates about sport and even promote debates about sport is very much needed in the twenty-first century, but so too is a more comprehensive understanding of sport in the world and not just sport in parts of the world. This study makes a contribution to our knowledge of sport, culture and society. It is hoped that the content of this study will help students of sport on that journey and help readers to reflect upon and inform public debates about sport and revolution, sport and the limits of capitalism, sport and poverty, sport and nation building and sport and human rights, but from the perspective of an 'other' community and through an interrogation of not only Western but also non-Western sources of information about sport in China.

The term 'other' sporting communities as it is used in this research is drawn from the post-colonial critique of the colonial or imperial worlds and consequently the way in which sport developed in many countries. The term at one level refers to something separate from oneself, but as it is used in this book it primarily refers to the articulation of differences between and within imperial, colonial and often-European stereotypes and actions associated with people, sports and places. Some writers have talked about the 'other' in terms of the regimes of truth that are produced by colonialism or imperialism. Such truths invariably view indigenous, non-European or non-Western forms of sport as inferior. This study of *Sport, Revolution and the Beijing Olympics* is sensitive to both internal and external forms of colonialism that have influenced the development of sport in China.

To view global and Western sport as a corpus of dogma allows us to question the values in the idea of an aspirant global sport rather differently. All major dogmatic systems, whether or not they are dogmatic about the free market or religion or political ideology or world sport, need to avoid the twin pitfalls of absolutist and relativist attitudes toward sport, both of which are forms of fundamentalism. Absolutist standpoints run the risk of regarding Western sport as a sacred set of commandments brought to the developing South and East by the developed North and or West. Those who lag behind are pressurized or compelled to convert to the faith of sport and modernity, thus raising barriers to encouraging a greater participation in international sporting festivals staged in or by the West. For example, it might be interesting to reflect on why Wushu has never been represented at the Olympic Games and who takes these decisions?

The relativist view, on the other hand, considers that Northern or Western sport is designed to suit only the Northern or Western sporting hemispheres and needs not have meaning for 'other' places or communities. There is no thought-crime greater today, it seems, than sympathy for relativism. To label an argument relativist is to dismiss it instantly, to imply that the argument's proposer has fallen into such moral jeopardy that no further rebuttal is required. If you say that different cultures are entitled to their own views on right and wrong, you are invariably proclaimed a relativist and yet, when did the West have a monopoly on wisdom? Our faith in Western liberal democracy and our belief that it possesses a superior moral truth have often blinded us to countries with other sporting traditions. One might have thought that the relativist position – to judge society by its own cultural, economic, social and ethical customs – was not only sensible, as our understanding of other societies will be severely limited if we do not take these customs into account, but also the genuine liberal position.

To assume that there can be no communication between major sporting doctrines from different parts of the world is in itself a form of fundamentalism that treats indigenous, national or local belief systems as closed and inflexible. Both variants of Western sporting dogma present other countries with a simple alternative, either to transform their sporting practices by denying who they are, or remain who they are, but give up any idea of transforming sport and them. Perhaps it is impossible for humanity to arrive at an understanding of the values that unite it, but if the countries of the North cease automatically to impose their own ideas on the rest of the sporting world and start to take due cognizance of other sporting cultures in a common exercise of critical self-examination, the aspiration of global sport may become more just and less charitable. If nothing else this study illustrates that other worlds of sport exist and have existed for a long time, and indeed may become an emergent force in the future as China's power unfolds.

Key Readings

Brownell, Susan (1995), *Training the Body for China: Sport in the Moral Order of the People's Republic.* Chicago: University of Chicago Press.

Brownell, Susan (2000), 'Why Should an Anthropologist Study in China', in Noel Dyck (ed.) *Games, Sports and Culture.* Oxford: Berg: 43–63.

Byrnes, Sholto (2005), 'New Statesman Essay', *New Statesman,* 3 October: 32–6.

Close, P., Askew, D. and Xu, X. (2007), *The Beijing Olympiad: The Political Economy of a Sporting Mega Event.* London: Routledge.

Dreyer, June (2003), *China's Political System: Modernization and Tradition.* Upper Saddle River, NJ: Prentice Hall.

O'Toole, J., Sutherden, A., Walshe, P. and Muir, D. (2006), 'Shuttle Cocks and Soccer: The State of Sport in China', *Sportbusiness* No. 119, December: 46–9.

Journal Articles

Brownell, Susan (2005), 'Challenged America: China and America – Women and Sport, Past Present and Future', *International Journal of the History of Sport* 22(6): 1173–93.

Brownell, Susan (1991), 'Sport in Britain and China, 1850–1920: An Explanatory Overview', *International Journal of the History of Sport* 8(2): 284–90.

Dong, Jinxia (2001), 'Women, Sport and Society in the Early Years of the New China', *International Journal of the History of Sport* 18(2): 1–35.

Hong, F. and Mangan, J. A. (2001), 'A Martyr for Modernity: Qui Jin, Feminist, Warrior and Revolutionary', *International Journal of the History of Sport* 18(1): 27–55.

Hong, F., Ping, W. and Huan, X. (2005), 'Beijing Ambitions: An Analysis of the Chinese Elite Sports System and its Olympic Strategy for the 2008 Olympic Games', *International Journal of the History of Sport* 22(4): 510–29.

Liu, Serena (2006). 'Towards an Analytical Theory of Social Change: The Case of China', *The British Journal of Sociology* 57(3): 503–20.

Qin, Hui (2003), 'The Stolypins of China', *New Left Review* 20, March/April: 83–113.

Other Readings

Brownell, Susan (2001), 'Making Dream Bodies in Beijing: Athletes, Fashion Models and Urban Mystique in China', in Nancy Chen, Suzanne Clark and Lyn Jeffrey (eds), *China Urban*, Durham, NC: Duke University Press, 123–42.

Hong, F. (1997), *Footbinding, Feminism and Freedom: the Liberation of Women's Bodies in Modern China*, London: Frank Cass.

Mackenzie, Hector (2004), 'Euro 2004 Fever Kicks Off in China', *Sunday Herald*, 20 June: 23.

Mitchell, Kevin (2004), 'Sport Focus: China – The New World Power', *Observer*, 23 May: 12.

Riordan, J. and Jones, R. (1999), *Sport and Physical Education in China.* London: E & FN Spon.

CHAPTER 2

Sport, Physical Culture and Western Faith Invaders

Introduction

The introduction of certain sports into China was influenced by the influx and diffusion of Western power in China. Western powers such as Britain, France and the United States of America have all attempted to consolidate their political, economic and religious foothold in China. Following the Opium Wars of 1839–1842 and 1856–1860, treaties were signed between China and imperialist countries, and major ports such as Shanghai, Ningbo, Fuzhou, Amoy, Canton, Tianjin and Hankou were opened to the West. Missionaries and merchants were granted the right to travel and purchase both property and land. The importing of opium was legalized, many foreign goods became exempt from the transit tax (*lijin*) and several Western countries received a substantial war indemnity from China. The Chinese government paid 21 million dollars to Britain as part of the Nanking Treaty of 1842; further significant payments were also negotiated with both Britain and France as part of the Beijing Treaty of 1860, while a further 333 millions dollars was paid to the Allied Powers as part of the Boxer Protocol of 1901. The Chinese regarded the negotiation of these treaties as being preferable to military confrontation with the Western powers.

Western imperialism has often been highlighted as a historical dynamic that has influenced the development of sport and physical culture in China. It is impossible to provide an exhaustive list of the ground that has been covered by researchers into areas such as sport, imperialism and the body, but it is crucial to realize that some of the orthodox questions have still to be tested against different forms of evidence from different time-frames and places. In providing a brief insight into one place between the period from 1860 to 1911, the material provided in this chapter is organized into the following sections.

- 'Sport, the West and China', establishes the fact that Western sports were imported into China during this phase of development;
- 'Exercise, physical culture and reform in China' reflects upon some of the factors influencing the development of Chinese physical culture;

- 'Missionaries and Western Faith Invaders' reinforces notions that the missionary school system was a key agent of western imperialism;
- The summary draws together key themes that have been presented in order to substantiate the part played by sport and physical culture in the diffusion of Western cultural imperialism between 1860 and about 1911.

Sport, the West and China

According to Blanchard (1995), in pre-modern China physical culture and activity was often incidentally associated with labour, military training and scholarly thought. No Chinese words existed for terms such as sport and physical education. Speculation continues to exist as to whether China was invited to the first modern Olympic Games in April 1896. It is clear that China did not participate in the Athens Olympic Games of 1896 or any other games until the Los Angeles Olympic Games of 1932. The first YMCA-sponsored athletic meeting took place in 1902 with the first intercollegiate athletic meeting being held two years later. The missionary schools and colleges initially had no formal physical-training courses but they did promote extracurricular forms of sport and as such were part of the incipient development of sport in modern China. While the development of sport in China is often attributed to the development of Western imperialism, it is crucial not to underestimate the part played by China in the making of its own history of sport.

It is hard to provide a complete explanation as to why Western people brought sport to China in the middle of the nineteenth century. Hobsbawm (1987: 56–83) argues that the era from 1875 to 1914 may be called 'the Age of Empire' not just because the period witnessed a new kind of imperialism, but also because it witnessed the emergence of a number of rulers who officially called themselves emperors. His analysis of imperialism noted not just political and economic spheres, but also cultural spheres. He emphasized that imperialism brought to both elites and potential elites of the dependent world 'Westernization'. In his view, Westernization initially occurred on the grounds of religion, morality, ideology and/or political pragmatism (ibid.: 77).

Hobsbawm did not discuss in detail the role of sport as an element of 'Westernization'; nonetheless, in his discussion of 'the bourgeois', he argued forcibly that sport was part of the newly invented tradition of general leisure activity that was valued as a criterion of middle-class lifestyle and culture (Hobsbawm, 1987: 174). Sport was seen as an important element in the formation of a new governing class modelled upon the public-school-trained British bourgeois "gentleman" who introduced it to the continent at the time (ibid.: 182). Much has been made of this thesis, but with specific reference to China all that can be said is that Western sport and forms of physical culture had been introduced to China by at least the 1860s. Sport in China may be viewed as a symbol or reflection of a particular image, way of life, badge of imperialism

closely associated with social class. At the time, sport was often the privilege of
many Western people in China, since many indigenous Chinese people were not
permitted to enter or join certain sports clubs.

Social exclusion is no modern phenomenon. Holt (1989: 207) claims that
sport was not just a symbol of education within the Empire but that it was also a
major source of recreation and entertainment for the colonialist. Sport in this
sense was viewed as symbolizing colonial relationships. The elite were not just
part of an incoming class, but also of a leisure class. Holt (1989: 212) adds that
sports may have been seen initially as training and amusement for a colonial elite,
but as the Empire expanded colonialists saw the value of using sport and games
to build a number of cultural bridges. When Holt compares the Western empires,
he observes that the cultural imperialism of the British tended to be more in-
sidious than that of the French or German empires. Guttmann (1994) argues that
the diffusion of Western sport was a phenomenon of cultural imperialism. He
concedes that the concept of cultural hegemony provides more than a merely cos-
metic conceptual improvement over the term 'cultural imperialism' (Guttmann,
1994: 5–6; 178–9). Gramscian theory stressed that cultural interaction was something much more complex than the domination of the powerful over the powerless. Whatever one's view on this issue, it is undeniable that the introduction of
Western sport in China could be seen as part of a process of Western imperialism.

Horse Racing

There is certainly some evidence to support this notion. Western sports – horse
racing, cricket, soccer, rowing, hunting, track and field athletics, golf, tennis,
and rugby – became increasingly popular as a result of changing patterns of
migration into and from China after the Opium Wars of 1860. Western agents
such as missionaries, traders, soldiers, administrators and diplomats started to
settle in the various leased territories, such as Shanghai, Ningbo, Fuzhou, Amoy,
Canton, Tianjin and Hankou. Many Western agents were British, although
French, German and American agents were also present. Horse racing (*pao-ma*)
was one of the more popular activities among Western peoples who settled
within the Chinese treaty ports.

The first racecourse in Shanghai was built in 1851, with races being held in
the spring and autumn of every year; a second race club was built in 1858, while
a further Shanghai Race Club had been built on the Jingansi Road by 1861
(Shanghai Library, 1998: 16). The seating arrangements were invariably segre-
gated. An exclusive stand for Western members was built at the Shanghai racecourse in 1862 (Yu, 1997: 64). Many local people were not allowed to enter the
club and could only watch races from the outside. In 1863, the owner of one
building near the Shanghai race club sold tickets to local people who wanted to
watch the horse racing from the top of the building (*Shanghai*, 2 October 1863:
1). A letter from Beijing revealed that British and Chinese customs officers were

betting on horse racing as early as 7 November 1863 (*Shanghai*, 25 December 1863: 1). It should be pointed out that gambling on contests (such as cockfights and cricket-fights) had already become deeply entrenched in Chinese Society centuries before. For the more affluent Chinese the British eventually built a wooden stand and charged admission fees of one and a half pounds Sterling for the upper seats and one pound Sterling for the lower seats (*Shanghai*, 22 October 1863: 1). Such a pricing system effectively produced a form of imperialistic class segregation and acted as a form of social exclusion for many.

Horse racing spread to other cities with, for example, Western merchants having developed horse racing in Hong Kong by 1872 (*Shanghai*, 16 March 1872: 2), and Hanko by 1864 (*Shanghai*, 2 October 1864: 2). Shanghai international merchants regularly held horse races. Westerners claimed that regular horse racing contributed to training strong horses for the purposes of war (*Shanghai*, 4 April 1870: 2). Some Western intellectuals criticized horse racing and questioned the ideology of selecting and training strong horses in order to promote gambling activity. Nevertheless, gambling on the horses had become popular by 1872. Chinese writers regularly noted the emergence of horse racing in the newspapers of the time. Such newspaper articles described horse racing in Shanghai as being exciting and attractive.

Boat Racing and Rowing

Horse racing was not the only popular sport practised in the Chinese treaty ports. According to Speak (1999: 72), by 1837 the Canton Regatta Club had organized boat races. The Western style of boat racing, with its use of oars and boat hooks, was an anomaly to local Chinese officials who described it as *tow sam pan*, literally the 'fighting boats'. As Crew (1940) points out:

> So far as amusements were concerned, the foreigners were left to their own resources ... They had the choice of growing morbid and melancholy through boredom and loneliness, or organising games, tournaments and parties which would help them pass the time between the infrequent calls of ships bringing new faces and letters from home. There were only a handful of foreigners in Canton before they built some small boats and organised yacht races, much to the confusion of the Chinese officials, who couldn't see any fun in a boat race which was not accompanied by the beating of drums, like the dragon-boat races. (Crew, 1940: 208–307)

In Shanghai one of the first races was held on the Whangpu River in 1849 (Shanghai Library, 1998: 21). Percival describes how the Shanghai Yacht and Boat Club's annual regattas in the spring and autumn of each year were in part rowdy affairs as Scottish, German and English crews pulled for their laurels (Percival, 1889: 8–12). A Rowing Club (Shanghai Library, 1998: 20–1) on the Wuchang Road along the Soochow creek was built in 1860. In 1870 both

American and British merchants extended the two-day boat racing games to the new West Water Gate. Victories recorded in local newspapers testify to the popularity of Western boat racing. The Americans won an eight-man boat race (*Shanghai*, 27 October 1870: 2). The Scots won on 14 October 1870. On one occasion, a scheduled boat race had to be postponed from 15 to 17 October because of rain. The race started at 3 p.m. and many foreigners and local people watched the boat race from the riverbank (*Shanghai*, 2 November, 1870: 2).

The examples cited here are merely mentioned to substantiate the fact that boat racing was practised within Chinese society prior to 1860. It too became associated with gambling. There was *Du chuan* (Boat Gambling) on Western sailboat races on the opposite shore of Jardine Matheson & Co, from 11:00 a.m. to 12:00 (*Shanghai*, 25 April 1872: 2). The boat race near the bridge of Soochow creek was described as being just as popular as horse racing (*Shun Pao*, 12 May 1872: 2). These newspaper articles show that Western boat races were popular in Shanghai following the arrival of Westerners in the latter half of the nineteenth century. Like horse racing, boat racing was also seen as the privilege of imperialists.

Cricket

The same attitude applied to cricket, which was viewed as a symbol of British cultural imperialism. Holt (1989: 203) asserts that sport played a major role in the transmission of imperial and national ideas from the late nineteenth century. Cricket in particular had a special meaning for the empire. Cricket was valued by certain British communities who settled around the world following the expansion of imperial power during the last quarter of the nineteenth century. Cricket in the Chinese language is called *ban qiu* (bat ball). During the nine-teenth century, cricket was also called *pao qiu* (throw ball), which created a slight confusion as to what activity was actually being played. In 1862 a Chinese news-paper featured the sale of a set of second-hand cricket and horse-riding equip-ment. The *Shanghai* described a carriage accident near the *pao qiu* (cricket) ground on 5 May 1865, and therefore it might be concluded that some sort of cricket ground existed in Shanghai around the 1860s. Chinese sports historians are not sure about what *pao qiu* involved. Hsu I-hsiung and Hsu Yuan-ming (1999: 70), for example, merely speculate that *pao qiu* was a kind of Western ball game. A Chinese artist's impression of the game of cricket, painted and pub-lished in Shanghai in the 1880s, not only describes how Western players played *pao qiu* (cricket) but also noted that the term '*pao qiu*' refers to the game of cricket.

Pictorial references show that members of the *Da Qing Pao Qiu* (Great Qing Cricket) clubs were at the Shanghai Cricket Club on 11 September 1907 (Shanghai Library, 1998: 55). This may substantiate the existence of early Chinese involvement in the development of cricket clubs.

Football

Football had established itself in China by the 1880s. The Chinese had their own traditional kickball game of *cuju*, which served as a form of military training. It is interesting that when the Chinese saw Westerners playing soccer in Shanghai in the 1880s, they thought soccer was the Chinese *cuju*. The term *cuju*, not football or kickball, was often used. One article with the headline *Cuju yu bin* (Playing football to entertain guests) featured Westerners in Shanghai hosting an invitation soccer match against officers and soldiers of the British Emperor's grandson at the racecourse in 1881. The host players were worried since they had not played football for a long time, so they had to practice in advance in order to pick the best men to play against the visitors (*Shun Pao*, 27 November 1881). The game started at 3:30 p.m at the racecourse on 1 December 1881. The weather turned and the game was moved indoors to the central house of the racecourse. The local Chinese were prohibited from entering the house. Many were not able to view the game because of the wet and muddy ground that rendered it difficult for carriages and horses to travel. They all felt disappointed and left (*Shun Pao*, 27 November 1881).

Other Sports

The majority of Western sports clubs hosted meetings on the grounds of the horse-racing courses. There were many different sporting events held by Western clubs. Crew notes:

> I believe the Shanghai Baseball Club is older than any similar organisation in America, for it was in existence before Lincoln was elected President ... Sports were organised along 'hong' (company) lines, and jockeys, golfers, bowlers, cricketers and oarsmen competed for the glory of the 'hong' just as college athletes compete for the Alma Mater ... Dozens of clubs connected with some sporting or athletic event flourished; clubs devoted to baseball, cricket, lawn bowls, bowling, billiards, golf, polo, hockey, rowing, swimming all emerged but the most important of all the Shanghai organisations was the Race Club. (Crew, 1940: 298–307)

An old picture shows that a rugby game between Shanghai and Tianjin foreigners was held in early 1908 (*Lao Shanghai*, 1998: 19). Western sport from open cities such as Shanghai and Tianjin spread to other cities. The Hongkou Recreation Ground was built in 1905 and included a golf club, hockey pitch, basketball court, soccer field, baseball field and bowling green. The Ground was opened to the Chinese in July 1928. In 1911 a tug-of-war was held at the Hongkou Recreation Ground (Shanghai Library, 1998: 31).

Sai-li in Chinese literally means 'strength competition' and could possibly be regarded as the early Chinese term for an athletic meet. One of the earliest

Sai-li took place in 1871. Newspapers described Western people exercising and training by jumping, playing a ball game, weightlifting and running, all of which was aimed to improve physical strength. The existence of the annual Western merchants' athletic meet may also be noted as having existed as early as 1871 (*Shanghai*, 11 May 1871: 2). The athletic meeting included activities such as jumping, ball games, weightlifting and running. The ball game could have been cricket since at this time soccer was still termed *cuju*. In 1872, *Xi Ren Sai-li* (Westerners' athletic meet) reported an athletic meet held on the Shanghai horse-racing course. The records of the various events were high jump 4 feet 5 inches, broad jump 17 feet 3 inches, ball throw (*pao qiu*) 106.5 yards, and running from 100 to 600 yards (*Shanghai*, 21 May 1872: 2). In '*Xi Ren Sai-li*', a further meeting was held on the annual Shanghai racing course in which all major events were held plus a tug-of-war. It is interesting to note from some reports that policemen gave entrance permits only to Western people and that local Chinese people were prohibited from entering and had to observe the proceedings from the opposite bank of the river (*Shun Pao*, 25 April 1882: 2). This situation was not too dissimilar to other Western sporting events, in that local Chinese people were often prohibited from entering the sporting clubs. It might be suggested that Holt (1992: 207) is correct to argue that 'Sport helped both to relieve the tedium of a distant posting and to integrate new arrivals into the small world of colonial society'. In China, Western sport was a symbol of both social class and imperialism.

When the Chinese first saw Western athletic meetings (*Sai li*) in Shanghai in 1871, many believed that the Westerners were stronger than the Chinese because Western sports cultivated people's martial spirit. After the Opium wars, the Chinese were allegedly defeated by Westerners not only because of their relatively weak military power, but also because of their alleged physical weakness and the lack of martial spirit. Some Chinese reformers thought their people must learn from Western physical culture in order to develop Chinese military spirit and power. They suggested revolutionary changes in both traditional Confucianism and the education system. To learn from the West became a popular slogan for Chinese reformers. Physical culture and organized sport was formally promoted in the school curriculum for the first time in Chinese history. As such, exercise and particular approaches to physical culture became subject to the process of reform.

Exercise, Physical Culture and Reform

China faced many internal social and political problems during the late nineteenth and early part of the twentieth centuries, such as corruption, overtaxation, famine and rebellion. The Chinese (Manchu) empire was unstable during the early 1860s and reformers claimed that China had to become a much stronger nation. Such a philosophy legitimated the adoption of

Western-style military drill. On the back of political enthusiasm for developing military strength, formal programmes of physical education emerged. The first course of physical training was established at the Nanking Military Academy in 1875. Similar programmes came into being at the Tianjin Naval Academy in 1881 under the patronage of Li Hung-Chang. Physical education courses were often influenced by German military ideology. Physical exercises using gymnastics, dumbbells, the horizontal bar, parallel bars, side horse, jumping, football, swimming, mountain climbing, pole climbing were all introduced as core aspects of physical training (Wu, 1981: 69). An English naval captain who helped to conduct the annual examination in 1890 suggested to Li Hung-Chang that the cadets be taught boxing, gymnastics and fencing in order 'to develop their pluck, nerve and self-confidence' (*North-China Herald*, 18 July 1890: 44). The influence of Western ideology in forming such early programmes had been relatively limited prior to about 1895 (Kolatch 1972: 4).

The loss of the Sino-Japanese war of 1895 was viewed as both a symbol of weakness and a failure of the reformation policies introduced between about 1860 and 1895. Reformers requested accelerated reforms, and the modernization of China's military, educational and financial systems. The development of new schools progressed rapidly, with new subjects including the expansion of Western forms of physical culture, exercise and education. Most physical-education teachers were not indigenous and were often from a military background. Military spirit and exercises were viewed as vital facets of any physical-education programme because of the influence of both Western and Japanese imperialism.

Prior to the 1870s strength to Confucian modernists had meant military strength. This narrow perception contributed to short-term objectives such as the maintenance of peace and the preservation of territorial integrity. The basic assumptions were that the people should acquire Western skills, that China had the natural resources for the fulfilment of her policy goals and that the bureaucracy should be supportive of these tasks. Reform along these lines was evident in cultural movements such as the self-strengthening movement. Its immediate objective was to build up military power. Its ultimate aim was to preserve and strengthen a traditional way of life. There was support for adopting Western methods among some of the new reformers. Feng Kuei-Fen (1809–1874) recognized the need for modernization and the importance of scientific studies when he was forced to take refuge from the Taipings in Shanghai. Here he was brought into direct contact with Westerner culture. As an advisor to the political elite, Feng demonstrated a grasp of both state and foreign affairs. Feng insisted upon the adoption of 'Western books on mathematics, mechanics, optics, light and chemistry (Bary et al., 1964: 48). He did not specifically mention Western physical culture, but he was a central figure during this period in encouraging the adoption of Western forms of teaching and learning.

Self-Strengthening Movement

Tseng Kuo-Fan (1811–1872) and Li Hung-Chang (1823–1901) were other exponents of the self-strengthening movement. Tseng was acclaimed as the conqueror of the Taipings, and as a Confucian practitioner he exemplified traditional values of industry, frugality, honesty, integrity in office and loyalty to the ruling dynasty. His teachings, learning and political thinking inspired the devotion of his subordinates and gave Confucianists a confidence that such personal qualities could meet the challenges facing China. In March 1871 Tseng and Li submitted a letter to the Tsungli Yamen, who was responsible for the handling of foreign affairs, in which he emphasized that China needed to learn from the West. They were convinced that Western methods could only be mastered through periods of prolonged and intensive study abroad. They pointed out that, in terms of education for the military and administration and commerce, technical education should be considered alongside those aspects of education that dealt with the mind, body, nature and destiny of a person. More specifically, 'now that the eyes of the people have been opened, if China wishes to adopt Western ideas and excel in Western methods, we should immediately select intelligent children and send them to study in foreign countries' (Bary et al., 1964: 50). The primary aim was to train an elite corps of intellectuals with a combination of both classical Chinese and Western studies that could be purposefully directed and managed in the interests of the state.

Yen Fu (1853–1921), one of the most influential writers during Mao-Zedong's boyhood (Teng and Fairbank, 1971: 113), studied at the Greenwich Naval Academy and translated Western works into Chinese. One of Yen's essays, 'On Strength' (Yuan Chiang), involved a discussion of Darwin's *On the Origin of the Species* in which he noted that while 'all species came from one origin they were gradually differentiated through surroundings and slight variations of physiology ... This is true not only of animals and plants but also of people ... The evidence is precise and strong' (Wang, 1966: 196). Commenting on Spencer, Yen stressed the philosopher's rigorous application of the evolutionary theory of social phcnomcna, and in particular he described the *First Principles*, the *Study of Sociology* and *Education: Intellectual, Moral, and Physical*. Yen pointed out the importance of physical training in education and argued, 'The principal aim of teaching is the development of intelligence, bodily vigour and moral virtues' (Wang, 1966: 197). He added that in 'any basic programme of development, bodily vigour was to be accorded first importance and that the academies in both Greece and Rome had their gymnasiums and that Plato himself was known for his physical strength' (Wang, 1966). Yen added that:

> Western scholars interested in statecraft always judge a nation by the physique, intelligence, and morals of its people. If by such criteria the quality of the people is high, neither their livelihood nor their status as a nation can be bad. If, on the other hand, the people are slow, unenlightened, and selfish, the group cannot last

and will be humiliated and annihilated when faced with stronger groups. The process does not need to take the form of armed conflicts but may come about through a gradual collapse as can be seen from many historical episodes. Hence the West accepts the self-preservation urge of all living beings as the fact in politics and education ... but extols the preservation of the species when it conflicts with the preservation of the individual ... In formulating a policy, the goal is always to improve the vigour, intelligence and virtue of people. (Wang 1966: 197)

He initially advocated the encouragement of people's power, the cultivation of their knowledge, and the revival of good conduct. After 1911, and especially after the European War, Yen Fu's ideas changed in that he subsequently asserted that both the Chinese government system and Chinese methods of learning were better than those of Europe. He asserted that the culture of the West since the European War had been corrupted and that three centuries of progress had only accomplished four things; to be selfish, to kill others, to have no integrity and to have lost a sense of shame (Teng and Fairbank, 1971: 151). Yen Fu became a conservative whose political *modus operandi* was to criticize the New Culture Movement. Such an ideological shift did not include a change in his thoughts about physical culture, exercise and health, in that he consistently argued throughout that the Chinese people must do more exercise in order to strengthen their bodies and that they should cease the popular practices of opium smoking and foot-binding (Yen, 1969: 55–6). Parks for public recreation and health were to be advocated and holidays once every seven days were to be introduced to enable civil and military officials to implement a way of life that recognized the need for periods of relaxation. The importance of health, recreation and physical culture for Chinese people was advocated, seen to be socially, politically and culturally important.

Liang Chi-Chao (1873–1929), escaped to Japan after the failure of Kang's regime and subsequently became one of the most influential advocates of reform in the years immediately before the Revolution of 1911. His writings dealt with a wide range of political, social and cultural issues. To many young Chinese studying abroad (most of them in Japan) he became an inspiration, a patriotic hero who combined Chinese classical learning with a sensitivity to Western ideas and trends. Liang advocated a view of world history that was strongly influenced by social Darwinism and the struggle for the survival of nations and races. In the 1890s, he and Kang urged China to go beyond the mere adoption of Western methods and ideas as a means of bringing about fundamental institutional change. He argued that such institutional change itself could only be effected through a transformation of the whole Chinese way of life and particularly its morals that were always considered to be the very essence of Confucianism. Morality was now to serve the interest of the official elites charged with the task of national survival. In *A People Made New*, Liang states that:

A state is formed by the assembling of people. The relation of a nation to its people resembles that of the body to its four limbs, five viscera, muscles, veins and corpuscles. It has never happened that the four limbs could be cut off, the five viscera wasted away, the muscles and veins injured, the corpuscles dried up, and yet the body still lives. Similarly, it has never happened that a people could be foolish, timid, disorganised and confused and yet the nation still stands. Therefore, if we wish the body to live for a long time we must understand the methods of hygiene. If we wish the nation to be secure, rich and honourable, we must discuss the way for the people to be 'made new'. (Bary et al., 1964: 94)

Liang argued that such terms did not necessarily mean that people must give up entirely what is old in order to follow the new. There are two meanings of *made new*: one is to improve what is original in the people and so renew it, and the other is to improve that which is originally lacking in the people and so make a new people. Liang's essay on 'Martial Spirit' was arguably one of his most significant contributions in which he analysed the reasons for the defeat of China by Western countries. It was suggested that the Chinese had martial form but lacked martial spirit. He pointed out that the human physical body had a strong relationship to the human spirit. The strength of the Europeans came in part from their addiction to sports in contrast to the Chinese who did not value sport but lived with poor hygiene, early marriage and weak offspring, and also cultivated bad habits such as smoking opium which further debilitated their bodies and souls. Liang not only emphasized physical culture and organized sport as one of most important parts of education (Gu, 1997: 187), but he also supported women's physical exercise in school. Liang's thoughts on physical culture were closely related to producing both a people and a nation.

In the years 1861 and 1862 a well-equipped foreign legion was formed in Shanghai to aid imperial troops against the Taiping rebels. The further demonstration of Western prowess produced a greater effect on the minds of some of the Chinese scholar-generals. Li Hung-Chang was convinced that in order to survive, China must accelerate its knowledge of Western learning in order to acquire further knowledge about Western methods. As early as 1872 a group of students were sent to the US, with the indirect result that those Chinese students who studied abroad were introduced to baseball. Li Hung-Chang sent 120 Chinese students to America between 1872 and 1881. Those students studied at Hartford where, writes Fairbank, 'they learned to tuck their queues under their caps and play very smart baseball' (Fairbank, 1978: 540). These 120 students from the Hartford project made their mark on China's foreign relations, industrialization and sports development (Fairbank, 1978: 540–2). The famous railway engineer Zhan Tianyou, who was one of those students, introduced baseball to China (Gu, 1990: 17). Liang Chang was also one of those students who played for the baseball team at the Phillips Academy in Andover. Liang won the final game with Exeter in 1881 and subsequently became the Chinese ambassador to the USA in the early part of twentieth century (Wu, 1981: 71). This was not to be the only time that sport was to become a factor in paving the way for diplomatic relations between China and the USA.

Modern Schools and Physical Culture

Modern schools established by the central and provincial governments between 1861 and 1894 fell into seven categories: (i) schools to train interpreters and foreign affairs specialists; (ii) schools to train interpreters and skilled workmen for the new shipyards and arsenals; (iii) schools to train deck and engine-room officers for the modern navy – these will be called naval academies; (iv) schools to train army officers – that is, military academies; (v) schools to train personnel for the telegraph administration; (vi) a naval and military medical school; and (vii) a school of mine engineering (Biggerstaff, 1972: 31). Physical culture and organized sport was a common part of the curriculum introduced to most if not all of these new schools.

Historically, physical culture had long been a major concern for Chinese traditional education. For example, the educational philosophy of the Chou Dynasty (1122–255 BC) is described in the *Book of Rites* as consisting of six virtues – wisdom, benevolence, goodness, righteousness, loyalty, harmony; the six praiseworthy actions – honouring one's parents, being friendly with one's brothers, being good neighbourly, maintaining cordial relationships with relatives by marriage, being trustful and being sympathetic; and the six arts – ritual, music, archery, charioteering, writing and mathematics. Archery, charioteering and dancing can be seen as contributing to some of the earliest known forms of physical education in traditional Chinese education. The *Book of Rites* gives in detail the model of a boy who 'at thirteen … learned music, and to repeat the odes, and to dance the *ko*. When a full-grown lad, he danced the *hsiang*. He learned archery and chariot driving' (Purcell, 1936: 4–5).

The *Book of Rites* had influenced Chinese traditional education and examination systems before 1860. In traditional China, examinations were divided into civil and military categories, but the former were more important than the latter in that the term 'examination system' itself referred only to civil-service examinations. The military examination system progressed through the same stages as its civil counterpart. To become a military licentiate, or *wu sheng-yuan*, a man had to pass the district, prefectural and qualifying military examinations. Then he was entitled to take the provincial military examination, after which came the metropolitan military examination. Those who succeeded in the latter became military graduates (*wu kung-shih*) and could compete in the palace military examination to become military *chin-shih*. The only difference between the two was that the military system lacked the extra re-examinations that had been interpolated in the civilian system. Miyazaki's descriptions of China's military examination system provides a brief illustrative insight into the place of physical culture and exercise in this examination process:

> People who hope to become army officers began with the district military examination, which was conducted by the magistrate and consisted of three sessions. In the first candidates had to shoot three arrows from horseback at a man-shaped

target about 1.6 meters high. If all three arrows hit home, the man received a perfect score; if two hit the mark, he was graded 'good'; and if only one reached the target he received a pass. Those who did not manage to do even that, or who fell from their horse, were eliminated. The rest went on to the second session. This consisted of a marksmanship test (*pu-she*) and a test of military talent (*chi-yung*). In the first the candidates had to shoot five arrows at a target at fifty paces. Those who made four or five hits were graded 'excellent', two or three earned a 'good', and one hit a 'pass', while anyone who did not hit the target at all was failed. The second part consisted of three tests: drawing a bow (*k'ai-kung*), brandishing a sword (*wu-tao*), and weightlifting (*to-shih*). In the first of these the men had to bend a bow into the shape of a full moon, with the bows graded by strength into 120-, 100- and 80-catty weapons (a catty, or chin, weighs approximately 600 grams, or about 21 ounces). A man who bent the heaviest bow received an 'excellent', the 100-catty bow earned a 'good', and the 80-catty bow gave him a grade of 'pass'. The next test involved grasping a halberd, ch'ing-lung tao, or 'green dragon sword,' brandishing it in front of one's face, swinging it around one's back and returning it to the front, and finally spinning it like a water wheel, all without once it touching the ground. Grades were assigned according to the weight of the halberd; men who used the 120-, 100- or 80-catty weapons were rated 'excellent', 'good', and 'pass', respectively. (Miyazaki, 1976: 102–3)

From 1898 onward, attempts were made to reform the examination system through the introduction of new material and by associating it with the schools of modern studies. By 1904, the complete integration of the school examinations with the state examinations and the gradual abolition of the old style of literary and military examination had occurred. By 1905, the examination system was abolished and represented a decisive break in the relationship between China and the West in terms of the influence of intellectual and cultural fields. Western military drill and physical exercise continued to be introduced as one of the major subjects in the new schools during the decades before and after 1900. Chen (1979: 124) states that Chinese schools in 1903 conducted three hours of physical drill and exercise every week.

The military-favoured physical exercise known as *ti tsao* (gymnastic) provided most of the physical training available in Chinese schools during the first decade of the twentieth century. It was this type of exercise prescribed by the Board of Education – the first organized government control over modern education – when it stipulated 2–3 hours per week of physical exercise for upper and lower elementary schools in 1905. Physical culture and organized sport was made a requirement in middle schools, higher schools, lower normal schools, and lower agricultural schools.

In 1907 a curriculum was devised for the women's normal schools. Periodic changes were made, such that physical culture and organized sport in lower elementary schools was raised to four hours per week by 1909. At that time, urban schools were expected to give physical training as a required course, and rural schools as an optional course. In 1905 only 102,767 Chinese children were in public schools out of a total school-age population of approximately 33 million. By 1910, the figure had risen to about 5 per cent of that figure. Among the government schools of that era, only Nanyang (Shanghai), Peiyang (Tianjin) and Haichün (Woosung) had formal sports programmes. The average programme in Chinese schools at that time was not dissimilar to the description provided by Martin Yang of physical education in the rural Shantung village of Taitou about 1915 (Kolatch, 1972: 5–6). The physical training provided there consisted mainly of military drill. Since the aim of the programme was to make the pupils good soldiers, marching, saluting and military terminology were prioritized so as to resemble a military camp. Teachers appealed to their students to train their bodies so that they would be able to defend their homes and their nation.

The first school dedicated solely to training physical educators was the Chinese Physical Training School (*Chung Kuo Ti Tsao Hsueh Hsiao*) opened in 1904, in Shanghai, by Hsu Fu-lin and his co-workers (Hsu Yi-ping and Liu Cheng-lieh). The teachers had been among those who had studied in Japan and brought back Japanese exercise systems. Outwardly, these people advocated a 'national physical education programme' (*kuo min ti yu*), while inwardly they also preached revolution and advocated the downfall of the Qing dynasty. Hsu himself translated a book from Japanese entitled *Swedish Curative Exercises*. By the time the school was forced to close down in 1927, 1,531 students had graduated from its two-year courses. The Chinese Physical Training School was extremely influential and produced most of the future heads of physical education departments until the government began opening physical education departments in its normal schools by about 1915. In 1905, Hsu Fu-lin's wife founded the Shanghai Chinese Girls' Physical Education School that continued to operate until the Japanese war. With the establishment of the Republic of China in 1911, the Board of Education gave way to the Ministry of Education (*Chiao Yu Pu*) which had little more machinery to implement its directives than had the Board. Nevertheless, it seemed to be more vigorous in its attitudes toward physical training. It reiterated earlier directives and called for three hours of physical culture and organized sport per week in both elementary and middle schools. By December 1912, it had stipulated the future direction of physical culture and organized sports programmes by stating: 'The essentials of physical exercise are to cause all parts of the body to develop equally, to strengthen the body, to enliven the spirit, and to cultivate the habits of discipline and harmony' (Wu, 1962: 330–7). This aim of physical culture and organized sport was very compatible with the missions of the Young Men's Christian Association (YMCA) and the Young Women's Christian Association (YWCA) and other missionary institutions.

Missionaries and Western Faith Invaders

The missionary system in China set up schools to aid in the propagation of Christianity. To many they may have been viewed as the pioneers of a modern education system .The nineteenth century witnessed a period of growth in relation to the setting up of Christian missionary schools. By 1844 as a result of the Treaty of Whampoa, the Chinese agreed to the free propagation of religion. By 1858, the Treaty of Tianjin had further provided for the freedom of movement for all missionaries. None of these early agreements conceded any rights to educate Chinese children, but Westerners bought land and opened schools. In the records of the 1894 convention of the Student Volunteer Movement for Foreign Missions, Fletcher Brockman, one of the early YMCA's Secretaries to China, claimed that the typical reason for this social and political movement emerging in China at this time was one of opportunism. One explanation for the oncoming of these Faith invaders was put in the following terms:

> One reason is [that] a million a month in that great land are dying without God. Can you picture what it is to die without God? Can you imagine it? – Because 300,000,000 in China are living without God. O brothers and sisters, can you picture what it is to live without God? Have you ever thought of it, to have no hope for the future and none for the present? (Lutz, 1971: 11)

Brockman's faith influenced the attitude with which he approached his work in China. Later he talked more openly about the goals of the missionary which in many ways would be viewed as racist today.

> [From the] *standpoint of the religious need of the missionary fields, I look upon all of the non-Christian countries as presenting the same problem. They were composed of heathens, and at the distance from which I viewed all heathens were alike. I believed sincerely that all non-Christian religions should be destroyed root, stock, and branch. The religious leaders of China were hostile to Christianity, I thought, and I must meet them with the same spirit. It was to be a fight to the finish between light and darkness. It is a fight for life. We must conquer them or they will conquer us.* (Brockman, 1935: 16–17 [italics added])

Missionaries were interested in the religious conversion of individuals' religious beliefs which they prioritized as separate from other aspects of culture. Griffith John spoke for many when he told a missionary conference in 1877 that:

> We are here not to develop the resources of the country, not for the advancement of commerce, not for mere promotion of civilization; but to do battle with the powers of darkness, to save people from sin, and conquer China for Christ. (Lutz, 1971: 11)

It might be suggested that the missionary's task was unsuccessful in that many failed to recognize the power of the Chinese gentry who viewed missionaries as a disruptive threat to Chinese orthodoxy and incited resistance against them. Some adopted alternative approaches. From the 1880s, Timothy Richards, W.A.P. Martin, Young J. Allen and other missionaries grew more sympathetic to Chinese culture and customs, and decided increasingly to:

'secularise' their work through the promotion of Western knowledge. From 'saving the hea-thens from the sufferings of hell', they moved to 'saving the heathens from the hell of suf-fering in this world and as such sponsored schools, libraries, hospitals, newspapers and magazines to promote Western culture and progress'. (Hook, 1982: 245 [italics added])

The growth of the Chinese Christian community facilitated the building of schools to educate Christians and the children of Christians. The missionary faith invaders hoped that by providing schools they could produce an informed Church membership and thus raise the status of Christianity in the eyes of the Chinese. The goals of missionary schools fell into three categories: (i) conversion of the upper classes in the hope that their conversion would influence the masses; (ii) the need for training Christian converts and workers in Christian schools, hospitals and churches and (iii) the hope of embedding a particular form of Christianity within the Chinese nation as a whole (Lutz, 1971: 19).

Physical culture and organized sport was an important part of the extra-curricular activities within the early missionary schools. In 1884 students of Zhen Jiang Christian Girls' School (Jiang Su province) were required to take part in gymnastics or physical exercise after their lessons at four o'clock every day (Gu, 1989: 63). These physical activities had an indirect influence on the liberation of women's foot-binding in China. Of equal significance from a historical point of view, as far as the development of Western non-military physical education in China is concerned, were the sports activities which were introduced through the Christian schools as early as 1888. Chinese youth became increasingly familiar with selected Western sports. In 1890, St John's University (Shanghai) introduced track and field athletics and formally adopted such sports, believing in the usefulness of sport in building both character and bodies. In 1904 the first inter-collegiate athletic meeting in the north of China was held between Beijing University and North China Union College. Military drill and callisthenics were emphasized in some colleges, with tennis, baseball and soccer proving to be so popular that they were subsequently introduced into the government schools. Both Ginning and Soochow provided physical-culture and organized-sport courses to train leaders in physical education and public health work for schools, colleges, the YMCA, the YWCA, and other missionary organizations (Lutz, 1971: 187). Christian colleges had a particular influence in promoting physical culture. Christian missionaries met with considerable opposition when they introduced physical culture and organized sport and recreation to students. At the mission school students had come to enjoy sports such as track and field, tennis and soccer. The Christian colleges organized intercollegiate athletic contests that included representatives from non-Christian institutions.

By this time the government had adopted the view that the development of a stronger physical culture through physical education could help China by strengthening its citizens. In 1909 a programme of modern physical education for China was organized under the leadership of M. J. Exner of the International Committee of the YMCA (Hoh, 1926: 90–3). Sports activity spread to many of the Church-affiliated schools while the government schools lagged behind. Development was so one-sided in favour of the Church schools that at the first National Athletic Meet in 1910 most of the athletes were from missionary schools and almost none of the participants were from government schools. A change occurred between 1910 and 1920 as the YMCA began to initiate sports programmes in government schools. The missionary schools initially conceived of physical culture and organized sport as something divorced from education, intended merely for recreational purposes. The faculty members who took charge of the programmes were not specialists in physical culture. Most had developed an interest in sports while attending school and gone on to serve as volunteer supervisors at the missionary schools.

YMCA Physical Culture and Education Programmes

The YMCA's physical-education and culture programme in China was not systematically introduced until the arrival of Dr. D. Willard Lyon to Tianjin in 1895. In 1898 three additional Foreign Secretaries, Robert R. Gailey, R. E. Lewis and Fletcher S. Brockman, were sent to China to join Lyon. They all had an interest in the popular power of physical culture and organized sport. C. H. Robertson arrived in 1902 to be the YMCA Secretary in Tianjin. He spent part of his time teaching specialist physical-education programmes in local Chinese schools. Both Gailey and Robertson took a particular interest in physical culture, in addition to their regular religious duties, while Tianjin took the lead among YMCAs in the development of physical-education programmes.

The YMCA sports effort in China developed along two broad paths. The first involved programmes initiated and run by the YMCA using its own facilities. As indicated earlier, such developments started in 1908 when M.J. Exner arrived in Shanghai and built the first Shanghai YMCA gymnasium. He developed a plan for physical-culture and organized-sport development and prepared the training course for physical-education teachers (Tsai, 1996: 156). The aim of physical culture and organized sports for him was to secure for the individual the physical basis for life. He opened a two-year course for the training of Physical Education Directors in October 1909. This course included training in all branches of sport, textbook work and lectures in anatomy, physiology, hygiene, tests and measurements, the history of physical training alongside compulsory Bible study. The trainees were to receive pedagogical experience at the Shanghai YMCA. His first class of trainees contained 14 students and by the spring of 1910 he was able to put on a sports demonstration in the Shanghai gymnasium before 200 spectators. A native Chinese student, Mr. C.G. Hoh from the original class, later became the YMCA's Physical Secretary. This YMCA's new programme produced some of the first Chinese-born muscular Christians inculcated in the values of both Western forms of physical culture and organized sports and religion (Kolatch, 1972: 10).

The direct link between physical culture and religion is born out in the following extract from an article written by Exner in 1911:

> There are several things that these First National Athletics Games should accomplish. In the first place they will call national attention to physical training and will stimulate interest in it all over China. They will do much to establish uniform standards and events in athletics; they will open an approach to many of the government schools, for we have found that the most ready opening into the government schools is through athletics; and they will do much to remove prejudice against Christianity. They will win respect for Christianity, especially in the minds of young men, in that they will cause Christianity to be associated with virile, manly elements. (Exner, 1911:19)

Exner and other leaders felt that by running a national athletic meet, nationwide attention and interest in physical culture and organized sport would be aroused. On the other hand, the YMCA and YWCA were also concerned about their image. They had found that their programmes gave them an inroad into government schools and groups that initially were prejudiced against Christian institutions. The associations were free to implement the gospel programme through physical culture and organized sport. It is important not to attach too great an importance to either of these aspects and yet it is important not to underestimate them either. The latter certainly had a more far-reaching effect in the long run. It was through the former that the associations first gained the confidence of others and thus made the Chinese receptive to their service programmes.

Geographically, the association's own programmes were limited to those cities where there were Association branches. It was thus available to rural areas only indirectly. The YMCA's first branch was set up in Tianjin, and from there it spread to Shanghai, Beijing, Foochow and Canton. Of the twenty-two associations in 1920, fifteen were coastal, five were located in central China, and only two were in west and south-west China. With the arrival of Exner in 1908, the Shanghai YMCA became the centre of YMCA physical-education work in China. The local programme, which was developed there between 1912 and 1917, became a model for physical work in other YMCAs.

Through personal-life teaching in the schools and hospitals and through printing presses and other institutions, the missionary became a propagator of ideals and customs associated with Western civilization. In opposition to the rights, privileges and teachings of Westerners, educated Chinese began to seek a conscious definition of their own state and nation. The Tung-meng Hui (Alliance Society), for example, was the Chinese revolutionary party founded under the leadership of Sun Yat-sen in July 1905 and had the aim of overthrowing Manchu rule. In the Republican Revolution of 1911 two of the influential leaders were Sun Yat-sen, a Christian, and Chiang Kai-shek were baptized in 1930 (Hook, 1982: 334). By 1912 more than 65 per cent of government officers in the province of Canton were Christians. A secular role was not eagerly assumed by the missionaries of the time; nor has their role in promotion of sport, exercise and physical culture in China been critically appraised by Chinese scholars. It was out of dismay for the indifference of the Chinese to the Christian message that missionaries in the nineteenth century founded schools and other institutions. The schools were considered evangelist agencies first and academic institutions second. As Holt (1989: 94) emphasizes, Christianity was one of the most important moral and intellectual forces behind the spread of sport. Sport did play a significant role in Chinese missionary schools during the last two decades of the nineteenth century and the early part of the twentieth century.

Summarizing Remarks

Sport and other forms of physical culture seems to have played an important role in the diffusion of Western cultural imperialism. Chinese sport was not simply assimilated into mainstream culture, but at times was actively marginalized and colonized by Western sporting traditions. The expansion of Western sports to China corresponded with the expansion of Western economic, social and cultural power. Western sports in China not only reproduced forms of imperialism, but also acted as a source of cultural power. In this sense, 'cultural power' may be thought of as a set of ideas, beliefs, rules and conventions concerning social behaviour carried throughout the empire by such servants as administrators, military officers, industrialists, traders, financiers, settlers and advisors of various kinds. The significance of these characteristics is that they were maintained within certain social circles and fostered within the colonial population more through systems of informal authority than through formal ones. The operation of this social power depended in part upon the ability of the imperial system to have its main social tenets accepted as appropriate forms of behaviour, being relatively accepted either by the bulk of the Chinese population or at least by sections of that population upon whom the British relied for the mediation of their ruling practices, objectives and ideology (Stoddart, 1998: 2). In the above cases, we suggested that some sectors of the local indigenous population consciously accepted Western sports as part of a cultural fantasy that reflected the power of forms of internal and external colonialism.

Sport played a role in the transmission of imperial and national ideas from the late nineteenth century. This chapter has attempted to provide an insight into some of the effects of cultural imperialism upon the development of sport and physical culture in China between at least 1860 and about 1911. It is has suggested (i) that Western sports and forms of physical culture were in part introduced to China through the agents of imperialism such as Western merchants, diplomats, teachers, soldiers and missionaries, and (ii) that while the emerging reformers of the time were receptive to Western ideology, they also tried to uphold the traditions of the Chinese Empire by promoting the adaptation of facets of Western physical culture and sport. The Western missionary-school system, the YMCA and the YWCA were not only influential in the early development of Chinese sport and physical culture, but they also served as agents of Western imperialism. This phase of development arguably lasted until the collapse of the Chinese (Manchu) Empire in 1911.

Key Readings

Blecher, Marc (1986), *China: Politics, Economics and Society*. London: Frances Pinter.

Brownell, Susan (1995), *Training the Body for China: Sport in the Moral Order of the People's Republic*. Chicago: University of Chicago Press.

Gu, Shiquan (1990), 'Introduction to Ancient and Modern Chinese Physical Culture', in H. G. Knuttgen, Q. Ma and Z. Wu (eds), *Sport in China*. Chicago: Human Kinetics: 3–24.

Hong, F. (1997), *Footbinding, Feminism and Freedom: the Liberation of Women's Bodies in Modern China*. London: Frank Cass.

Said, Edward (1993) *Culture and Imperialism*. London: Vintage.

Riordan, James and Jones, Robin (1999), *Sport and Physical Education in China*. London: E & FN Spon.

Journal Articles

Brownell, Susan (1991), 'Sport in Britain and China, 1850–1920: An Explanatory Overview', *International Journal of the History of Sport* 8(2): 284–90.

Supiot, A. (2003), 'The Labyrinth of Human Rights', *New Left Review* 21, May/June: 118–36.

Other Readings

Bickers, Robert (1999), *Britain in China: Community, Culture and Colonialism 1900–1949*. Manchester: Manchester University Press.

Blanchard, Kendall (1995), *The Anthropology of Sport: An Introduction*. Westport, CT: Greenwood.

Brownell, S. and Wasserstrom, J. (2002), *Chinese Femininities and Chinese Masculinities*. Berkeley: University of California Press.

Lutz, Jessie Gregory (1971), *China and the Christian Colleges 1850–1950*. London: Cornell University Press.

Xu, Guoqi (2008), *Olympic Dreams: China and Sports 1895–2000*. Cambridge, MA: Harvard University Press.

CHAPTER 3

Sport, Physical Culture, Nationalism and the Chinese Republic

Introduction

A further phase of development of sport and physical culture in China lasted from about 1911 until about 1949, and three important processes may be highlighted. First, the continuing influence of imperialist and patriarchal power exercised through the Young Men's Christian Association (YMCA) and the missionary school system. Western agents were requested to respect the sovereign rights of education (which included physical education and sport) in China during a period of anti-imperialism between 1919 and 1927. Second, the Chinese Nationalist Party (Kuomintang or KMT) launched a critical debate on both indigenous and Western forms of sport and physical culture between 1915 and 1937. Mao Zedong's article 'A Study of Physical Education' (*New Youth*, 1 April 1917: 66–8) informed some of the thinking about sport and physical culture during this period. Third, the defeat of the Chinese nationalists in 1949 resulted in the KMT fleeing to Taiwan. The emergence of 'Two Chinas' will be covered later in this text but several questions will be addressed in this chapter in relation to how sport developed before 1949, under early Communist control.

The Rise and Fall of the YMCA

The YMCA continued to exercise a relative degree of control over the development of physical activity and sport. From 1908 to 1911, Exner's influence proved to be the incipient beginning of a constructive programme of physical education and culture in China. Four secretaries arrived in China between 1911 and 1913 to continue this work, namely J. H. Crocker, A. H. Swan, C. A. Siler and C. H. McCloy. Crocker took over the position of national director while Swan continued to develop training programmes under the umbrella of the Shanghai YMCA. In 1912 two steps were taken to broaden the appeal of the programme. First, boxing was introduced as a core sport. It was thought that men might be willing to attend boxing classes and subsequently develop an interest in other sports such as volleyball (Swan, 1913). Second, YMCA members were entitled to sports privileges and were accommodated within the training programmes free of charge. The YMCA sports programmes increased the popularity of the movement with the typical opening hours being some ten hours a day, six days a week. By 1915, this involved some 3,000 participants per week. A 'typical day' was as follows:

9:30 am	Gym practice for Physical Director's trainees
11:00 am	Gym class for students in YMCA day school
1:00 pm	Gym class for students in YMCA day school
3:00 pm	Gym class for students in YMCA day school
4:00 pm	Boys full-members gym, bath and swim
5:15 pm	Businessmen's exercise class
5:30–7:00 pm	Swimming pool open for men
8:00–9:00 pm	Orphan boys' gym and exercise classes
9:00–9:30 pm	Evening school students' gym, bath and swim

The budget in 1916 for such a programme was $13,921. There was a constant struggle to meet operational expenses. Despite the YMCA being a service organization it did not cater for the lower class of Chinese who could not afford the costs of membership (Swan, 1916: 537–46). Growth in other YMCA Physical Education Departments was just as steady as it was in Shanghai. In 1917, there were 130,890 attending gymnasium classes; by 1918, this had increased to 229,197 and by 1922 to 725,062 (Hoh, 1926: 208–20). By 1923, the staff membership of the YMCA Physical Education Departments was estimated to be 46 full-time directors (36 of them Chinese), most of whom had a middle-school education plus a technical qualification in physical education.

To encourage the participation of boys and young men in its programme, the National Office of the YMCA Physical Education Department devised several programmes which were run on a national scale. One of the most successful was the 'Hexathlon championships' adapted from a YMCA programme developed in the United States. It involved competition among the YMCA city associations, with each association being divided into a junior and senior (aged 18 and over) division. Some of the events included: (i) 60-yard potato race, (ii) 160-yard potato race, (iii) standing broad jump, (iv) running high jump, and (v) shot put. Each city association entered as many competitors as it wished, but only recorded the six best scores in each event. Each member competed individually, with the results being forwarded to the National YMCA Office. The Hexathlon Championship began in China in 1915 and continued into the mid-1920s. By 1917, the National Committee of the YMCA of China published a 'Standard Programme for Boys' which provided five rankings for boys aged 12–20 in each of the following four categories: mental, physical, religious and social. The five physical standards were (i) health, (ii) swimming or walking, (iii) jumping, (iv) running and (v) games. By 1918, a 'Four-Fold programme' was established in which physical fitness and healthy living were included (Wu, 1956: 156). Both of these programmes viewed physical training as being an integral part of the development of a complete Christian.

The YMCA as a Christian organization was interested in the expansion of its various programmes as a means of gaining a foothold in areas and among groups that would ordinarily be closed to the influence of missionaries. This, in turn, was meant to facilitate conversion to Christianity. Had the YMCA restricted itself to programmes in its own centres, then its influence would have been limited. A relative positive factor in the YMCA's development was the freedom that its secretaries enjoyed to travel relatively free from the suspicion that often greeted locally based organizations. The YMCA became known as a coordinator and sponsor of significant athletic events. Although perhaps best known for initiating two important series of sports meetings during the Nationalist period, the National Athletic Meeting and the Far Eastern Championship Games, the YMCA spent a much greater proportion of its funds on more localized meetings.

The first YMCA sponsorship of an athletic meeting had taken place as early as 1902 in Tianjin (Wu, 1956: 96–7). At the outset, the YMCA usually fielded a team in the competitions that it had arranged with local schools. In subsequent years, however, the YMCA devoted itself increasingly to the management of meetings. In the same vein, the YMCA hosted 'athletic days' whereby people interested in a particular sport, on an informal level of competition, would come to the YMCA athletic field for several hours of recreation (*Tientsin Young Men*, 1903). During the first quarter of the century, no group other than the YMCA carried on the continuous sponsorship of small-scale athletic meetings and informal recreation through sports. This was one of the main reasons why more formal athletics on a large scale were subsequently able to develop in the Republic of China. Without these opportunities, the skills necessary for national and international competition could never have been developed.

As mentioned above, the top YMCA physical-education directors spent substantial time travelling and promoting the idea of sport. They gave many lectures throughout China, both urban and rural. Consequently, the YMCA became synonymous with sport, and when a government school or a municipal government began to think of initiating a sport programme, it was only natural for them to turn to the YMCA for advice. The YMCA was able to help in several ways. If it was a school seeking advice and it was located in the geographical area of a YMCA branch, the physical-education secretary of the branch sometimes taught a course. At other times, the YMCA supplied government schools with teachers of regular subjects from the West who, by virtue of their athletic background, were able to organize sports programmes. The YMCA was also able to supply in-service training for PE teachers in government schools.

During the 1913/14 school year, eleven schools in Shanghai sent staff members to the Shanghai YMCA once a week for PE training. From 1914 to 1916, YMCA secretaries were constantly approached to organize PE programmes in various schools, especially in Beijing and Shanghai. By 1914, the

Beijing YMCA directed PE programmes in the Beijing Union Medical College and other local schools. By 1915 the Chinese government, in conjunction with the YMCA, had decided to organize departments of Physical Education and Culture in five normal universities. The first was founded in 1915 in Nanjing, with the YMCA's Charles H. McCloy heading the department. In 1916, similar departments had been founded in Beijing, Sichuan, Wuchang, and Guangdong (Wu, 1956: 141–4).

The success of the YMCA effort in passing over the leadership of Chinese athletics to the Chinese gradually contributed to a reduction in its own influence. It was largely, if not completely, through the chain of events started by the YMCA that the Amateur Athletic Union and National Amateur Athletic Federation were founded. As these organizations gained in strength, they gradually took over control of domestic physical education and sport that had once been the province of the YMCA. Thus the YMCA, which had gained so much of its status as an organizer of athletic meets, lost a primary source of influence.

The Anti-Christian Movement

Although the Anti-Christian Movement and the Restore Education Rights campaigns emerged in the 1920s, the core of Chinese nationalism remained anti-imperialist and anti-capitalist. Chinese intellectuals tended to define China in terms of what it was not. What they generally agreed upon was that China was not a China of simply one strong sporting tradition, nor was it to be simply a replica of the West. Though many aspects of Western civilization were considered essential to the new China, China as a nation was being defined in contrast to Western civilization, nation-states and ideologies. For a number of Chinese intellectuals, the rejection of Christianity was part of the process of defining China, as well as part of the search for a blueprint for China. There were two movements, one directed against Christianity and one directed against the mission schools, both of which expressed Chinese nationalist sentiments during the 1920s. One of the effects of Chinese nationalism was that the YMCA's work on sport declined. In the final analysis, thereafter, it was the times themselves which drew the curtain on YMCA influence in China. Anti-foreign, anti-Christian and anti-imperialist feelings began to grow across China during the mid-1920s.

The YMCA, with its national offices in Shanghai, suffered accordingly. With the establishment of the Nationalist government in 1927/28, provincial and national physical education institutes began to be established in large numbers, while at the same time the private control of physical education and sport by groups such as the YMCA was discouraged (Wu, 1956: 178). With the return of J. H. Gray (leader of the YMCA, 1920–1927) to the United States in 1927, the YMCA ceased its active role as being an agent in the formation of Chinese physical education, and an era was brought to an end. During this stage, the

YMCA had been one of the most influential institutions in the incipient development of physical culture and sport in China. This does not mean that all Chinese could recognize the efforts of Western missionaries to develop facets of Chinese physical culture and sport. As argued in the last chapter, the YMCA and missionary schools' role was as partial agents of forms of Western imperialism that enhanced Western culture and ideals. The introduction of Marxism during the second decade of the twentieth century and the emergence of the May Fourth Movement contributed to the first Cultural Revolution in modern Chinese history. Through this movement, Chinese people reconsidered their own national identity and cultural reform. A number of scholars discussed the importance of sport, but the debates on developing military training or physical education in schools and developing Western or Chinese indigenous sport were also now and essential part of the dialogue surrounding the development of physical culture and sport in China. They both were about to experience the impact of a particular form of nationalism.

Sport and the Chinese Republic

The development of sport from 1911 was not isolated from the military, economic, political and social change that characterized the period. The period from 1911 to 1927 was transformative, during which time the country became fragmented and ruled by a number of regional military dictators or warlords. The first Chinese Republic was established in 1912 but had collapsed by 1916. National government ceased to exist. Throughout China, warlords carved out autonomous districts with their own armies and tax systems. These warlords were involved in a series of land wars. Dr Sun Yet-Sen reorganized the Chinese Nationalist Party (Kuomintang or KMT) and established a power base in southern China with the support of several local warlords in Canton. Sun set up the Whampoa Military Academy and appointed Chiang Kai-Shek as its superintendent. By 1925, the KMT had begun a military campaign against the warlords north of the capital of Beijing, thereby uniting the nation under Nationalist rule. There remained external problems and tensions resulting from the extension of Japanese imperialism and the continuing influence of Western imperialism. The May Fourth Movement of 1919 and the May Thirtieth Incident of 1925, two of the most important historical events in the development of early Chinese nationalism, were effectively protests against both Japanese and Western imperialism. These events not only strengthened Chinese nationalism but also influenced critical debates about the nature and development of sport. It is necessary in the first instance to briefly comment upon the impetus for Chinese nationalism.

Chinese Nationalism

Modern Chinese nationalism came of age on 4 May 1919, when more than 3,000 college students from a dozen institutions in Beijing endorsed a manifesto denouncing the decision of the Paris Peace Conference to transfer Germany's rights in Shantung Province to Japan. The student demonstration of 4 May erupted into violent action that brought police repression, but the students' patriotic example inspired similar demonstrations in other major centres by the merchant class, other patriots and students. May Fourth was a milestone in the growth of incipient Chinese nationalism. Marxism at the time challenged any subsequent interest in the West and Western notions of democracy, science and modernization. This was partially due to the impact of the October Russian Revolution of 1917. During this period an organic political division between the Nationalists and Communists manifested itself. The May Fourth Movement is often cited in relation to the New Culture Movement in Modern China. The notion implies an attempt to destroy what remained of the traditional Confucian culture of the Republican era and to replace it with something new, such as Enlightenment from the West. The collapse of the old dynastic system in 1911 and the failure of Yuan Shih-kai's Confucian-garbed monarchical restoration in 1916 meant that politically the power of Confucianism had weakened. However, it had been much more than a political philosophy in that for many it had been a complete way of life, which Nationalism and Republicanism only supplanted in part. There were some Republicans who felt that aspects of the old culture, Confucian ethics especially, should be preserved and strengthened, lest the whole fabric of Chinese life fall apart and the new regime itself be seriously weakened. Others, with far more influence on the younger generation, drew precisely the opposite conclusion. For them nothing in Confucianism was worth salvaging from the debris of the Manchu dynasty, the argument being that whatever vestiges of the past remained in daily life needed to be rooted out, otherwise the young republic would rest on a shaky philosophical and political foundation and its progress would be retarded by an ill-informed citizenry. The new order required a whole new culture, and thus political revolution had to be followed by a cultural revolution.

During and just after the First World War the intellectual spearhead of this second revolution went on the offensive, launching a movement that reached out in many directions and touched many aspects of Chinese society. Initially it may be considered as involving six major phases in more or less chronological order: (i) the attack on Confucianism; (ii) the Literary Revolution; (iii) the proclaiming of a new philosophy of life; (iv) the debate on science and the philosophy of life; (v) the 'doubting of the antiquity' movement; and (vi) the debate about Chinese and Western cultural values. These aspects of an emerging Chinese politics and culture overlapped one another considerably and certain leading writers figured prominently in more than one phase of the movement. Sport featured in the debates about Chinese and Western cultural values.

From their anti-traditionalist character one may infer that the leaders of the movement looked very much to the West. Positivism was an inspiration, while science and materialism were their great slogans. Writers and thinkers such as John Dewey and Bertrand Russell proved to be influential. The leaders themselves were in many cases Western-educated, though not necessarily schooled in the West, since Western-style education had by now been established in the East, in Japan and in the new national and missionary colleges of China. Above all, they had a new audience, young, intense, frustrated by China's failures in the past, and full of eager hopes for the future.

Sport, Nationalism and the Nationalist Government

The development of sport and physical culture may not have been a mainstream political concern but, between about 1912 and 1945, forms of nationalism and nationalist thinking impacted upon national sport, physical culture and traditional sport in China in a number of different ways.

Nationalism and Military Training

During the early stages of the Chinese Republic, nationalism was more or less the only panacea in the Chinese imagination powerful enough to save the nation from imperialism. Chinese intellectuals regularly raised debates about military training and the need to develop a martial spirit in the interests of the nation. Militarism was a core concept driving the development of physical culture and education in schools. There were divergent points of view about the nature of this activity. Xu Yibing argued that military training must be abolished in schools because the context of military exercise, such as attention, at ease, fall-in, trail arms, sling arms and shoulder arms, failed to inspire the majority of students (Hsu, 1996: 13). Training courses were standardised at all levels within the school. Military training teachers were attacked as soldiers who had lower levels of education than other teachers.

In one of Dewey's speeches given at Nanking University in 1919, the philosopher claimed that

> [m]ass physical education development is the most urgent problem for every country today. Can China approach this mission? It is better to improve personal and mass hygiene, teach a knowledge of physical education in society rather than focus on military education and military training which only applies to military schools... (*Physical Culture Weekly*, 23 June 1919: 6–7)

Dewey's thoughts had influenced a number of intellectuals on the nature and purpose of military exercise in schools. Hu Shih, one of the principal leaders in both the May Fourth Movement and the New Culture Movement, as a student was influenced by Dewey's ideas, which were often in contrast to the solutions offered by Marxism. On account of Dewey's visiting lectures covering eleven provinces in China from 1919 to 1921, this specific philosophy of pragmatism was recognized as one of the influential Western ideas imported into modern China.

Dewey believed that education was necessary for democratic citizenship, social efficiency and social experience. He considered mind and body to be integrated parts of the human whole and that the body or physical aspects of humans served as the conductor of experience. The philosophical position of the body relative to epistemological considerations and the nature of our existence became an important issue, since Dewey believed play to be purposeful activity that directed interest through physical means. Play was not a physical act that had no meaning. Rather it was an activity that integrated mind and body. The philosophy of Dewey was used to justify team sports in physical-education programmes because they allegedly promoted democratic activities and social interaction. The societal benefits derived from participation in physical education were very significant and did much to ensure strong support for physical education and athletics in China (Mechikoff and Estes, 1998: 240–1).

Neither Dewey nor his student Hu Shih considered the problem of imperialism and nationalism in China. Under the trends of anti-militarism and anti-military drills, one physical-education teacher, Chang Bao-chen, held an opinion different from that of the majority of intellectuals on the issues of the day. Chang argued that while Dewey's suggestion for democratic education of the masses and socialism was fine for China, Chinese people were unable to pick themselves up at that moment. Therefore, the Chinese needed military education to discipline themselves. Chang doubted that Western ideas of democracy could satisfactorily bring about human happiness and well-being. He argued:

Why don't the English give freedom to India? Why cannot Koreans be independent after the peace conference at Versailles? Why don't colonial countries donate some of the pervading benevolence to indigenous people in their colonies instead of carrying on a punitive campaign and slavery? What are colonists thinking and doing about their colonies today? While Europeans advocate humanism, their humanism is merely for strong nations, not for weak nations in the world. If we abolish military drill in schools, we are giving up our defence power and binding up our own body ... recently, a lot of scholars insist on abolishing military drill and building up formal physical education. Their reasons for abolishing military drill in schools are (i) military drill is mechanical, partial, forced with no freedom of speech; and (ii) military drill is incompatible with the human body physically and psychologically. However, what kind of sport is 'formal physical education'? If military drill is mechanical, forced and disciplined, then I want to emphasis that gymnastics has rules and words of command, hasn't it? If military drill is partial, then I wish to illustrate that sport is not partial to the human body ... Military drill is only 1–2 hours in a school curriculum, it will not affect a student's physical development. Therefore, in my view, if China wants to progress on physical education, it should improve the methods and context of physical education ... It is not necessary to debate the problem of military drill. (*Physical Culture Weekly*, 24 November 1919: 5–8)

Chang was one of the very few educators who supported military drill in schools, not only because China needed militarism to strengthen itself, but also because the world as he saw it was dominated by forms of imperialism. Chang argued that improving physical education and abolishing military drill were different issues. If Chinese physical educators wanted to reform physical education in schools, they should focus on teaching the methods and the context of physical education and organized sport. Chang was one of the earliest Chinese educators to make the political link between physical culture and imperialism.

The debate on militarism was further complicated by one of the founders of Chinese physical education. Xu argued in 1920 that

As early as 1904 and 1905, revolutionary thinking among the people had been spreading by the day ... everyone said that without a martial education it would not be enough to save the nation from extinction. So in school ticao [callisthenics and gymnastics] classes, martial spirit was established as the main goal, and military-style callisthenics became the standard. But with this trend came a multitude of corrupt practices, with young, average, unintelligent, immoral soldiers coming right out of the barracks and in one swoop becoming teachers, ineffective and not worth a damn. These are people that do not even know what a professor is or where a school is, excessive drinkers and mad gamblers, who love to fight like wolves and for whom nothing would be below. Not a year goes by that the schools' reputation is not soiled, that society's faith is not lost, that students and their fathers and brothers do not hate ticao classes even more, to the point now where it is seen as poison. (*Physical Culture Weekly Special Edition*, 5 January 1920: 61–6)

In Xu's view, military-style callisthenics were not suitable for the school curriculum, not only because of the context of military callisthenics, but also because of what in his view were unintelligent and immoral soldier-teachers in the schools. Some historians (Hsu, 1996: 100–3; Gu, 1989: 114 and 175) have explained anti-military callisthenics as merely the logical result of a Western 'tide of thought' brought to China by the modernist May Fourth Movement of 1919, or a reaction to the First World War defeat suffered by Germany which was seen as a failing symbol of militarism in China. The discussion above drawing upon Dewey's pragmatism, physical education and the concern over military callisthenics has illustrated that such developments were not divorced from the political and social concerns of the time. The debates about physical education military callisthenics and physical culture were not the only facets of culture to be influenced by the period since the very nature of indigenous sport in China was also a concern.

Nationalism and Indigenous Sports

Ancient Chinese physical culture consisted of a large number of different selected activities and events. The relationship between Chinese nationalism and martial arts and Jingzuo (to sit still with a peaceful mind or to sit as a form of therapy) needs to be commented upon. 'Martial arts' is an English translation of several classical Chinese terms adapted to Japanese language and culture. The terms came to Europe and America primarily from Japan, not China. This was in part because of the high level of development of martial-arts culture in Japan and its subsequent migration, as well as a greater Western familiarity with the Japanese selection of tradition. In China, the English term 'martial art' was introduced from Japan in the early part of the twentieth century. Chinese martial arts, currently known as *wushu* or *guoshu* (national arts), were in earlier times called *wuyong* (military valour) or *wuyi* (military skill). Both Japanese pronunciation 'bu' and Chinese pronunciation 'Wu' use the same character, which is commonly translated as 'martial' or 'military'. Traditionally, Chinese martial arts were a form of military training or military sports. Generally speaking, the Chinese used the term 'martial arts' relative to a fighting system in Chinese culture. Historically Chinese martial-arts exercise was prohibited in civil society during the alien dynasties.

There seems to be a certain degree of agreement among Chinese historians concerning why Chinese martial arts may have been seen to reflect a high degree of Chinese nationalism and religious culture before the twentieth century: (i) that martial arts was a form of Chinese cultural nationalism; (ii) that martial arts was an informal form of religious Buddhism and Taoism; (iii) that martial arts aroused the imagination of Chinese nationalism; (iv) that martial-arts exercise was a traditional gathering for subordinate classes; (v) that martial arts was a core part of Chinese traditional physical culture; (vi) that martial arts was a kind of physical, spiritual and mental training; and (vii) that martial arts was not in any sense scientific.

During the early period of the Chinese Republic, promoting martial spirit was one of the aims of education (*San Pao*, 5 April 1915: 6–7). In 1915, the Ministry of Education proposed that military education should be put into effect. All schools were to teach traditional Chinese martial arts and martial-arts teachers were to be educated at teacher-training schools (*San Pao*, 30 May 1915: 3). A proposal for promoting traditional Chinese martial arts as a gymnastic course in schools was introduced to inspire people's martial spirit. Thus, in 1915, it was recognized that

> [the] world is dominated by social Darwinism. People shall have a martial spirit in order to struggle for their country. China has promoted her martial spirit and has added gymnastic exercises in the tri-balance of education on wisdom, morality and the body over the last two decades. Today the Chinese people are still weak after learning from Western forms of education. The traditional Chinese martial arts are

over thousands of years old. Therefore, it is necessary to promote traditional Chinese martial arts that are more suitable for the Chinese people. All schools shall put martial arts in the gymnastic courses. (*San Pao*, 31 May 1915: 3)

Most Chinese educators still thought of gymnastics courses as 'physical education'. This was the first time that martial arts were promoted as part of the school curriculum. Chinese martial-arts teaching methods had changed from traditional individual teaching to group teaching which stipulated instructional command and movement.

A number of martial-arts societies were organized after 1915. The Jingwu Physical Culture Society was the largest and most popular Chinese martial-arts society that spread through China and south-east Asia from 1917 to 1929. In 1929 there were forty-two branches and over 400,000 members. The Jingwu Physical Culture Society was the first sports society to combine Western and Chinese physical culture, which taught not only Chinese martial arts and military training but also Western sports such as gymnastics exercise, athletics, football, basketball, volleyball, tennis and swimming. The headquarters of the Jingwu Physical Culture Society in Shanghai was destroyed twice by the Japanese invasions of 1932 and 1937 because of its sympathies for Chinese patriotism and anti-Japanese imperialism (National Research Institute of Martial Arts, 1996: 335; Gu, 1989: 273).

Although martial-arts development was part of the school education curriculum as early as 1915, critical debates about the nature and influence of indigenous and Western sports were raised by the New Culture Movement. Chen Tu-hsiu, one of the Chinese Communist Party's founders and editor of a magazine *New Youth*, led the assault on Confucianism which began in 1916. He compared the individual in society to the cell in a body. Its birth and death are transitory. New ones replace the old. This, he argued, is as it should be and need not be feared at all. In one of his articles, he criticized the objectives of the classical feudal education system for over-emphasizing literary memorizing and neglecting physical exercise. Thus, he advocated the tri-balance of wisdom, morality and the body. In this sense, his idea was similar to that of Yen Fu. Although Chen Tu-Hsiu argued that a student's physical strength is one of the essential elements in the present educational policy (*New Youth*, 15 October 1915: 128–32), he disagreed about putting martial arts in the school curriculum because of his support for anti-traditionalism and anti-militarism. His view was that sport should contain no martial drill, no boxing and no violent competitive games (*New Youth*, 1 January 1920: 319).

Another anti-martial-arts writer, Lu Xun, argued that the propaganda of traditional Chinese sport was based on superstition, feudalism and anti-science. Lu said

I do not mind if some people think martial arts is a special skill and enjoy their own practice. This is not a big matter. However, I disagree with the propaganda of traditional Chinese martial arts because educators promote martial arts as a fashion, as if all Chinese people should do the exercise, and most advocators promote martial arts in a ghost-like spirit. This social phenomenon is dangerous. (*New Youth*, 15 February 1919: 241–4)

In Lu's view, over-emphasizing the orthodox function of Chinese martial arts might promote patriotism and give rise to a movement similar to that of the Boxer Rebellions in 1900.

Quiet Sports and Active Sports

The debates about Chinese martial arts were essentially between what Lu viewed as 'quiet sport' and 'active sport'. 'Active sport' was seen as physical activities such as gymnastics, swimming, ball games, and athletics. There is no clear definition of 'quiet sport', but it generally referred to a kind of traditional Chinese breathing exercise – *Jingzuo* (sitting in silence or meditation) means to sit still with a peaceful mind or to sit as a form of therapy. In ancient China, Jingzuo was often combined with Buddhism, Taoism and Zen. Some physical-culture intellectuals promoted Jingzuo as a form of national legacy.

One such Jingzuo supporter was Huang Xing who was the founder of *Physical Culture Weekly* (*Tiyu Chou Pao*) 1918–1920. Huang emphasized the reasons why he promoted 'quiet sport':

The first reason is that quiet sport made people's minds clear. Especially today there are only about sixty to seventy percent of physical educators' minds that are pure in China ... The first condition of quiet sport is to curb one's temper and desire. If one can take away his/her temper and desire, then certainly his/her mind will be clear. (*Physical Culture Weekly*, 24 February 1919: 2–3)

Later, Huang argued:

Over the last decade or more, sports development has not been successful ... there are many complicated reasons. The major reason is that most leaders are not interested in physical culture in our society ... A healthy mind is based on a healthy body. Now everyone considers that it is necessary to advocate physical culture and a number of people have searched for the method of promoting physical culture. However, except in developed provinces, most people still do not know anything about the completed proposal of the Physical Culture Promotion Plan over the last six months ... This obstacle is from the old custom of Chinese society that thought that those leaders must enjoy high rank and live in ease and comfort. Therefore, those leaders do not want to do physical exercise that will affect their high rank's status ... They also misunderstand that physical culture merely belongs to military men. As a result, quiet sport is very suitable for individuals and leaders. (*Physical Culture Weekly*, 3 March 1919: 2–3)

According to Huang, most physical educators needed quiet sport in order to facilitate clear minds. Leaders needed quiet sport to help change individual minds and should therefore support and promote quiet sport. Huang's idea of quiet sport was an exercise to make soul-searching an essential part of sports development for physical educators and social leaders in China. Huang explained that Jingzuo was a kind of exercise to cultivate people's physical and mental capabilities. He pointed out that the four essentials of Jingzuo were (i) posture, (ii) breathing, (iii) avoiding closed eyes and sleep, and (iv) the prevention and treatment of diseases (*Physical Culture Weekly*, 26 January 1920: 2–3; 2 February 1920: 2–3). Jingzuo was popular in eighteen provinces and rural areas during this period. One of its advocators, Jiang Wei-qiao, was a teacher at Beijing University where Jiang's studies on the method of Jingzuo were reprinted more than fourteen times in a period of not more than four years (Hsu, 1996: 235).

Other intellectuals raised different views on Jingzuo. Lu Xun argued that children and youth needed more physical activities than sitting in silence. Lu criticized Jingzuo as not being scientific and causing passive thinking. An article published in 1920 complained that:

[after] eight years of the 1911 Revolution, education, economics and politics have shown no progress and are even worse than before ... but only two things show progress – poker and Jingzuo. Except for proper labour, everyone is skilled in the field of poker and Jingzuo in China today. (*Physical Culture Weekly Special Edition*, 5 January 1920: 109)

During the New Culture Movement Jingzuo was blamed not only for being passive but also for being a symbol of traditionalism. Martial arts or Jingzuo is a kind of traditional Chinese physical exercise that has a particular set of cultural values. Among those critics of the New Culture Movement, no matter whether they were anti-traditionalist or anti-Confucianist, there were also those who supported and advocated Chinese indigenous physical culture. They all acknowledged that China must strengthen the nation and race through physical culture. Chinese people, it was argued, needed more physical exercise to strengthen themselves and save their nation from the threat of imperialism. After these decades of critical debates about the influence of Western and Chinese culture, Western sport continued to influence indigenous development. The arrival of Western sport forced the Chinese to reassess selected martial traditions. Chinese martial arts both absorbed and resisted methods of Western culture and, through scientific study, made improvements in teaching, competition and games. In the 1920s, the influence of Western physical culture led to a standardization of competition and regulations in Chinese martial arts. The first national martial-arts games were held in 1923 in Shanghai. Martial arts continued to play a significant role in the development of Chinese nationalism and sport after the Chinese Nationalist Party reunified most of China in 1928.

Nationalism and Physical Education

The formation of the Nanking Government in October 1928 brought with it an entirely new era in nationalist thinking about physical education, physical culture and sports. Physical training became a key concern of government, and the emphasis shifted to introducing legislation that would provide for physical education and sport. The research here will focus upon three aspects: (i) the government's drive to promote sports as a facet of education in schools; (ii) the ways in which government used sports in schools to promote feelings of nationalism and patriotism; and (iii) the continuing influence of Western imperialism.

The German-Japanese military tradition which was to dominate Chinese thinking about PE at the beginning of the century did not go unopposed. However, The National Athletic Meetings of 1901 and 1914, and the Far Eastern Championships, held in Shanghai in 1915, served further to introduce Western sports to many Chinese young people. Gradually, sport was incorporated into the curriculum of all Chinese government schools. A twin-track school physical-education system was developed in which military exercises were stressed in class time and Western sports dominated the after-school curriculum. Between 1910 and 1920, there was a growth of PE-teacher training schools. The Chinese government and the YMCA jointly developed physical-education departments in five higher normal schools. In 1915, the YWCA established a two-year physical-training course for women that by 1925 had become part of Ginling College in Nanking (*China Mission Yearbook*, 1925: 292–3).

As the 1920s approached, the Japanese influence in education started to wane as American influences increased while progressive Chinese educators at the same time began to pay more attention to the role of sport. At the Fourth Annual Conference of the National Federation of Educational Associations in 1928, it was suggested that men and women be sent abroad to study PE and that courses in the subject be required in all normal government schools. The conference recommended the establishment of PE associations in all provinces and municipalities. In order to extend the impact of military training, it called for boxing, fencing, and physical drill to be a compulsory part of the school experience. The Ministry of Education endorsed these recommendations (Speak, 1932: 83–4).

As Chiang Kai-shek progressed toward the unification of China during 1927 and 1928, sport for the first time began to receive formal legislative government attention. The changes introduced established total official government control over sport in the school curriculum. The first step in this process took place in December 1927 when the University Council – which had been created in 1927 – established a National PE Committee. It was composed of well-known athletes and specialists in PE whose collective aim was to promote physical culture on a large scale. The Committee was largely ineffectual, partly because its members were spread throughout China and it could not easily be convened, and consequently it was abandoned in 1928 (Wu, 1962: 344–9; *Chinese Yearbook* 1935/36, Chapter I: 543–4).

In May 1928, the University Council convened the First National Educational Conference. The outstanding resolution of this conference was that education would conform to the Three People's Principles of Sun Yat-sen. The two-week conference resolved 'to promote nationalism and that education should seek ... to raise the general level of moral integrity and physical vigour of the people ...' (*China Yearbook*, 1929/30: 521). The third point of the conference's 15-point resolution noted the importance of 'stressing the training of national physical strength' (Wu, 1962: 325–30). The Three People's Principles – People's Nationhood, People's Power, and People's Livelihood, or Nationalism, Democracy and Socialism (or Communism) (Chien, 1970: 112–15; Sharman 1968: 271–300) – were concerned in part with stimulating a national spirit, a spirit of sacrifice and a sense of discipline. The Kuomintang wanted to marginalize individualism and help to promote activities that would forge group consciousness. They paradoxically supported the elitist ideology of athleticism. They endorsed the idea by encouraging people to work together and to learn to endure physical hardship through physical training and athletics in order that a national sense of unity might be forged. It was hoped that strengthening the body would increase the intellectual capacity of the nation.

The Three People's Principles PE programme was developed in order to

- emphasize training of character and disposition
- advocate military PE
- expand mass PE
- advocate PE for women
- stress development for physical toil and intellectual thought
- contribute to family life, education and aesthetic education (Wang, 1967: 104–11).

The National Physical Education Law of April 1929 enforced the Nationalist Government's ideas in the area of sport and physical culture. It can be argued that it was the first step taken by the nationalist government toward the formal institutionalization of sport in schools. At least three processes – codification, organization and legitimization – can be mentioned. As Gruneau argues:

Codification simply refers to the process whereby sports pastimes have gone from informal regulation by local and, in many cases, oral traditions, to a system based on written rules that have a more universal acceptance. The emergence of modern sport is often said to have been dependent on a movement from local variations in rules, games, and styles of play to more universal and widely accepted practices. Formal organizations, such as clubs, leagues, or national associations, have been the primary vehicles for this transformation. The codification of rules required the establishment of formal bodies that could act as the custodians of sports regulations and provide 'proper' channels for their modification. It was also necessary for those organizations to legitimise particular practices in an attempt to build public support for particular ways of playing. (Gruneau, 1988: 14)

The law was amended in September 1941, but its main provisions, as ratified by the Legislative Yuan (administrative body) and presented in their entirety below, remained in effect until 1949. The 1929 National Physical Education Law stated that:

- The young men and women of the Chinese Republic have a responsibility to be the recipients of PE and parents or guardians have the responsibility of enforcing it.
- The aims of PE are to bring about orderly development, suitable health, as well as physical power and the power to resist, together with the growth of all faculties of the body so as to be able to endure every type of labour and exceptionally telling tasks.
- In planning PE programmes, whether for boys or girls, age and individual bodily strengths and weaknesses must be paid attention to; its management and methods should follow the declarations of the Training Commissioner's Department and the Ministry of Education.
- All customs and habits which hinder regular growth of the bodies of young men and young women should be strictly prohibited by the administrative organs of counties, municipalities, town, villages and hamlets and its programme should be fixed by the Ministry of Education Committee and the Training Commissioner's Department.
- Each self-governing hamlet, village, town and municipality must erect public sports grounds.
- Schools at the upper middle school level and above must all establish PE as a required subject and must, at the same time, comply with the previously announced military PE programme.
- All PE committees established among the people must be registered under the supervision of the local government, and make application to the Ministry of the Interior, and consult with the Training Commissioner's Department. However, those people who are serving the people's PE in scientific research and in investigation of teaching materials are not bound by this limitation. In matters of budget, all PE authorities should be closely controlled by the local government that must watch its financial situation and call in higher government control bodies to help it in making decisions.
- PE organized in each county, municipality, village, town, and hamlet must accept the control of local government and be under that organization which controls education.
- All PE personnel responsible for school or people's PE committees must have proper credentials. The regulations regarding the nature of the credentials are to be fixed by the Training Commissioner's Office.
- All PE personnel who have served for three years or more in good standing

should be given suitable rewards by the Training Commissioner's Department, with the Department to work out details.

- The Training Commissioner's Department should set up a special high level physical education committee to deal with the research findings of special organizations and to examine foreign situations so as to serve the objective of people's physical education.
- All physical education groups must inject group traits into the government programme.
- This law takes effect from the day on which it is issued (Wang, 1967: 100–1; Wu, 1981: 115–16).

The KMT, the government of the nationalists, saw sport as a means of developing a national spirit of unity which would enable China to emerge as a modern state and defend itself. The 1929 law stressed the need for national control of sport. The phrase 'group traits' mentioned in article 12 refers to the national feeling of oneness that the KMT hoped to foster. Article 4 addressed itself to the need to work against traditional attitudes that would undermine attempts at a successful sport programme. Articles 5–12 showed that the government monopolized national sports organizations and school physical education. Sport was said to function as a vehicle for political socialization (helping to forge particular ways of thinking and behaving) that reflected and reinforced the value preferences and beliefs of the ruling elites. Government sport programmes and legislation can be seen to be representative of official nationalist interests. In compliance with the 1929 Law, many provincial and municipal educational administrative bodies (e.g. Beijing, Shanghai, Shantung, Hupei, Ankwei, Chekiang and Kansu) began to establish physical education committees staffed by sport specialists (Wu, 1962: 325–30).

From the 1932 National Physical Education and Culture Conference there emerged more than 280 resolutions among which was a statement of the broad aims of physical education and sport, together with recommendations for specific actions that should be taken to achieve these broad goals. It was decided (i) that people must receive sufficient opportunity to develop their bodies; (ii) that they be trained to exercise in order to adapt to external conditions; (iii) that the spirit of cooperation and unity be cultivated together with courage, endurance, and nationalism through physical education and sport; and (iv) that the habit of participating in sport as recreation be developed among the people. Most of the progressive steps taken in this area during the next few years resulted from the resolutions of this Conference. These included the appointment of a national Director of Physical Education and an advisory committee; the organization of physical-education committees within provincial bureaux of education and municipal boards of education; the sponsorship of in-service summer school sessions by the Ministry of Education; the planning of physical-education curricula for primary and middle schools; the government to control and organize a series of National Athletic Meetings and support for annual meetings to be provided in all the provinces, counties and municipalities (*Chinese Yearbook*, 1935/36: 542).

The National Government, Athletic Meetings and War

Following the completion of the 1924 National Athletic Meeting, plans were made to hold a further meeting in Canton in 1926. The civil war in China delayed these plans with the result that only four meetings were held between 1924 and 1930. The surrogate government agency, The China National Amateur Athletic Federation, was responsible for the meetings. The provincial government also took an active part and provided a budget of between $100,000 of the $260,000. The Chinese took complete charge of directing and organizing this event. Chinese schools also took an increasing part in the meet as the majority of athletes came from Chinese government schools (*North China Herald*, 8 April 1930: 45). Chinese government leaders were impressed with the potential that the event had for fostering feelings of national unity among youth and took steps to put its control under the Ministry of Education. The Ministry set up an organizing committee, and voted to hold the fifth meet in Nanking, in 1931. The Mukden Incident, in which the Japanese invaded Manchuria, forced it to be delayed until 1933. Both the fifth and the sixth (in 1935) National Athletic Meetings were run by the Chinese government. The previously unmatched scope of the meets, and the money spent on making them a success in times of increasing national tension, seem to indicate an effort on the part of the government to enhance morale and convey a feeling of normality.

President Wang Ching-wei expressed the government's feelings about the national meetings in formal terms at the 1933 opening ceremony when he stated that

[in] the present-day world the struggle for survival depends not only on human energy but also on the utilization of material forces. That China at the present moment needs more adequate material resources there can be no doubt whatsoever, but this utilization of material forces depends essentially on the vigour of the human spirit. We can utilize these forces only when we are in healthful spirits, otherwise we shall be simply utilized by them instead. A healthy mind always dwells in a healthy body. With a sound body, one can carry on any struggle to the finish, and not give up midway, but an unswerving spirit in an unhealthy body cannot lead us to ultimate victory. In this lies the significance of athletics. Though in past athletic meets the training and health as well as the skill of our students have been amply demonstrated, yet, according to the reports of the Ministry of Education, the number of Senior Middle School graduates who are able to fulfil the requirements of the military physical examination is still not very large. The reasons for this state of affairs are manifold, but neglect of sports is one of the chief causes. My hope for the present National Athletic Meet is that the occasion may reveal both our strong and weak points in the matter of physical health, in order

that we may promote the former and rectify the latter. The aim of the athletes present today should be not merely to win personal honours, but more especially to contribute towards the strengthening of the country and the race. To impart this new spirit, this desire to fortify the country and the race, to the masses of the people, is therefore the primary aim of the National Athletic Meet. Over 100,000 are present at this Meet today, and I hope that every one of them will become strong and healthy, so that they may with greater advantage share the responsibility of overcoming the national crisis. (Tang, 1935: 104)

The 1933 meet attracted 2,248 athletes (including 706 women) from thirty-three provinces and municipalities, including athletes from the provinces of Manchuria. For the occasion, the country's largest steel-and-concrete sports arena was constructed, near the Ming Tombs, at a cost of around $1.5 million. Some 300,000 spectators filled the stadium during the ten days of competition. They were joined by over 300 newspaper correspondents and 100 photographers from 134 newspapers and agencies, as well as several film companies. Management of the event by China's top sports administrators – Po-ling Chang, C. T. Wang, Gunsun Hoh, and Shou-yi Tung – ensured a smooth completion (Wu, 1956: 183–5).

Although the seventh meeting had been planned for 1937 in Nanking, the Marco Polo Bridge Incident and the subsequent Japanese occupation meant the postponement of this meeting until May 1938, when it was held in Shanghai (Wu, 1962: 186). Chiang Kai-shek apparently used this meet as a show of strength for his government. Although he was able to secure fifty-eight teams (more than 2,000 athletes) from provinces, municipalities, overseas Chinese and the military, the attendance was only about 10 per cent of that of the sixth meeting in 1935 (Wu, 1962: 424–5).

China's sport suffered setbacks during the period of confrontation with Japan (1937–1945). The Nationalist government, because it saw sport as a means of strengthening the people, continued to give its support throughout this period. In 1937, the Physical Education Committee of the Ministry of Education was responsible for the coordination of all matters dealing with physical education, the Boy Scouts, hygiene education and student military training. The early 1940s were years in which the Physical Education Committee was actively trying to plan for the future. At the same time, it had to take into account the limitations imposed upon it by the war. In October 1940, the Second National Physical Education Conference was held in Chungking with the emphasis on deciding upon a national PE programme sensitive to China's war needs. It was not until the 1940s that the Nationalist government took its first effective step toward enforcing its new PE directives. In 1940, the Ministry of Education published the official methods of athletic skills and bodily growth. Testing groups were sent to schools to examine weight, height, bodily development, and athletic skills. The China National Amateur Athletic Federation made an effort to continue with its programmes during the war years. Beginning in 1941, it co-operated with the referee's associations and formed branches in rural areas. In 1943, there were 12 branches of the Federation in the provinces, counties and municipalities, and nine referee associations. The China National Amateur Athletic Federation remained active in China until 1949 and thereafter continued its work in Taiwan (Wu, 1962: 337–40).

The development of sport in China during the period 1928–1949 is complex. Western and Japanese imperialism continued to influence China. The KMT government ruled over China in name, but not in fact, with the Japanese controlling some areas and Nationalists and Communists other areas. The country was divided politically. This element of disunity drained the already weak potential for sporting development. Instead of developing a unified administrative command that could tap into China's reservoirs of athletic power and establish a central physical-education institute to train the badly needed leadership, each faction was left to fend for itself. Teachers reflected Japanese, German and American influences. But no influence was sufficiently evident to establish the basis of a lasting tradition (Kolatch, 1972: 50). Eichberg (1973) has argued that physical exercise did not become a mass movement until the beginning of the nineteenth century, when its association with nationalism was a result of the achievement motive common to both sports and nationalism. In China, physical training was pursued for the goal of helping establish a new healthy state. The linkage of physical culture with the strength of the state is ancient and strong with modern sport and modern nationalism simply giving it a new twist. This link is a natural result of the fact that victory in sports can symbolize physical and natural dominance. The control and ordering of physical bodies in time and space was the goal in establishing a new regime, and sport and physical education provided a potent metaphor for the process (Brownell, 1991: 284–90). Although Chiang Kai-shek tried to unify a country in which control was shared from time to time and place to place by the Nationalists, the Japanese, and Mao's Communists, his efforts deteriorated into a brutal and bitterly anti-Communist dictatorship. Chiang tried for a unified national sports programme modelled on that of the early social democratic republic, but in a chaotic situation in which 'the vast majority of Chinese had not only never participated in regular sports but had never even been to school' (Kolatch, 1972: 50), his efforts rarely got far beyond formal resolutions and bureaucratic structures.

Sport and Early Communism

The Chinese Communist Party (CCP), founded in Shanghai in 1921, began its quest for revolution among China's proletariat. This was the terrain prescribed by Marx's own works, and its revolutionary potential had been confirmed by the Bolshevik revolution in the Soviet Union. Because of a combination of its own newness, the formidability of the fluid and confusing political situation in China and advice from the Soviet Union, the Party entered into a 'united-front' agreement with the KMT in the early 1920s. At the time it remained the leading revolutionary force in the country with the agreement further reducing the need for the CCP to expend its energies on forming its own military organization. Many of its members joined the KMT army, often as political commissars. The alliance allowed it to concentrate its early efforts on organizing unions and strikes. The united-front strategy was sensible for the new party so long as the KMT leadership remained pluralistic and reliable, with Soviet aid helping to guarantee the CCP's safety. But it left the communists defenceless when the KMT moved decisively and ruthlessly to the right. In April 1927, Chiang Kai-shek in a surprise move broke the alliance with the CCP by slaughtering communist activists in Shanghai. The 'white terror' of April 1927 taught the CCP a lesson that decisively influenced its future and in particular the fact that the CCP needed its own armed forces.

Communist Party leaders learned from the April events the impossibilities of making a proletarian-based revolution within the prevailing conditions in the China of the time, though it took the Party Central Committee some time to reach this conclusion. The Party continued to lead urban uprisings through the rest of 1927. There are several reasons for this: the continuing importance of Marxist and Leninist theories; a still extant organizational base in other Chinese cities; the hope that the non-communist left of the KMT might yet triumph over the right led by Chiang Kai-shek; and a steady stream of advice from Moscow not to abandon the cities or the KMT. Thus, the centre of gravity of the decimated CCP did not shift away from the cities until about 1931, when the Central Committee moved its headquarters out of hiding in Shanghai and into the Jiangxi countryside. Orthodoxies die hard, sometimes harder than the people who carry them (Blecher, 1986: 18).

Mao Zedong and a few like-minded comrades were able to liberate themselves from the failed orthodoxy sooner than others. By March 1926 Mao was urging the Party to pay attention to the peasants, sharpening his position with the publication of a report on his rural investigation in Hunan in March 1927 (Mao, Vol. 1, 1967: 13–59). Consequently, the Party put him in charge of the Autumn Harvest Uprising in the autumn of that year. When the revolt was crushed by the KMT, Mao and his small-armed band retreated to the remote mountainous region of Jinggangshan, on the border of Hunan and Jiangxi.

In the early months in Jinggangshan, Mao and Zhu De looked for their first base of support in alliances with local outlaws, bandit gangs and secret societies that operated in the area. Initially these alliances had as much or more to do with the need to survive in a hostile area as with revolutionary strategy. The Chinese agrarian structure posed serious obstacles to any communist efforts to effectively organize peasants in their villages. The Party would eventually solve this problem, but only with patient effort and much experience. In the interim, Mao and Zhu found their early allies among marginal groups who lived outside the landlord-dominated agrarian structure.

Gradually, the communist movement in Jinggangshan began to broaden its support. Communist cadres who had survived KMT attacks in 1927 joined it, and it recruited local miners and railway men, peasants and soldiers from other Northern Expeditionary armies. A radical land policy was adopted, under which all land was to be confiscated and redistributed. This frightened off many rich and well-to-do peasants, who were the mainstays of production in this very poor section of the countryside. Mao favoured a more moderate policy under which only landlords would be expropriated and others with surplus land would be permitted to sell it. Implementation of the radical policy moved slowly, and was not completed before the Jinggangshan base had to be abandoned in early 1929 under the pressure of a KMT blockade that gave rise to serious food shortages. The Jinggangshan Communists moved eastward to a new base straddling the border between Jiangxi and Fujian Provinces and established their headquarters at Ruijing. During the period of Jinggangshan, the CCP's main problem was survival.

Mao, Physical Culture and Sports Development

The CCP's sport development programme was combined with military exercise. One reason for this was that the majority of Red Army soldiers were from among workers, peasants and lumpen-proletarians, who ordinarily needed six months' or a year's military training before they could fight (Mao, Vol. 1, 1967: 81–2). The other reason was the influence of Mao's thought on physical culture inherited from one of Yen Fu's essays 'On Strength' (*Yuan Qiang*). Mao's first article on physical culture was published in the April 1917 issue of *New Youth*. This article was written long before he was exposed to any Marxist influence. However, it reveals many personality traits, and many strands of thought that can be subsequently followed through. This article was concerned about the Chinese people suffering the catastrophe of *wang-kuo*, which means losing state, then becoming 'slaves without a country'. This theme was widespread in China in the late nineteenth and early twentieth centuries, but also later. Mao argued that

[the] country is being drained of strength. Public interest in martial arts is flagging. The people's health is declining with each passing day. These phenomena are deserving of serious concern. Exponents of physical education have over the years failed to accomplish anything because they have never got to the root of the problems. Our country will even weaken if things are allowed to go on unchanged for long. It should be noted that athletic feats such as accurate shooting and long-distance throws are something external that results from training, whereas muscular physical strength is something internal that causes good performance. How can a person shoot accurately or make a long-distance throw if he has a poor physique and shies away from weapons? Muscular physical strength comes from training, which must be done conscientiously. Physical educators of today have

devised not a few methods, yet they failed to achieve the desired results. This is because external forces can hardly appeal to the public that is not aware of the real significance of physical education. What are its effects and how should one go about it? Since people are all at sea with these questions, it is only natural that little result has been attained. To make physical culture effective, it is imperative to activate the minds of the people and make them sports-conscious. (*New Youth*, 1917: 166–8; Mao, 1996: 3–4)

Mao's advocating of physical and mental fitness was to prepare people for their social duty. The purpose of physical culture and exercise was to save the country, since traditional culture provided neither an adequate method, nor an adequate philosophy. On the other hand, Mao also expressed two basic themes of thought and action throughout the whole of his subsequent career, namely nationalism and an admiration for the martial spirit. Mao claimed that a human being had to fulfil social duties, which included productive labour and fighting for survival of the state.

Sports development was very difficult for communists during the Jinggangshan period. The major physical exercise was military activities, such as mountain climbing, marching and military operations. Once in training, Mao told soldiers, 'You all shall have intensive military training, good exercise in military field operations and train well your body. Then we can fight our enemy' (Gu, 1989: 366; Gu, 1997: 299). There was a military field operation exercise every three to five days. Mao also trained soldiers to climb mountains. In the mountain-climbing competition, normally, two red flags were put on the top of mountain and three bullets were put under the flags. Soldiers would stand at the foot of the mountain and start to run up to the top of mountain at an order. Whoever reached the flags first would be the winner and get the three bullets. The Red Army, which was stationed at Jinggangshan, climbed Buyun Mountain often in the winter of 1927. The additional prizes for competition in climbing Buyun Mountain were two pieces of tobacco and a pair of straw sandals.

The Central Committee of the Party moved its headquarters to Ruijing and established the Jiangxi Soviet that undertook a series of agrarian reforms which on the whole were quite radical. The 1930 policy agreed by Mao was less extreme than that of the Jinggangshan years. All land was to be confiscated from the landlords and rich peasants, but rich peasants, their dependents and even some landlords were allotted shares of redistributed land equal to those received by the 'masses'. This principle of protecting the interests of rich peasants in order to help assure their continuing contribution to production was to be upheld by Mao beyond liberation. At this time, though, it was controversial within the CCP. This policy was reversed by the 1931 land law, drafted by a group of Moscow-trained CCP leaders known as the '28 Bolsheviks', who were influenced by Stalin's stringent anti-kulak policy. It provided for the redistribution of only the poorest land to rich peasants, and none at all to landlords who were also subject to being drafted for forced labour.

The radicalism of agrarian policy in the Jiangxi Soviet was coupled with difficulties in its implementation. The CCP first began to recognize the complexity and difficulty of mixing leadership and mass participation in order to carry out agrarian reform effectively. It was a problem with which the Party would continue to struggle for many years, and the experience garnered in Jiangxi proved to be invaluable in refining and defining its distinctive mass style during the Yanan period. For the time being, the Chinese Soviet Republic was established in Ruijing in November 1931. The Soviet government launched a policy of sport and sports leadership. Mao set the principle of physical education: 'Training iron bones and muscles of workers and peasants, then, defeating all our enemies' and 'Developing red sports, cultivating a team spirit and strong physique for the masses of workers and peasants necessary for the class struggle' (Gu, 1997: 300).

According to Gu, the first and only whole Soviet-area athletic meet of the Chinese Republic was held in Ruijing from 30 May to 3 June 1933. The goal of the sports meet was to spread the revolutionary war, to promote Soviet propaganda, develop anti-Japanese, anti-imperialism and anti-KMT propaganda in White areas. In the struggle of the worker and peasant masses, the aim was partly to build physique for the class struggle and cultivate team spirit (Gu, 1997: 311). The organizing committee of the sports meet was Bo Gu, Deng Yingchao, Wang Sengrong, Xiang Ying, Zhang Aiping, He Changgong, and Yang Shangqun. Most were leading members of the CCP. Sports events in this meet included track and field, basketball, volleyball, football, table tennis and tennis. Over 180 athletes participated from the Red Army, the Jiangxi and Fujian Young Pioneers, mass organizations of the Soviet area and the Central Committee. This meet was the biggest and most significant in the development of sport in the Soviet area (Gu, 1997: 311–12).

The Young Pioneers and Female Participation

After the tournament, Zhang Aiping was critical, arguing that sport had not involved enough Young Pioneers and young labour masses, that there had been a bureaucratic style of work in the preparation, and that the records of track and field were worse than those of the sports meet of the Red Army School the previous year. Furthermore, there were no female athletes (Gu, 1997). Zhang Aiping's critique was influential on the later development of female participation in sport under the CCP (Hong, 1997: 172). Being one of the chief leaders of the Young Pioneers, she wrote a song called 'The Gymnastic Song of the Young Pioneers'. This song reflects upon the purpose of sport in the Jiangxi Soviet.

Young Pioneers come to develop their bodies,
They are doing gymnastics, playing games.
They are strong, active and good at military skills.

Young Pioneers come to develop their bodies.
They are playing war games.
They are fighting against the white dogs [the KMT army].
Young Pioneers come to develop their bodies,
They defend the Soviet.
They are young, but strong.
They are great heroes and heroines. (Gu, 1986: 29)

The Young Pioneers' main duty was to consolidate Red Army strength. Accordingly, Young Pioneers were encouraged to extend and improve their military and athletic activities, and hence athletic meets were popular. A sports tournament called 'The First General View on Young Pioneers of the Chinese Soviet Republic' was held at the Red Army School near Ruijing from 4 to 8 September 1932. Sports events included the high jump, long jump, the 1,600-metre race, obstacle race and swimming. There were twenty-one teams and 688 athletes in this competition. According to Zhang, the track and field records of the Red Army School in 1932 were better than in the whole Soviet area meet of the Chinese Soviet Republic later in 1933 (Gu, 1986: 30).

The Chinese Soviet Republic Red Sports Committee was founded in 1933, and was the leading organization in the Jiangxi Soviet. However, the work of the Chinese Soviet Republic Red Sports Committee was terminated along with the Jiangxi Soviet in October 1934 after the KMT fifth encirclement. The CCP moved out of its Jiangxi-Fujian area and started the 'Long March', which caused huge damage to the CCP's Red Army: of the 100,000 or more who left the Jiangxi base, only 8,000 arrived in Shanxi Province in late 1935. It was a miracle that the CCP survived after this Long March. Even today, it is associated with so much heroism and so much death that it has an awesome status in Chinese historical consciousness (Blecher, 1986: 22).

After the Long March, the major focus and direction of the Chinese revolution underwent two major shifts. The first was the formation of a united front with the KMT against Japan. The second was the development of a new class constituency, an agrarian policy, a set of political institutions and a form of leader-mass relationship that came to be known as the 'Yanan Way'. The CCP's class policy in the Jiangxi Soviet was now seen as excessively radical, but it had failed to promote broad mass support and a level of economic production needed to sustain the revolutionary base. The '28 Bolsheviks' were blamed for the mistakes of their military and agrarian policies in the Jiangxi Soviet period. The CCP policy now called for the support not only of the poor and middle peasantry and the working class, but also of rich peasants, the petty bourgeoisie, intellectuals, national capitalists and landlords opposed to Japanese imperialism.

The greatest innovations and most decisive break with past practice came in the area of political organization and leader-mass relations. The 'mass line' development in Yanan was a radically new approach that involved closer and more democratic leader-mass relations. It reduced the underlying distinctions between party, state and army on the one hand and citizens on the other – that is, between state and society. In Yanan the mass line took several concrete forms. First was the reduction and streamlining of government administrative apparatuses, and decentralization of political authority. Second was the campaign to send cadres to the rural villages. Third was the effort to enhance the democratic and representative character of local governments by separating them clearly from the Party and ensuring definite and significant representation of non-party people in them. Fourth was the broadening of the forms of popular political expression and the range of issues on which such expression could take place. Fifth, in a continuation of practices developed during the Jiangxi Soviet, was the armed forces playing an important role in civilian affairs, in a way that subordinated them to civil authority (Blecher, 1986: 24–7).

The Yanan Sports Society

Under the guidelines of the mass line, the Yanan Sports Society was founded by the CCP between 1939 and 1940 (so far there is no evidence that can provide the date). Li Fuchun was the honorary chairman. The aims of the Yanan Sports Committee were to organize mass sporting activities for organizations, schools, armies and factories to strengthen physique and enhance the efficiency of work, production and study. At the same time, the Yanan Sport Society promoted 'ten-minutes exercise' every day, organized a demonstration of sport and an exhibition of sport photos, and held the city's regular sports competitions during weekends and holidays. Sport developed progressively in Yanan under the advocacy of the Yanan Sport Society (Gu, 1997: 318).

In Yanan, the public engaged in several different sporting activities, such as gymnastic exercises, running, swimming and hiking in the morning. At midday, the basketball and volleyball courts in schools, organizations and factories were crowded. After dinner, all sports fields were even more crowded than during the daytime. In the summer, the Yan River provided a natural swimming pool for water sports. In the winter, the River was a natural ski field. A ski competition was held in front of Yanan University on 7 March 1943. The New Yanan Sports Society was established on 25 January 1942 for promoting sport, translating and editing physical-education textbooks, and encouraging sport research and surveys. General Zhu De, the honorary chairman, made a speech at the inaugural meeting of the New Yanan Sports Society, saying that

> Today Chinese sport is not yet widespread. In particular, sport was ignored in Yanan. From now on, every school, organization and army shall advocate and organize sport. Gymnastic exercise is the main sport, and ball games and instrumental exercise are the assistant sports in schools and organizations. It is necessary to establish a formal instrumental exercise in the Red Army. We need to start all sports competitions, advocate dancing, hunting, ice skiing, swimming and combine sport with hygiene. (*Liberation Daily*, 28 January 1942: 2)

Zhu's thought of sport was quite similar to that of other CCP leaders who believed sport could be used to enhance the Red Army's military strength against Japanese imperialism. General Zhu De held a sports tournament during an anti-Japanese war campaign, in Yanan from 1 to 6 September 1942. The aims of this meet were 'to support the anti-fascist war and revolution', 'Develop mass sport' and 'provide the opportunity for every citizen to strengthen [his or her] physique as a duty against Japanese invasion and to save our nation' (Gu, 1997: 323). A song about the meet describes this in the following way:

Soldiers of the nation and warriors of revolution,
Come! Let's show off our agility in sport.
The international robbers and the bloody Fascists
Will be trembling before us.
Climb to the top, run to be first,
Shoot on target, throw a hand grenade far,
Look! General Zhu is on the viewing stand guiding us to go forward!

Soldiers of the nation and warriors of revolution,
Come! Let's show off our agility in sport.
The international young anti-invasion comrades
Will cheer us with jubilation and applause.
Like a dragon in the water, like a tiger on the land,
Winners are not elated by victory,
Losers are not discouraged by failure.
Look! General Zhu is on the viewing stand guiding us to go forward!
(*Liberation Daily*, 31 August 1942: 3)

The song illustrates a close relationship between sport and military thought in the CCP. Military drills were the core events of the CCP's sports meets. There were also many sports competitions for track and field, basketball, volleyball and swimming. Other events such as tennis, football, baseball, horse riding, diving, gymnastics, dance and martial arts were demonstration events. More than 130 athletes joined this meet, the biggest in the Yanan period during the anti-Japanese war. The need for suitable physical-education cadres who could organize events, train athletes and teach physical education in schools was an urgent problem during the Yanan period. To meet this need, in the spring of 1941 a physical-education training class was set up in the Yanan Youth Cadres School, which was directly under the supervision of the Central Youth Military Sport Committee. A few months later, in September, this physical-education class was integrated into Yanan University as a department of physical education. The first group of PE students only graduated from Yanan in the summer of 1942, owing to the shortage of PE teachers in Red Army and rural schools. The Physical Education Department of Yanan University was the first and most influential academic institute training PE teachers for the CCP during the Yanan period.

The CCP's popularity during the Yanan period stemmed in part from its innovation and flexible strategies on class relations, agrarian policy, political organization and leader-mass relations. Its stature was also enhanced by the leading role it took in the anti-Japanese war. The CCP armies concentrated their military effort on fighting the Japanese. They used mobile guerrilla tactics they had developed during the Long March to wage coordinated offensives, while also engaging in sustained harassment behind Japanese lines. Though the CCP could not really damage the powerful Japanese war machine until the latter had been weakened by its declining position in the Pacific War, its efforts did help to keep the Japanese armies at bay in many areas. More important than their military effect was the positive political image of establishing the CCP as the leading anti-Japanese force in China.

There is much controversy among analysts of the CCP concerning the reasons for its rapid growth in power and popularity between 1937 and 1945. Some have argued that the Communists owe their popularity to their nationalism, not to their programmes of agrarian and political change (Johnson, 1962). Discussing the tasks of the Chinese revolution, Mao said

> Insofar as imperialism and the feudal landlord class are the chief enemies of the Chinese revolution at this stage, what are the present tasks of the revolution? Unquestionably, the main tasks are to strike at these two enemies, to carry out a national revolution to overthrow foreign imperialist oppression and a democratic revolution to overthrow feudal landlord oppression, the primary and foremost task being national revolution to overthrow imperialism. (Mao, 1967, Vol. 2: 318)

In Mao's thought nationalism was the core social force behind the Chinese revolution. Sport was viewed as one of the CCP's major avenues for promoting the tasks of the Chinese revolution. Mao wrote a few words of encouragement in 'Exercise the Body to Fight the Japanese' in 1942 (*New China Daily*, 9 September 1942: 1). Under Mao the notion of nationalism and sport was very popular in the Red Army. A 'Song of Sport' describes sport in the army:

> In the moment of sunset and the cold wind of evening,
> Let's go to the sports field to do exercise together.
> Playing baseball, exercising on the parallel bars, doing the high jump and long
> 　　jump,
> Throwing a hand grenade, shooting on target and practising gun-bayonet arts.
> Look! Whose shoulder is bigger! Look! Whose body is stronger!
> Do exercise continually, crude iron cloud shift to steel,
> Do physical exercise continually; a weak man could become a strong man.
> Training our body intensively, killing our enemies in battle bravely.
> Everyone's body is as strong as a tiger,
> No one wants to be as weak as a lamb. (*Journal of Sport History and Culture* 3,
> 　　1984: 2)

In Mao's view, the principal form of struggle in the Chinese revolution was armed struggle, and hence physical exercise could strengthen the Red Army to win the CCP's armed struggle. Sport development in the CCP's revolution base had some significant characteristics. This chapter has shown that the CCP's sports organizations were affected by a group of Moscow-trained '28 Bolsheviks' during the Jiangxi Soviet period. Under the campaigns of mass-line, the CCP introduced modern sport to masses of workers and peasants, and to rural areas in China. They established the Physical Education Department in Yanan University in 1942, which helped to train the major group of PE teachers for rural schools and Red Army under CCP control. CCP sport was imbued with the ideology of a military spirit. Most sports activities were combined with military drills in the Red Army. CCP sport suffered from poor equipment and facilities, since the CCP was always faced by the KMT military 'extermination' and economic blockade, and the rural areas that it controlled were poorer than China's industrial and financial centres, the richest farmlands in the coastal areas and in the north-east under the control of KMT.

There were many reasons behind the CCP's victory in 1949. Sport in relative terms did not contribute directly to the successes of the CCP revolution. However, sport was an effective form of training for the Red Army and a useful medium for carrying social and political messages of the time. In practical terms the CCP had the problem of a shortage of sports staff and poor equipment and sports facilities within their village bases. The CCP's military leaders were quick to advocate sporting activities and supported holding events as a means of raising military spirit, developing a team spirit and nationalism. The strategy of mass sport and physical culture was not only an effective tool in attracting mass participation in athletic activities, but also a popular means of reinforcing notions of national identity, communist democracy and the ideal of a healthy peasantry working for China.

Summarizing Remarks

This chapter has broadly covered the period of development from about 1911 to about 1949. At least three important processes affected the development of sport and physical culture in China during this stage: (i) the continuing influence of Western imperialism; (ii) the emergence of communism and a popular form of nationalism, and (iii) the failure of the Chinese Republic. Imperialism has often been described as the common tendency of political units to grow the units until they encompass the earth, and in the sense that all political units seek expansion, the imperial nations that impacted upon China during this period need to be viewed as problematic. Both missionaries and the military had an ideological agenda in encouraging and adopting Western sports and forms of physical culture. The natural reaction to imperialism has invariably been nationalism. Although the Anti-Christian Movement and the Restore Education Rights campaigns emerged in the 1920s, the core of Chinese nationalism remained anti-imperialist and anti-capitalist. Chinese intellectuals often tended to define China in terms of what it was not. What they generally agreed was that sport and physical culture in China was not to be simply a replica of that of the West but a statement about national intent.

By 1920 the International Olympic Committee (IOC) had recognized the Far Eastern Athletic Association; by 1922 the first IOC member from China had been elected; by 1924 the All-China (Amateur) Athletic Association had been founded; and by 1928 China had sent a diplomat to observe the 1928 Olympic Games in Amsterdam. The National Physical Education Law was introduced in 1929. The Yanan Sports Society was founded by the CCP in 1939 just six years after the formation of the Chinese Soviet Republic Red Sports Committee of 1933. Having athletes participate in the 1932 Los Angeles Olympic Games paved the way for a formal recognition of both potential domestic and international importance of the Olympic Movement to the KMT government. China sent a 117-strong delegation to the Berlin Olympic Games of 1936 but poor performances meant shame for the nation. Despite investment in preparation, China fared little better at the 1948 London Olympic Games.

As with other areas, what the history of sport in China shows is that it is vital to restore any interpretation of sport in China to the complexity and impurity of the historical situations in which it is caught. Chinese commentators have been curiously absent from international discussion about sport, physical culture and, in particular, the impact of sport and physical culture in different revolutionary political movements of the first half of the twentieth century. If this was the case in relation to this period it was even more the case during the period up to 1976. During the whole epoch of the period from 1911 both the French and Russian revolutions were central models for China, and orientations toward them often defined the political divisions. The new culture movement of the May Fourth period championed the French Revolution and its values of liberty, equality and fraternity while first-generation Communist members often took the Russian Revolution as a model. However, as we have shown in this chapter British and American imperialist thought often impacted upon both the development of sport and physical culture in China and was often a contributory factor to the evolution of a nationalist response.

Key Readings

Bale, John and Cronin, Mike (2003), *Sport and Postcolonialism*. Oxford: Berg.

Guttmann, Allen (1994), *Games and Empires: Modern Sports and Cultural Imperialism*. New York: Columbia University Press.

Hong, Fan (1997), *Footbinding, Feminism and Freedom: the Liberation of Women's Bodies in Modern China*. London: Frank Cass.

Mao, Zedong (1996), A *Study of Physical Culture*. Beijing: People's Sport Publishing House Press.

Mechikoff, Robert A. and Estes, Steven G. (1998), *A History and Philosophy of Sport and Physical Education: From Ancient Civilizations to the Modern World*. New York: McGraw-Hill.

Stoddart, B. and Sandiford, A. (1998), *The Imperial Game*. Manchester: Manchester University Press.

Journal Articles

Chow, Rey (1997), 'Can One Say No to China?', *New Literary History* 28(1), Winter: 147–51.

Exner, Max J. (1911), 'Physical Training in China', *Physical Training* 8(6), April: 19.

Gu, Shiquan (1986), 'The Development of Sports in Lenin Primary School, Junior Groups and Young Pioneers during the Chinese Soviet Republic Period', Beijing, *Journal of Sport History and Culture* 6: 28–30 (in Chinese).

Hong, Fan (2000), 'Blue Shirts, Nationalists and Nationalism: Fascism in 1930s China' in J. Mangan (ed.), *Superman, Supreme: Fascist Body as Political Icon-Global Fascism*. London: Frank Cass.

Other Readings

Gu, Shiquan (1990), 'Introduction to Ancient and Modern Chinese Physical Culture', in H. G. Knuttgen, Q. Ma and Z. Wu (eds), (ed.) *Sport in China*. Chicago: Human Kinetics: 3–24.

MacFarquhar, Roderick (1972), *China Under Mao: Politics Takes Command*. Cambridge, MA: Massachusetts Institute of Technology Press.

Stoddart, B. (1998), 'Other Cultures', in B. Stoddart and K. Sandiford (eds), *The Imperial Game*. Manchester: Manchester University Press, 135–49.

Wu, Chih-Kang (1956) 'The Influence of the YMCA on the Development of Physical Education in China'. Ann Arbor, MI, University of Michigan unpublished PhD thesis.

CHAPTER 4

Socialism, Health, Soviet Sport and the Cultural Revolution

Introduction

As leader of the Communist Party of China from 1934 until his death in September 1976, Mao Zedong is in part remembered for two mass campaigns, namely the Great Leap Forward of 1958 and the Great Proletarian Cultural Revolution of 1966. The first ended with famine while the second ended in chaos. Both movements began from a rational and intellectual attempt to create a humane and to some extent democratic alternative to what Mao viewed as the problem of Stalinism. The Communist Party under Mao seized control of mainland China in October 1949. Mao's experience of power was not unlike that of Lenin since both were devoted to the idea of communal socialism and both to some extent were involved in building an alternative state. While Lenin died early, Mao lived to launch a protest against the system he had helped to create. From the 1950s to the 1970s China could be represented as a patriarchal family in which the state controlled everything under the rule of the Party, compared to say the 1980s when the family could no longer be completely held together and the parsimonious division of the family assets becomes inevitable.

Anti-Imperialism and the New Democratic Physical Culture

The CCP divided the future development of Chinese society into at least two successive stages, namely the bourgeois-democratic revolution and the socialist revolution. The 'new democracy' was the term used to describe the first of these phases. Its policies and orientation emanated from an essay by Mao Zedong first published in 1940 and titled Mao's writing *On New Democracy* (Mao, 1967, 2: 339–84). This outlined the principles of a transitional system in which a temporary alliance of workers, peasants, petty bourgeoisie and national bourgeoisie would co-exist under CCP leadership. The period of New Democracy effectively came to an end with the socialist transformation of industry and the drive for collectivization in 1953. Mao explained why China needed to build a new society, state and nation in the following terms:

> For many years we Communists have struggled for a cultural revolution as well as for a political and economic revolution, and our aim is to build a new society and a new state for the Chinese nation. The new society and new state will have not only a new politics and a new economy but also a new culture. In other words, not only do we want to change a China that is politically oppressed and economically exploited into a China that is politically free and economically prosperous, we also want to change the China which is being kept ignorant and backward under the sway of the old culture into an enlightened and progressive China under the sway of a new culture. In short, we want to build a new China. Our aim in the cultural sphere is to build a new Chinese national culture. (Mao, 1967, 2: 339–84)

Sport was seen as an important part of new Chinese national culture. In 1952, at the June inaugural meeting of the All-China Sports Federation, Mao called upon the Chinese people to 'Develop physical culture and sport, and strengthen the physique of the people'. In 1952 the People's Committee of the Central Government of the Communist Party of China established the Physical Culture and Sports Committee of the Central Government. By 1954 the committee had been relocated in the sense that the Physical Culture and Sports Committee belonged to the Ministry of Civil Affairs.

Physical Culture, Health and Hygiene

It is clear that Physical Culture and its association with health, hygiene and exercise meant much more than just sport. Its importance was such that, while it was closely linked with mental education, Mao often prioritized physical culture over mental culture. Thus the notion of Physical Culture within communist ideologies included the notion of record breaking, but in terms of social policy the much broader concerns of physical education and people's health were more important to the Cultural Revolution. Physical Culture stood for clean living, progress, good health and rationality and was regarded by the authorities as one of the most suitable and effective instruments for implementing new social policies as well as the relative degrees of social control implicit within many programmes. In 1953, Mao talked to the Second National Congress of the New Democratic Youth League of China, asserting that:

> Young physical people between fourteen and twenty-five need to study and work, but as youth is the age of physical growth, much is lost if their health is neglected. The young need to study much more, for they have to learn many things older people already know. However, they must not be overloaded with either study or work. And the fourteen- to eighteen-year-olds in particular should not be made to work with the same intensity as grown-ups. Young people, being what they are,

need more time for play, recreation and sport. Otherwise they won't be happy ... I would like to say a few words to our young people: first, I wish them good health; second, I wish them success in their study; and third, I wish them success in their work ... The revolution has brought us many fine things, but also one thing that is not so good. Everybody is much too active and enthusiastic, often getting tired out. Now we must make sure that everybody, including workers, educationists, soldiers, students and cadres, can keep fit. Of course, it does not necessarily mean that if you are in good health you will be good in study, for study must be done in the proper way ... Now it is necessary to arrange some recreation for which there must be time and facilities, and this end should be firmly grasped too. The Party Central Committee has decided to cut down the number of meetings and study hours, and you must see to it that this decision is carried out. Challenge anyone who refuses to do so. In short, young people should be enabled to keep fit, study well and work well. Some leading comrades are interested only in getting work out of young people and pay little attention to their health. In the new China of today we must change our approach and think more about the interest of our children and youth. (Mao, 1977, 5: 96–7)

In this statement Mao illustrates his earlier views concerning young people, in particular, those who needed more time for play, recreation and sport. Mao saw in them the hope of building a new China. He used the slogan 'Keep fit, Study well, Work well' (Mao, 1977, 5: 97). In the body of a speech of 27 February 1957 on the correct handling of the contradictions among the people, he stated that 'We should enable everyone who receives an education to develop morally, intellectually and physically and become a worker possessed of both a socialist consciousness and a general education' (Mao, 1977, 5: 405). The significance of these statements lies in their constant citation and, combined with Mao's 1917 essay, contain much of the substance of Chinese Communist Policy on physical culture during Mao's era. Though Mao did not mention sport directly in *On New Democracy*, he signals the direction of the new democratic culture:

New democratic culture is national. It links up with the socialist and new demo-cratic cultures of all other nations and they are related in such a way that they can absorb something from each other and help each other to develop, together forming a new world culture; but as a revolutionary national culture it can never link up with any reactionary imperialist culture of whatever nation. New demo-cratic culture is scientific. Opposed as it is to all feudal and superstitious ideas, it stands for seeking truth from facts, for objective truth and for the unity of theory and practice. On this point, the possibility exists of a united front against imperi-alism, feudalism and superstition between the scientific thought of the Chinese proletariat and those Chinese bourgeois materialists and natural scientists that are progressive, but in no case is there a possibility of a united front with any reac-tionary idealism ... New democratic culture belongs to the broad masses and is therefore democratic. It should serve the toiling masses of workers and educa-tionalists that make up more than 90 per cent of the nation's population and it should gradually become their very own ... A national, scientific and mass culture – such is the anti-imperialist and anti-feudal culture of the people, the culture of New Democracy, the new culture of the Chinese nation. (Mao, 1967, 2: 380–2)

In line with Mao's philosophy, Feng Wenbin, the inaugural President of the All-China Sports Federation, spelled out the task of physical culture at the 1949 meeting of the Federation. He stated that the New Democratic physical culture motto was 'to develop sports for people's health, New Democratic construction, and the people's national defence' (*New Physical Culture*, 1 July 1950: 8–9. Feng defined the New Democratic physical culture as national, scientific and mass. In terms of national physical culture, Mao argued that Chinese sport was national and that 'It opposes imperialist oppression and upholds the dignity and independence of the Chinese nation. It belongs to our own nation and bears our own national characteristics' (Mao, 1967, 2: 380). Chinese sport needed a national character, but it also needed to combine with other advanced sport systems, such as that practised in the Soviet Union. Chinese sport was to be a part of the 'New Sport' in the world. In terms of scientific physical culture, Chinese sport was scientific inasmuch as it was opposed to all feudal and superstitious ideas and stood for seeking truth from facts, for objective truth and for the unity of theory and practice (Mao, 1967, 2: 381). Sport, then, was viewed as being united and progressive, it had to contribute to Communist political action aimed at forming a systematic united front against imperialism and feudalism. Both the body and the mind must be seen to be kept in balance in terms of overall human development. In terms of mass physical culture, sport was viewed as serving and belonging to the masses. From the schools to the factories, from the cities to the villages, and from the intellectuals to the labourers, sport had to be viewed as spreading to all masses (*New Physical Culture*, 1 July 1950: 8–9).

In Feng's description, the New Democratic physical culture was one of the core themes of Mao's New Democracy (Mao, 1967, 2: 380–2). The vision of a national physical culture was characterized by Mao's thoughts about Chinese nationalism. The argument about scientific physical culture did not mention that sport should conform to the principles of science or that all sports programmes would adhere to the principles of physiology, hygiene, anatomy and physics, but should maintain a close relationship between physical culture and scientific research. It accommodated Mao's thoughts on anti-feudalism rather than those on scientific method. Accordingly, a national, scientific and mass physical culture was based upon the anti-imperialist and anti-feudal culture of the physical education, the culture of New Democracy, and the new culture of the Chinese nation. In other words, New Democratic physical culture meant *New Physical Culture*, while *Old Physical Culture* meant sports development in China before 1949.

Xu Yingchao in a critique of the Old physical culture argued that:

Modern Chinese sport methods, organisations and theories have been copied from the USA, which is a capitalist state, its politics, economics, military and education all serve the bourgeoisie. The American imperialists spread their sport not because they were concerned about the health of the Chinese people, but because sport was an ideal tool of cultural imperialism. The American imperialists emphasised to the Chinese people that American sports equipment was the best, their athletes were the fastest and their basketball team was the top one in the world. American sport was perfect in every field. The Chinese Old physical educators always believed that American sport was superior to China's. American sport served the dominant classes and was not for masses. (*New Physical Culture*, 1 July 1950: 10)

Concerning Xu's statements on Old Chinese sport, it must be noted that sport was not only copied from the United States of America (USA), but that its advocates also spread the superior image of American sport, and that American sport methods, organizations, theories and equipment were to be viewed within the overall context of a form of cultural imperialism. Basketball had been introduced to China by about 1895, but during the introductory period from about 1895 to 1948 few people paid attention to the game. A game was held in 1949 as part of the celebrations of the New China being emancipated from KMT control. The New China participated in the 10th Universiade basketball tournament in Hungary and has been a regular contributor to this tournament ever since. Certainly, as has been indicated here, New physical culture accompanied Mao's thoughts on Chinese nationalism and its characteristics of anti-imperialism. This is one of the reasons why New China developed a *New Physical Culture*. How were Chinese martial arts or indigenous sport to be viewed within this new historical epoch?

Martial Arts and Anti-feudalism

While Chinese Old Physical Culture was partly seen to be influenced by American imperialism, Chinese martial arts were condemned as being feudalist. A particular case was the Chinese martial art of Wushu, which, according to Fan Hong (2001: 158), was seen as a tool of the counter-revolutionaries who had set up anti-revolutionary organizations which threatened the stability of society, taught young people to be thieves and provided shelter for the people's enemies. Hong's argument agrees unconditionally with the government's official claim that these Wushu organizations in the countryside and cities should be banned and that the Youth League and the local governments should reorganize the Wushu groups in schools, factories and government departments. She adds that the Sports Ministry pointed out, 'In journals we do not encourage Wushu activities among the masses. Provincial and local sports commissions do not need to have offices to promote Wushu activities' (Hong, 2001: 158). Furthermore, Hong cites the case of Wang Xinwu, a martial-arts expert, who was criticized as a counter-revolutionary and rightist who used Wushu as a means to attack the Party and New China. Wushu thus clearly symbolized an undesirable component of the class struggle (ibid.). Hong does not explain what the exact meaning of this counter-revolutionary movement actually was or how they intended to overthrow the New China or the stability of existing society. The charge of counter-revolutionary was officially vague enough that it could easily be used as an all-purpose tool or slogan to discredit or wipe out those organizations or people who challenged or questioned official government policy.

Fan Hong's comments on Wushu draw heavily upon the interpretation of Wushu presented through the Chinese book *Sports History of the People's Republic of China 1949–1999* (Wu, 1999) edited by Wu Shaozu, the former director of the State General Sports Administration of China and President of the international Wushu Federation. The position adopted might have mentioned the government's attack on Wushu's development during the Anti-Rightist Campaign. Wu and other Chinese writers regarded Chinese Leftist thoughts as having unreasonably interrupted the development of Wushu in 1955 (Wu, 1999: 92–5; National Research Institute of Martial Arts, 1996: 365–6). Hong (2001: 158 and 165) cites Wu and notes that 'the reinstatement of Wushu started in the 1950s and ... Wushu was now regarded as a legacy of Chinese culture'. A study of this reference (Wu, 1999: 92–5) demonstrates unconditionally that there are no sentences that may reasonably be translated in the way quoted by Hong. In fact, there do not appear to be any statements consistent with the translation on this issue. Hong's view is different from that presented in *The History of Chinese Martial Arts* (1996), edited by the National Research Institute of Martial Arts in China, although she quotes this book as one of the important and essential Chinese sources (Hong, 2001: 150). According to this book, the Sports Ministry interrupted the development of Wushu in 1955 since some Wushu organizations: (i) did not register; (ii) were filled with feudalism and superstition, and destroyed the social order; (iii) cheated people to make money; and (iv) provided shelter for hiding counter-revolutionaries. The government started to put an order on Wushu organizations. Under the leftist policy, the Chinese martial arts activities were stopped and consequently suffered a setback (National Research Institute of Martial Arts, 1996: 365).

Liu Shaoqi, a senior CCP figure and Chairman of the People's Republic from 1959 to 1969, talked to the Sport Ministry on 9 March 1956, pointing out that 'We shall strengthen our research on martial arts and improve martial arts, qigong and traditional Chinese sports. We also shall study the scientific value of Chinese martial arts and promote them' (National Research Institute of Martial Arts, 1996: 365–6; Wu, 1999: 100). In the same year, 'The Draft Temporary Rules of Sports Competition in the People's Republic of China' listed martial arts as a performance event and therefore officially approved of the activity. A martial-arts display was held in Beijing, 1–7 November 1956. A new method of scoring for martial arts was used and thus began to elevate martial arts to a competitive sport in China. From 1957 to 1959, the Sports Ministry held national martial-arts-education meetings for martial-arts enthusiasts. At these meetings, martial-arts exponents were to learn of the CCP's policy on sports, to develop martial arts from different schools and to discuss the problems of martial arts teaching. A Chinese Wushu Society was established 19–22 September 1958. The first 'Rules of Wushu competition' were approved by the Sports Ministry and used at the national youth sports meet and the first national sports competition in 1959. At this stage, Wushu was thriving and a lot of different schools of Wushu thought were published. Nonetheless, martial-arts development did suffer a setback during the Cultural Revolution from 1966 to 1976 (National Research Institute of Martial Arts, 1996: 366–7).

Socialist Sport and the Soviet Gaze

While writers claim that the principles and methods of sport in Communist China were not directly borrowed from the Soviet Union, but were developed during the communist years in Jiangxi and Yanan – the so called 'Red Sports' and 'New Sports' respectively – from 1929 to 1948, it is important to explain the impulses for Chinese sport to borrow directly from the Soviet Union. China did copy a great deal of the Soviet sports system in the early years of the Chinese People's Republic. The editor's comment in *New Physical Culture*, for example, declares that in order 'To establish New Physical Culture, we must learn from the Soviet Union and other People's Democracies' (*New Physical Culture*, 1 July 1950: 6). In a speech at a preparatory meeting of the National Physical Culture Committee in 1950, Vice-Chairman Chu Teh insisted that 'we shall learn well from the sports experience of the Soviet Union" (*New Physical Culture*, 1 July 1950: 7). When the first Soviet sports delegation visited China, Chu Teh emphasized again that 'Chinese sport should learn from our Russian comrades and struggle for Chinese people's sport' (*New Physical Culture*, 25 February 1951: 2).

There are at least six facets of Maoist thinking about physical culture and sport which are consistent with socialist ideologies about sport in other Communist countries, notably the former Soviet Union, and as such they exercised what might be termed the Soviet Gaze although not control over sport in the New China. These six facets of thinking about Physical Culture and Sport were, broadly speaking:

- to raise physical and social health standards;
- to socialize the population into the new establishment system of values;
- to rationally supervise workers' recreation and to identify sport (like other amenities) with the workplace so that the Party Leadership and its agencies could observe and plan pragmatically the practices of the workforce and identify with wider communities to encourage a population to be healthier;
- to link sport ideologically and even organizationally to military preparedness,

stemming from a fear of war and the necessity to be prepared to meet such an eventuality;

- to facilitate an all-pervasive presence throughout society of forces of control such as the military and security forces, providing the option of imposition from above should the construction of the New Democracy flag from below;
- to cultivate popular attitudes toward physical exercise through a military effort and organization, deploying scarce resources in what was actually an efficient method in the most economical way, in a vast country with problems of communication and few sports facilities.

A Soviet youth delegation visited China in August of 1950 and introduced the Soviet model of sports development. At the same time, the first Chinese sports delegation visited the Soviet Union and observed sports development, in particular the Soviet sports organizations (Gu, 1997: 343). The first sports delegation from the Soviet Union to visit China on 20 December 1950 returned on 31 January 1951. It visited eight cities in China and played thirty-three basketball games with local teams. Soviet sports experts gave talks and held fourteen meetings with Chinese sports officials. They described current methods of sports development in the Soviet Union, basketball organization and the functions, principles and steps of basic training, basketball refereeing and the organization and duties of sports personnel. It was seen as an essential step for the Chinese to learn from Soviet sport during the early days of the People's Republic (*New Physical Culture*, 25 February 1951: 3). He Long, who was the first Sports Minister of the People's Republic, led a Chinese delegation to the Soviet Union in 1954. It is true that New China certainly learned from the Soviet experience. It was natural that China should learn, as in other areas, from a fellow socialist state that already had thirty-three years of socialist sporting experience.

Physical culture, according to Marx and Lenin, was an integral part of the socialist system. Marx advised that the system would consist of three elements combining training of mind with training of body:

> First, mental education, second, bodily education, such as is given in schools of gymnastics, and by military exercises and third, technological training, which acquaints the pupil with the basic principles of all processes of production and, simultaneously, gives him the habits of handling elementary instruments of all trades. (Marx and Engels, 1969, 2: 81)

Marx placed physical education on an equal footing with intellectual education, productive labour and polytechnical education. In the *English Factory Acts*, Marx had seen the germs of the prototypical education of such a system in which mental and physical education would be combined with manual labour to improve social production and all-round individuals:

From the Factory system budded, as Robert Owen has shown in detail, the germ of the education of the future, an education that will, in the case of every child over a given age, combine productive labour with instruction and gymnastics. (Marx, 1965: 483–4)

If Marx had made scant direct reference to sport, Lenin was scarcely more prolific on the subject – despite the sixty volumes of his writing in the last Soviet edition. Lenin was an active practitioner of physical fitness and sport in his own lifetime. He stated that he did 'gymnastics with great pleasure and value every day' (Lenin, 1963, 4: 72). Like Marx, Lenin's educational philosophy favoured a combination of training of the mind and the body:

It is impossible to visualise the ideal of a future society without a combination of instruction and productive labour, nor can productive labour without parallel instruction and physical education be put on a plane required by the modern level of technology and the state of scientific knowledge. (Lenin, 1963, 2: 485)

Lenin took a position on the character-building effects of sport that was not too far removed from that of the British ideological notion of Muscular Christians. Lenin argued that

Young people especially need to have a zest for living and be in good spirits. Healthy sport – gymnastics, swimming, hiking, all manner of physical exercise – should be combined as much as possible with a variety of intellectual interests, study, analysis and investigation ... that will give young people more than extraneous theories and discussions about sex ... healthy bodies and healthy minds. (Zetkin, 1955: 84)

Lenin spoke to the Third All-Russia Congress of the Russian Communist Youth League in October 1920 and stated that

The physical culture of the younger generation is an essential element in the overall system of communist upbringing of young people, aimed at creating harmoniously developed human beings, creative citizens of communist society. Today, physical culture also has direct practical aims: (i) preparing young people for work; and (ii) preparing them for the military defence of Soviet power. (Chudinov, 1959: 43–4)

This was a clear-cut official statement on the aims of Soviet physical culture that made unreserved qualifications about the rational use of physical education for the purposes of work and defence. It is perhaps not surprising then that a Marxist-Leninist interpretation of culture (both mental and physical), including the interdependence of the mental and physical states of human beings, provided the general framework within which physical and mental recreation was viewed in many communist states, including China.

As in other spheres, the Soviet sports influence on China until the late 1950s was quite substantial. The 'Labour-Defence System' was a 1931 Soviet innovation that China adapted from the Soviet Union as a national fitness programme. Early school physical-education manuals were translated from Russian, and Communist China's first international sports contacts were also with the Soviet Union. The Soviet influence was evident in the creation of physical culture institutes, government financing and control of sports, trade-union sports societies, national ranking for individual sports, armed forces, clubs and sponsorship to enable talented athletes to train full time, as well as sports boarding schools and sports programmes for women. It is not surprising that Communist China, which considered itself an orthodox socialist state, drew on the statements of the early Soviet theorists to justify its efforts in physical culture and sport.

The decision to make the 'Labour-Defence System' a formal programme ratified by law was reached during the first plenary session of the Central People's Government Commission on Physical Culture, held 16–22 January 1954 in Beijing. This meeting included all the members of the Commission, members of the Physical Culture Committees of the six administrative regions, and representatives of the Political Department of various military regions. During this meeting, Vice-Chairman Chu Teh clarified the connection between national defence and physical culture. He argued that 'In the field of national defence, powerful and skilful bodies are needed by the country. Because of this it was deemed that young people had to be strong in physique, bright, lively, courageous, sharp, tough and unyielding' (*South China Morning Post* 748, 9 February 1954: 14). The Labour Defence System (called 'Prepared for Labour and Defence' in the Soviet Union) was an essential part of the Soviet sport influence on Chinese sport and physical education in schools.

Sport and Physical Education in Schools

Sport and physical-education policy reflected important aspects of Mao's thinking on physical culture and sport. Physical education became a compulsory subject in schools during the early 1950s. Ma Hsu-Lun, the Minister of Education, reported in 1951 the policy and tasks of educational work in China:

> The adoption of effective steps for carrying out Chairman Mao's principle of 'Health above all' to improve the students' state of health, and, on the prevailing foundation, to improve the remuneration of middle school and elementary schools teachers ... The Physical Culture Committee should be established to guide all schools in faithfully carrying out the policy of 'Health above all', in reducing the students' amount of class work and after-class activities, to promote sports activities and recreation activities, to strengthen health education, to improve environmental hygiene and medical facilities, to improve the food of students, and to promote the people's athletic and health activities, so as to improve the state of health of people. (Ma, 1951: 5–12)

Mao's principle of 'Health above all' developed into an early policy directive relating to physical education in schools. In a speech 'On the Correct Handling of Contradictions Among the People', Mao announced that 'our educational policy must enable everyone who receives an education to develop morally, intellectually and physically and become a worker with both a socialist consciousness and culture (Mao, 1977, 5: 405). Physical education became a significant part of socialist education in schools. Each of China's two constitutional documents made reference to physical culture. The Common Programme – the legal guidelines before the adopting of a Constitution in 1954 – refers indirectly to physical culture. In Article 41 it states that: 'Culture and education in the People's Republic of China are New Democratic, which is, national, scientific and popular. The main reasons for raising the cultural level of the people are: training of personnel for national construction work, liquidation of feudal, comprador and fascist ideologies and development of the ideology of serving the people' (*Current Background* 9, 21 September 1950: 11). Physical culture was also alluded to in Article 48: 'National sports shall be promoted. Public health and medical work shall be extended and attention shall be paid to safeguarding the health of mothers, infants and children' (ibid.: 12). The aims of New China's physical education were seen as part of the entire New Democratic culture and education system that was viewed as being national, scientific and popular.

In order to achieve the goals of the New Physical Culture, New China partially relied on the Soviet model. A study of the Soviet experience in physical education began in the early 1950s. The Soviet guidelines for physical education for grades 1–4, 5–7 and 8–10 were translated into Chinese as a physical-education teacher's guide. Soviet manuals on physical education were studied to aid China in setting up its own physical-education system. This included the aims and responsibilities of physical education, the different physiological traits of various age groups, basic methods and problems of physical-education school testing and planning of physical education, the nature of female physical education and the organization of school physical education. Through this study of Soviet experience, Chinese educators concluded that physical education should be considered a subject on a par with all others. Liu Ai-Feng, Deputy Minister of Education, set out the characteristics of Chinese physical education:

Physical culture is one of the important aspects of school education. We must implement universally the Party's educational guidelines, follow the instructions of morality, intelligence as well as physique, and cultivate them to be cultured labourers with socialist consciousness so as to become firm revolutionary successors. The middle school and primary school students are in the stage of growing physically and gaining knowledge, therefore it is more important to pay attention to their normal development and improvement of their health. Physical training has a close connection with moral and intellectual development. How they are physically developed and whether they are strong or weak at this stage, not only has an direct effect on their mental outlook and their smooth completion of study tasks, but also has effect on whether they will be able to make greater contributions and play their part in the three revolutionary movement of class struggle, production struggle and scientific experiment in future. This is a big problem in relation to the health growth of our next generation as well as the Socialist revolution and Socialist construction. It is precisely because of this that the Party and Government have all along shown concern to the health development of our younger generation. In 1958 Chairman Mao not only appealed to the young men to be 'good in health, study and work' but has also repeatedly instructed us to pay attention to the physical health of students. (*Extracts from China Mainland Magazines* 434, 14 September 1964: 34)

This statement points out the close relationship in schools between health and the physical-education programme. The improvement of school physical education called for doing a good job in three aspects: (i) to handle physical education properly; (ii) to make the students persistently and painstakingly do morning exercise and break exercise; and (iii) to encourage extracurricular physical training activities among students to fit in with their timetable for work, self-study and recreational activities (ibid.: 35). Military sports were also considered an important means of intensifying 'proletarian consciousness' among Young Communist League (YCL) organizations in schools, defined as:

> [an] intense comprehension of enemy activity and national defence and constant awareness of the fact that class and class struggle exist throughout the transitional period, that class enemies and new and old bourgeois elements at home and elsewhere are always attempting a restoration of capitalism. (*Survey of China Mainland Press* 3435, 8 April 1965: 7)

YCL organizations were encouraged to develop mass military sports, such as firing practice, mountain climbing, military camping, grenade throwing and swimming with a heavy load, so that the youth of the country knew that they should be ever ready to fight as long as class enemies exist (ibid.).

The Labour Defence System was largely confined to schools above middle school level in the first half of the 1950s (*New Physical Culture*, 30 July 1951: 18–20). The content of the Labour Defence System was very similar to the Soviet Prepared for Labour and Defence system (Riordan, 1977: 410–15). Accordingly, five basic aspects of Chinese physical education during this stage were recognized: (i) the most basic was exercise – the core of the physical training programme – and participation in a varied set of exercises was viewed as preparation for all other aspects of physical education; (ii) physical education involved both games and dance which were included in the middle-school programme; (iii) sports were seen as an extension of basic exercises with competition; (iv) physical education involved training for labour and defence: the Labour Defence System was the main focus of the upper-school physical-education programme, and always had a military flavour; and (v) physical education involved complete patriotic and socialist education.

Some sports historians have condemned some Western writers for their ill-informed interpretation of the Chinese system and practice of sport as explained in the young Mao's article (Hong, 2001: 156, 165) and yet they too are guilty of not providing a complete picture. Many for example overlook Mao's early thoughts on physical culture, claiming it as not being relevant to China's Constitution in 1954. Yet in referring to the early achievement of the CCP – for example, in the preparatory meeting for the Eighth National Congress in 1956 – Mao said that:

> China used to be stigmatized as a 'decrepit empire', 'the sick man of East Asia', a country with a backward economy and a backward culture, with no hygiene, poor at ball games and swimming, where the women had bound feet, the men wore pigtails and eunuchs could still be found, and where the moon did not shine as brightly as in foreign lands. In short, there was much that was bad in China. But after six years' work of transformation we have changed the face of China. No one can deny our achievements. (Mao, 1977, 5: 313)

Mao's speech states how Chinese physical culture and sport had been part of the process of changing the face of China between 1949 and 1956. Mao believed in the importance of physical culture in China from an early age. In one of his early articles, he stated that:

> [the] country is being drained of strength. Public interest in martial arts is flagging. The people's health is declining with each passing day. These phenomena are deserving of serious concerns. Exponents of physical culture have over the years failed to accomplish anything because they have never got to the root of the problems. Our country will become even weaker if things are allowed to go on unchanged for long. (Mao, 1996: 3)

Sport and the Great Leap Forward

Mao's thoughts on physical culture were coloured by his view on nationalism from 1917 to 1956. It was not until 1956, however, that Mao questioned the validity of the Soviet model as a guide to Chinese development. In a speech entitled, 'On the Ten Great Relationships', Mao emphasized the importance of light industry and agriculture, industrialization of the countryside, decentralization of planning, labour-intensive projects, the development of inland areas, and the use of moral incentives rather than material ones in stimulating revolutionary commitment (Mao, 1977, 5: 284–307). This collection of strategies, in Mao's view, was to lead to rapid economic development and allow China to overtake the capitalist West. The Great Leap Forward campaign was launched in 1958 to realize this aim, but it also represented Mao's utopian vision of creating a specifically Chinese form of socialism which entailed a renewed emphasis on the key role of the peasantry and the ultimate achievement of a 'collectivist cornucopia'

(MacFarquhar, 1972: 467). This resulted in a setback not just for sport and physical education but also for the Labour Defence System.

The Ten-year Guidelines for Sports Development

Following the announcement of the Great Leap Forward, participants in the Labour Defence programmes and mass sports increased manyfold but, more significantly, the State General Sports Administration of China issued in 1958 'Ten-Year Guidelines for Sports Development'. This contained certain elements, namely (i) competitive sports; (ii) school physical education; (iii) labour sport; (iv) rural sport; (v) sports playgrounds and (vi) scientific research into sport.

The aim of the competitive-sports development plan was to approach world and international levels within a decade. The ten major targeted sports were basketball, volleyball, football, table tennis, track and field, gymnastics, weightlifting, swimming, ice skating and shooting. The specific target was to have five million people achieve the basic sports standard (later upgraded to 50 million), some 150,000 active athletes and at least 3,000 international athletes (later upgraded to 10,000). In terms of international competition the 1968 Olympic Games were set as a specific target. The plan aimed for Chinese athletes to be in the top three positions in track and field, swimming, ice-skating, gymnastics, table tennis, basketball and volleyball, and in the top six in football. At the same time, the guidelines projected 700 youth sports schools with levels of involvement being set at 140,000 members within five years, extended to involve 12,000 schools with 360,000 members within the Third Five Year Plan (*Archive of the State General Sports Administration of China*, 'The Ten-Year Guidelines for Sports Development 1958–1967', 9 February 1958).

Sport and physical education were set different standards at various levels of school. At the university standard, 10 per cent of students would be in the first class, 50 per cent in the second class and 40 per cent in the third class within the Second Five-Year Plan. In the Third Five-Year Plan, 20 per cent of students would be in the first class, 60 per cent in the second class and 20 per cent in the third class. In the Second Five-Year Plan, at senior high school standard there would be 1 per cent of students in the first class, 9 per cent in the second class, 50 per cent in the third class, and 40 per cent in the junior class. In the Third Five-Year Plan, there would be 3 per cent of students in the first class, 20 per cent in the second class, 60 per cent in the third class and 17 per cent in the junior class. At the junior high school standard in the Second Five-Year Plan, 1 per cent of students would be in the second class, 20 per cent in the third class and 79 per cent in the junior class. In the Third Five-Year Plan, proportions would be 3 per cent in the second class, 30 per cent in the third class and 67 per cent in the junior class. By contrast, in the Labour Defence System, the Guidelines projected all university students to attain the second standard, all senior high school students the first standard and all junior high school students attaining to the junior standard by 1960 (*Archive of the State General Sports Administration of China*, 'The Ten Year Guidelines for Sports Development in basic unions', 9 February 1958).

Labour sports programmes were developed at factories and included track and field, gymnastics, weightlifting, swimming, ice-skating, handball, shooting, chess, Chinese wrestling, exercises, basketball, volleyball, football, badminton, martial arts, cycling, mountain climbing and hiking. The Guidelines projected ninety-three organized sports teams with 930,000 members among 3 billion workers. The Labour Defence System would be promoted among 80 per cent of the trade unions, and 2.79 million workers would achieve the standard level; 279,000 would become standard athletes; 28,000 would become Level 3 referees and 930,000 workers would become primary instructors and referees with 200,000–260,000 sports meets to be held by trade unions every year up to 1962 (*Archive of the State General Sports Administration of China*, 'The Ten Year Guidelines for Sports Development in basic unions', 9 February 1958).

Rural sports in co-operative farms included exercises, hand-grenade throwing, middle- to long-distance running, high jump, long jump, weightlifting, swimming, horizontal-bar or parallel-bar gymnastics, wrestling and traditional sports activities. The targets projected 1.32 million sports teams with 13.2 million members, 450 trade-union sports societies with 11.81 million members; 67,500 trade-union societies promoted the Labour Defence System which involved – for 1.32 million primary instructors and referees – 400,000 farmers achieving the first class level and 400,000 sport meets to be held by trade-union societies every year by 1962. Provincial cities' sports grounds were to be increased in number from 434 in 1957 to 1,023 in 1967. The Guidelines on sports research called for ten major research centres to work on sports theories and organizations, sports skills and training, sports hygiene and physiology, sports medicine and therapy, sports psychology, Chinese sports history, sports organizations and systems, sports-instructor training and school physical education, research on sports equipment and fields and international sports (*Archive of the State General Sports Administration of China*, 'The Ten Year Guidelines for Sports Development', 9 February 1958).

The Guidelines called for '40 million people to achieve the standard of the Labour Defence System, 8 million people to achieve the basic sports standard, and 5,000 people to become top sports people' (*Archive of the State General Sports Administration of China*, 'The Report about The Ten Year Guidelines for Sports Development', 8 September 1958). Furthermore, they aimed to make the basic standard of labour defence widespread: the first target was 150 million and the second 200 million. In the number of active sportspeople, the first target was 50 million and the second 70 million. In the number of top-class athletes, the first target was 10,000 and the second 15,000 (*Archive of the State General Sports Administration of China*, 'The Report about The Ten Year Guidelines for Sports Development', 8 September 1958). These high targets for sports devel-

opment were almost impossible to achieve or verify, partially because of the tendency to report false information (Gu, 1997: 350). This tendency ceased in
1960 when the CCP and Mao admitted the errors of the Great Leap Forward.
In order to solve the crisis of the Great Leap Forward, the CCP launched a new
policy of recovery and readjustment from the end of 1960.

Sport, Socialist Education and Schools

The Labour Defence System, mass sport and sport in socialist education were
three essential elements of school education. Tung Tsun-tsai's two major
reforms on General Education highlight the importance of sport in schools
during the Great Leap Forward:

> The physique of students will be improved through labour discipline. 41 per cent
> of the students in the Third Middle School in Changke, Honan, were afflicted
> with stomach trouble in 1955, which dropped to 9 per cent in 1956, and now
> there is not one such patient. At the sports meeting arranged in the Hsu-Chang
> administrative district, the students of the school won 21 championships in 35
> events. Many instances prove that in those schools where the work-and-study pro-
> gramme has been launched, not only the incidence of diseases among the students
> is lower, but also they often lead in athletic events. (Tung, 1958: 14–22)

Tung argued for the importance of labour discipline and sport in the schools.
This was common under the Soviet Prepared for Labour and Defence system
aimed at strengthening production and introducing a programme of work combined with school education that was part of the 1958 educational reforms in
China. A delegation to the All-China Conference of Advanced Socialist Workers
in Education, Culture, Heath and Physical Education made the following
remarks:

> The education and cultural task of our country is a task of socialism. It is an
> instrument for the consolidation of proletarian dictatorship, and it is at the same
> time an instrument for the Communist education of our people. The fundamental
> principle is that education and cultural work must serve proletarian politics and
> socialist economic construction. In order to accomplish this, education must be
> led by our Party. Within the realm of education and culture, the struggle between
> capitalism and socialism has manifested itself in many forms. Over a long time,
> the focus of contention has always been on the fundamental problem of party
> leadership. Prior to 1957, despite the fact that we had made great gains in educa-
> tional and cultural work, we were not able to consolidate, in time, the leadership
> of the proletariat. As a result, the bourgeois rightists, taking advantage of this con-
> dition, began to challenge the Party on all fronts, shouting such slogans as 'the
> Party is incapable of leading educational work', 'education for education's sake',
> and 'separate labour from mental work' ... The thorough crushing of the vicious

attacks by the bourgeois rightists has firmly established the indisputable correctness of our Party's educational and cultural policy, has paved the way for even greater progress, and has made possible the Great Leap Forward on all fronts. (*People's Daily*, 2 June 1960: 1)

Although such comments from the Conference do not mention physical education directly, the CCP's education policy was fundamentally focused on the anti-rightist campaign and the Great Leap Forward, and consequently neglected the problem of famine. As a result, sports teams witnessed a reduction in training time while schools ceased to hold physical activities and physical-education courses because of a shortage of food. According to sports statistics, 1962 was the worst year for sports development between 1958 and 1965 (Gu, 1997: 356–8). The political and ideological framework of *Red and Expert* was still seen as an important educational policy of the CCP's campaign. *Red* referred to the political criterion for socialism and serving the people, while *Expert* referred to the vocational level for working hard and making contributions to society (Su, 1983: 39). In 1962, the Universities Committee of the Beijing Municipal Committee of the Young Communist League (YCL) of Tsinghua University arranged separate forums on the question of Redness and Expertness. The view was to provide better guidance to students in becoming both Red and Expert and promoting all-round development. Most of those taking part in the forums were senior students successful in solving the problem of Red and Expert. Based upon their own experience, they expressed their views on the question of Red and Expert. The term Red and Expert is, in this sense, particularly pertinent and revealing, for being Red was viewed as being more important than being Expert, and the objective of education was to train a new generation of ideologically trustworthy and technically competent people (MacFarquhar, 1972: 248).

Physical health was viewed as having a very important bearing on both Redness and Expertness. All the students taking part in the forums agreed that, in order to train oneself and become both 'Red and Expert', one must have good physical health. Without good physical health, one would find it difficult to become Red and Expert. In particular, Lu Kuo-pao, a sixth-year student of Beijing University, talked about his own personal experience and offered the following comments:

Physical health has a very important bearing on 'Redness and Expertness'. Take myself for instance. My health was very poor when I was in middle school. This affected my studies. Later, I began to pay attention to physical training. For several years, I kept on doing physical exercises and such things as long-distance running. In this way, my health has been able to give me considerable help. In the university, I have been working for a Party branch for several years. I often work and study till very late, but I never feel tired. Even after studying throughout the night, I would still feel quite energetic when I went to class the following day. My experience shows that, in order to train oneself and become the kind of useful person needed by the Party, one must pay attention to physical training. (Lu, 1963: 2–5)

Lu Kuo-pao's experience was quite different from that of others at that time. Although China's economy in 1962 was better than that in 1961, the basic place of physical activities in society was still poor. The government did not organize physical exercise, such as long-distance running and the labour defence events. The principle of school physical education meant taking part in fewer or no physical activities at all (Wu, 1999: 122). Yet Lu's experience shows that physical heath was one of the important elements of being 'Red and Expert' in Mao's socialist education movement. In the 'Red and Expert' campaign, physical culture became an important aspect of school education, particularly at primary- and middle-school levels, and was considered a means of carrying out both political and ideological education:

> Physical culture is one of the important aspects of school education. We must implement universally the Party's educational guidelines, follow the instructions of Chairman Mao, enable the students to develop vigorously and actively in respect of morality, intelligence as well as physique, and encourage them to be cultured labourers with socialist consciousness so as to become firm revolutionary successors ... it [the physical culture movement] will enable students better to complete their study task so that in future when they participate in productive labour, enter into military service, or join other construction enterprises, they will be vigorous and firmly determined to shoulder the heavy task. (Liu, 1964: 34–6)

According to Liu Ai-feng, then Deputy Minister of Education, improvement in school physical education required three elements: (i) to handle the physical education course properly ... according to physiological plans, that is, to correctly understand the significance of physical training; (ii) to make the students persistently undertake morning and break exercises; and (iii) to actively promote extracurricular physical-training activities, so as to fit in with their timetable for work, self-study, and recreational activities. Liu emphasized that diversified sports methods should be used for physical training in middle and primary schools. He argued that in order to enable every student to have a chance of physical training, they must do more physical training without using any equipment, make do with what is available, and use all available conditions (Liu, 1964: 35). Liu concluded that the key point in improving school physical training was the strengthening of leadership and socialist thought. More specifically he argued that:

> The Party Central Committee has instructed us that we should not only regard physical culture as an important means to improve health and strengthen bodily constitution, but also as an important measure for carrying out communist education for students. The task of our socialist revolution and socialist construction requires our next generation to possess high political consciousness and iron revolutionary will, to master the necessary cultural and scientific knowledge and technique, and have a strong body to obtain a revolutionary will and undertake construction. (Liu, 1964: 36)

Although the Sino-Soviet split brought the Labour Defence System to an end (Hong, 2001: 157), military sports were still considered an important means of intensifying 'proletarian consciousness', defined as:

an intense comprehension of enemy activity and national defence and constant awareness of the fact that class and class struggle exist throughout the transitional period, that class enemies and new and old bourgeois elements at home and elsewhere are always attempting to restore capitalism. (*China Youth Daily*, Editorial, 25 March 1965: 1)

YCL organizations were encouraged to develop mass activities of military sports (firing practice, mountain climbing, military camping, grenade throwing, swimming with a heavy load, etc.), so that the youth of the country could be made 'to know that they must be ever ready to fight as long as class enemies exist' (*China Youth Daily*, Editorial, 25 March 1965: 1). Hong argued that this was to concentrate all the resources on a few elite athletes in order to produce high performances in the international sports arena. It was a turning point from mass to elite sport in China (Hong, 2001: 157). During the pre-Cultural Revolution, in the stage from 1963 to 1966 Mao's socialist education movement of *Red and Expert* called for mass mobilization to attack capitalist workers who were supporters of Liu Shaoqi and Deng Xiaoping during the Cultural Revolution and were accused of following the capitalist road.

Sport, Communes and Famine

There is very little detailed information on how exactly sports development in the people's communes started. The emergence of the people's communes in rural China occurred during the Great Leap Forward. The people's communes were the final stage in the collectivization of Chinese agriculture and were created by merging existing agricultural co-operatives. Communes were the fundamental administrative unit of the socialist social structure of the Chinese countryside, combining industry, agriculture, trade, banking, child care, retirement homes, medical centres, road and bridge building and maintenance, education and military affairs. At the same time, the commune was the basic organization of socialist state power. Sport was frequently associated with education and military affairs in the people's communes.

The first task of each new commune was to carry out the programme of the Great Leap Forward. It is asserted that sport began to bloom in the countryside from about 1956 as the movement to encourage individual farms to become part of larger co-operatives gained momentum. Physical culture and sports committees mushroomed at the basic level of the People's Committees. Sports teams were organized according to production brigades and teams. Special attempts were made to organize sports activities according to peasant work schedules. Thus, much sporting activity took place during rest periods, before work, and especially during slack seasons. The nature of the programme in the communes coincided with that of the factory. Through the people's communes, mass sports made great headway in rural areas. With greater resources at the commune's command and with the labour force more effectively organized, the development of mass sport was accelerated. It is said that through the establishment of common dining halls and crèches peasants were freed from daily chores so that they had more time for recreation and sports.

The people's commune transformed the social structure, local administrative systems, traditional values of the peasantry and the personal relationships among villagers for more than 550 million human beings (about one-quarter of the world's population at that time). Changes within the commune to mass sports, the Labour Defence System and military exercise profoundly affected many sport institutions in rural China. A people's commune in Suiping *Hsien* (county) Honan Province approved the 'Draft Regulations of the Weihsing (Satellite or Sputnik) People's Commune' in August 1958. Article 21 of the Draft Regulations stated that

The Commune is to expand mass cultural, recreational and sports activities so as to develop mental and physical opportunities for Communist citizens. Step by step, a library, theatre and film projection team is to be set up for the Commune; clubs, amateur troupes, song groups and ball teams are to be created for big teams; small reading rooms and radio listening facilities will be provided for production teams. (*Contemporary China 3*, 1958/59)

Article 21 addressed recreation and sports activities that were important components for the communist citizen. Along with mass sport and the Labour Defence System, military training was an integral part of the commune's daily life. The emphasis on the popular militia as an essential part of the commune suggests that what Mao had in mind was the dissolution of the 'bourgeois' state. Article 10 of the Draft Regulations states how military training was held in the commune:

The Commune is to arm all the people. Able-bodied young men of military age and demobilized and retired servicemen are to be enrolled in the militia to undergo regular military training and shoulder the tasks assigned by the State. During the period of military training and execution of tasks, the militiamen are to receive their wages as usual. (*Contemporary China 3*, 1958/59)

The Great Leap Forward and the Anti-Rightist Campaign disrupted the national economy between 1958 and 1962. The Anti-Rightist Campaign profoundly shocked China's intellectuals, as well as the millions who had agreed with the criticisms made by the Party during 1957. Many sports coaches, physical-education teachers and sport officials were seen as rightist during this stage, and this affected the development of sport. The famine that occurred between

1959 and 1961 put an end to many sports activities. In the official view, there were three years of natural disasters. Gu has noted the official view that the famine must be seen as a result of the three years of natural disasters and diffi-culties (Gu, 1997: 349). Wu Shaozu not only agreed with this official view, but also conceded that the number of abnormal deaths increased during this period (Wu, 1999: 112). Fan Hong's essay mentions the great famine, the shortage of finance and food, and reduction of sports teams, but is silent on the disaster of millions of people dying. In the last few years, a growing number of Chinese living abroad have written memoirs shedding more light on the subject (Jin, 1999: 200–12). It has become clear that one of the greatest traumas suffered by the Chinese people was not the Cultural Revolution but the famine (Becker, 1999: xi). The impact of the famine has not yet been given sufficient attention by Chinese sports historians. Historians today, both Western and Chinese (Becker, 1999; Hutchings, 2001; Jin, 1999), concede that the 1958 policies were a complete disaster and that there were at least 20 million deaths attributable directly and indirectly to famine. Some commentators suggest that 40 million is the more precise figure – according to official Chinese statistics, the country's population in 1959 was 672.07 million.

Dissatisfaction with the policies of the Great Leap Forward meant that Mao's political influence declined. Even today the CCP refuses to acknowledge that a famine took place, and forbids investigation into or public discussion of what it called the 'three difficult years'. This makes the tragedy that swept through almost every part of China between 1958 and 1962 almost invisible. It also exposes a grim reality behind the exercise of power in communist China based on an ability to suppress the truth, and to force people to say – perhaps even believe – things that were evidently untrue (Hutchings, 2001: 164). In terms of sport, the nationwide sports system was established through the political cam-paign from 1957. Sports recovered from the Great Leap Forward and developed rapidly during the pre-Cultural Revolution between 1963 and 1966. However, the Cultural Revolution created further conflicts between the radicals and the pragmatists on sport. It is necessary therefore to outline a broader approach to sport and the Cultural Revolution.

Sport and the Great Proletarian Cultural Revolution

Sports historians and writers have put forward a number of arguments in rela-tion to the Cultural Revolution. Most of them agree with the official resolution of the Cultural Revolution in 1981, with the arguments below representing some of the common ground. Gu Shiquan indicates that the Cultural Revolution was ten years of unprecedented disaster for sport (Gu, 1997: 364). In martial arts, as previously mentioned, experts were condemned as vestiges of feudalism, monsters and academic reactionaries who were ruined during the Cultural Revolution which set Chinese martial arts back ten years or more (National

Research Institute of Martial Arts, 1996: 368–9; Yu, 1985: 195). Wu Shaozu, the former Director of the State General Sports Administration, agrees with the official resolution on Party history of 1981 and condemned the Cultural Revolution for destroying sports development. He wrote that during the Cultural Revolution (i) tragedies occurred among the top table-tennis players who committed suicide; (ii) the sports level declined because most athletes were involved with the Cultural Revolution and ceased their training programmes; and (iii) the entire sports system was at a standstill or near standstill (Wu, 1999: 171–200). Chen (1999) argues that the Cultural Revolution was also an unprecedented disaster for ideology in contemporary China.

Under the influence of cultural dictatorship and with metaphysics on the rampage, sport scholarship was extremely distorted by leftist sport thought, and sport was put to the service of politics. Chen criticized the policy of 'Friendship first, competition second' because in practice it expressed Mao's revolutionary line of 'friendship first' meaning 'politics first'. Accordingly, sport was weak and was used as a political tool during the Cultural Revolution (Chen, 1999: 7).The very idea of applying a rational approach to the management of cultural nationalism through sport is intriguing, and only Maoist China made a serious effort to curb such feelings. Prior to the death of Mao-Zedong in 1976 such feelings were eroded, but prior to this date Maoist sport specialized, according to Hoberman (1987), on an etiquette involving, at least from the outside, the eradication of overt hostile or aggressive feelings toward an opponent, thus upholding the notion of friendship first and competition second. Foreign athletes and spectators were often reported as being in awe of the emotional self-control of Chinese athletes and spectators.

Table Tennis, Da-zi-bao and the Red Guards

During the early stages of the Cultural Revolution, argues Hong (2001: 158), competitive sport was damaged, the training system was dismantled, sports schools closed, sports competitions ceased, Chinese teams stopped going abroad; outstanding athletes were condemned as sons and daughters of the bourgeoisie, and suffered mentally and physically (Hong, 2001: 158). Many sports leaders, officials and workers were also persecuted and falsely incriminated (Wu, 1999: 172). There is evidence to substantiate these claims in Chinese sports between 1968 and 1970. A few Da-zi-bao can still be seen as important sources of Chinese sports history during the Cultural Revolution. Da-zi-bao had been customary in the People's Republic of China, with official newspapers displayed on walls generally associated with the Cultural Revolution. They were used to attack individual CCP members. One of Mao Zedong's own Da-zi-bao 'Bombard Headquarters' (People's Daily, 5 August 1966: 1) was interpreted by all delegates as an attack on Liu Shaoqi, Deng

Xiaoping and other prominent leaders of the Party apparatus. During the early stages of the Cultural Revolution, the struggle among the top leadership intensified with the Maoist position becoming increasingly radical.

In a Red Guard Da-zi-bao, He Long, the CCP's commander and first Sports Minister, was attacked for supporting Liu Shaoqi's and Deng Xiaoping's revisionist sports policy and sports news publication. Many of his colleagues were attacked as revisionists and counter-revolutionaries (Tan and Zhao, 1996: 403–4). Most sports officials, including three Deputy Sports Ministers – Jung Kao-tang, Li Meng-hua and Li Ta – plus Wang Ling in the State Physical Culture and Sports Commission were attacked (Robinson, 1971: 307–12). Sports development was threatened, mass sport was ruined, sports training programmes were replaced by 'political struggle' and both the *New Physical Culture* and *Physical Culture News* ceased publication. The national sports system was stigmatized as an independent realm beyond proletarian politics and CCP control. In a Da-zi-bao *My Accusation*, Zhuang Zedong, who won the 26th World Table Tennis Championship in Beijing in 1961, accused He Long and Jung Kao-tang of promoting revisionist policy ideals within the independent realm of table tennis and stated that (i) he was both mentally and physically injured and ruined over the preceding eight years in the table tennis team; (ii) he became a prototype of the typical revisionism under Jung Kao-tang's education; and (iii) he wanted to revolt, he wanted to rebel and he wanted to be a people's servant (Tan and Zhao, 1996: 332–5). The slogans 'Bring down Liu Shaoqi, Deng Xiaoping, He Long and Jung Kao-tang! Long Live Mao Zedong's thought! Long Live Chairman Mao!' (Tan and Zhao, 1996) were often seen at the end of these Da-zi-baos. He Long suffered torment from ill treatment both physically and mentally and died on 9 June 1969 (Gu, 1997: 360–1).

Further tragedies included the suicides of three of the top table-tennis players during the *Clean Up the Class Ranks Campaign*. This particular campaign targeted six factories and two universities in Beijing, which were under Mao's personal supervision (Chang, 1993: 496). Fu Qifang, a famous table-tennis coach and player, came from Hong Kong with Jiang Yongning to join the Chinese National Table Tennis Team in 1952, and Rong Guotuan had won the first world table-tennis championship in Chinese sports history in 1959. Since they were all from Hong Kong, they were viewed as spies and targeted during the *Clean Up the Class Ranks Campaign*. Fu Qifang was tortured in denunciation meetings and beaten by other sportspeople, and hanged himself on 16 April 1968. The second table-tennis player, Jiang Yongning, was seen as a Japanese spy and hanged himself on 16 May 1968. The third table-tennis player, Rong Guotuan, hanged himself nine years after his championship win, on 20 June 1968. In Rong's last letter, he wrote: 'I am not a spy. Please do not suspect me. I am sorry to you all. I love my honour more than my life' (Yan and Gao, 1989: 411–12). These were the most notorious but not the only tragedies of Chinese sport during the Cultural Revolution.

The Chinese sports management, training and competition systems were totally abolished in 1967. Most sports teams were dismissed. There were 47 province and city football teams, involving some 1,124 players and 115 professional coaches, disbanded. Sports training equipment and facilities were destroyed while sports stadiums became the gathering places for denunciation meetings (Wu, 1999: 175). As Jung Chang comments, the People's Sports Stadium no longer hosted any kind of sport since Mao condemned competitive games. Athletes had to devote themselves to the Cultural Revolution (Chang, 1993: 494). Certain forms of activity were spared. Following Mao's own characterization of the Cultural Revolution, ideological education was imposed upon some 'loyal' activities to Chairman Mao. 'Loyalty dances', for example, was a physical exercise that followed the melodies of Mao's Quotations to illustrate people's loyalty to Chairman Mao. Everyone had to dance the 'Loyalty Dances' during the early period of the Cultural Revolution (Yan and Gao, 1989: 386). As Chang testified:

> In the autumn of 1968 a new type of team took over my school; they were called 'Mao Zedong Thought Propaganda Teams'. Made up of soldiers or workers who had not been involved in factional fighting, their task was to restore order ... The old textbooks had all been condemned as 'bourgeois poison', and nobody was brave enough to write new ones. So we just sat in classes reciting Mao's articles and reading People's Daily editorials. We sang songs of Mao's quotations, or gathered to dance the 'loyalty dance', gyrating and waving our Little Red Books. Making 'loyalty dances' compulsory was one of the major orders issued by the Revolutionary Committees throughout China. This absurd decision was mandatory everywhere: in schools and factories, on the streets, in shops, on railway platforms, even in hospitals for patients who could still move. (Chang, 1993: 502–3)

Although sports competition was halted during the early stage of the Cultural Revolution, sports performance and mass sport competition became part of celebration activities among the revolutionary communities. For instance, after the Ninth Party Congress of 1969 athletes had to dance the 'Loyalty Dances' before competitions and recite Mao's Quotations loudly when players violated a sports rule (Wu, 1999: 188). Martial arts were not allowed to hold formal competitions, while 'Loyalty Boxing' was developed and promoted as an alternative form of martial art (Yu, 1985: 195). Many martial-arts experts were condemned as ministers and sons of the preceding feudalism, monsters and reactionaries of academic authorities who were ruined during this stage. Martial-arts competition was attacked as a medium of feudalism and superstition, with the result being that weapons and equipment were confiscated (National Research Institute of Martial Arts, 1996: 368–9; Yu, 1985: 195). This was the second major setback for traditional martial arts in China since 1949.

Mass Sport, Restoration and the Gang of Four

The intensity and violence of the Red Guard movement almost brought China to the brink of internal war between 1966 and 1969. At the same time, Mao swept away most 'capitalist roaders' and 'hidden enemies', such as President Liu Shaoqi, the Party General Secretary Deng Xiaoping, Sports Minister He Long and their followers who had disregarded Mao's policy following the Great Leap Forward (Blecher, 1997: 75–7). Mao gradually increased the political status of the People's Liberation Army and reconstructed the Party to re-establish its control over society. This was done in part by reorganizing most of the previous state and mass organizations following the Ninth Congress of April 1969. Premier Zhou Enlai worked to restore scientific and educational standards and this included the restoration of a positive all-round attitude to sports.

Premier Zhou recognized the sports achievements between 1949 and 1966 at the first national physical culture and sports conference during the Cultural Revolution in July 1971. Zhou's positive support for sport inspired many sports officials and experts. He gradually restored sports training, competition, schools and organizations and the level of sports administration that had all been discontinued between 1966 and 1970. Sports officials returned to the State Physical Culture and Sports Commission that was now dominated by the PLA. National countryside sports development meetings, national labour sports meetings and the national spare-time physical education and sports schools conference were all held in 1972 (Gu, 1997: 361–2).

Mass sports development became an important policy of the Chinese government in 1972. A traditional mass sports activity – round-the-city running race – was held in the Beijing Chungwent District during the Spring Festival of 1972. The Beijing No. 26 Middle School was said to have had the highest number of participants when more than 100 boys and girls formed some 20 teams to take part in a middle-school cross-country run race. An article 'Mass Physical Training' describes sports development in this school:

> Upon our arrival at 6:30 in the morning, we saw some 500 students training on the sports grounds – some practising throwing the javelin, discus, hand-grenade and other objects, some running or practising the high jump and long jump, and some playing ball games. At 7:30, the students gathered on the large field or in the courtyards, doing setting-up exercises to music broadcast over the radio. Classes began at 8:00. From 8:00 through 4:00 p.m., we saw over a dozen classes taking physical training lessons on the grounds. During the interval after lunch and after 4:00 o'clock in the afternoon, the students played ball games and engaged in various other activities. So keen are the youngsters for ball games that they throng the sports grounds even on Sundays.
>
> The No. 26 Middle School has 3,070 boy and girl students in 54 classes, with five full-time and three part-time physical training teachers. The school has adequate

sports facilities, including nine basketball courts, one volleyball court, one football field and ten table tennis tables. Apart from school teams for football, boys' and girls' basketball, volleyball, table tennis and track and field, many grades and classes have their own teams.

How to organize such large contingents in regular training? What ideology should be used to guide their activities? What results have been obtained from mass physical training? And what is the relationship between moral, intellectual and physical development? A physical training teacher whom we interviewed gave answers to these questions.

Through the Great Cultural Revolution, the teacher began by way of introduction, we have come to understand that in physical training there is also the question of 'For whom?' Since the purpose is to build up the people's health, we should stress the mass character of such training. It is wrong to train just a few 'stars'; our duty is to help the majority of students take an interest in physical training and actively participate in sports activities ... First of all, we do our best to popularize those sports that give a comparatively large amount of exercise but require no particular skill, such as running, tug-of-war, skipping and throwing the hand grenade ... Secondly, we pay proper attention to combining sports contests with everyday sports activities, using competition to stimulate training. It is natural that an upsurge in mass activity precedes every such meet. (*Beijing Review* 14, 7 April 1972: 11–13)

The first National Middle School Sports competition was held one year later in 1973 (Gu, 1997: 362). However, the process of building up all-round sports development and physical culture was again affected when Zhou's restoration work was attacked in subsequent political campaigns. On 18 January 1974, with Mao's approval, the Party circulated a document prepared under the direction of Jiang Qing (Mao's wife) entitled 'The doctrines of Lin Biao, Confucius and Mencius'. This marked the formal start of the official campaign to criticize Lin Biao, re-interpret Confucius (*pi Lin, pi Kong*), all of which was covered extensively in 1974 New Year's Day editorials of the *People's Daily*, the *Hongqi* (*Red Flag*) and the *Liberation Army News* (Yan and Gao, 1989: 671). This campaign was led by Jiang Qing, Wang Hongwen, Zhang Chunqiao and Yao Wenyuan, subsequently referred to as the 'Gang of Four'. The purpose of the campaign was to undermine Zhou Enlai (MacFarquhar, 1993: 286–7), and again Leftist thought between 1974 and 1976 disrupted the development of sport.

During the restoration period, Zhou had appointed Wang Meng as chair of the State Physical Culture and Sports Commission and permitted *Physical Culture Daily* to resume publication. Nonetheless, in the campaign to criticize Lin Biao and Confucius, Zhuang Zedong, who had won the World Table Tennis Championship three times, replaced Wang Meng, became a confidant of Jiang Qing, and was said to have organized his own 'gang' to support the 'Gang of Four' in the State Physical Culture and Sports Commission (Yan and Gao,

1989: 678). Under the slogans of 'sports revolution' and 'sports reform', the former leaders of the State Physical Culture and Sports Commission were attacked by the 'Gang of Four' as third-generation revisionists who had failed to denounce both bourgeois sports and capitalists. Gradually they took over the State Physical Culture and Sports Commission between 1974 and 1976. Zhou made concessions in relation to the hiring of personnel in the State Physical Culture and Sports Commission and the Ministry of Culture. He kept a handle on power in the Ministry of Education during the Party's power struggle in 1974 (Yan and Gao, 1989: 718). Chinese sports were not brought out of chaos until Mao's death on 9 September 1976 and the arrest of the 'Gang of Four' in October 1976, which was considered as the official end of the Cultural Revolution.

How can we fairly judge sports development in the Great Proletarian Cultural Revolution? In terms of official statements, as late as 1977, even after the purge of the 'Gang of Four', Chinese leaders continued to portray the Cultural Revolution in glowing terms. Premier Hua Guofeng declared at the Eleventh Party Congress that 'Beyond any doubt, the Cultural Revolution will go down in the history of the proletariat as a momentous innovation which will shine through the passage of time' (The Eleventh National Congress of the Communist Party of China – documents, 1977: 51–2). He promised that further Cultural Revolutions would take place many times in the future as a way of continuing the struggle against bourgeois and capitalist influences within the Party (MacFarquhar, 1993: 231).

The official line completely changed within two years. By mid-1979, Chairman Ye Jianying had described the Cultural Revolution as an appalling catastrophe suffered by all the people. The interpretation that has prevailed more recently is that China was never in danger of capitalist restoration, that Mao's diagnosis of China's political situation in 1966 ran counter to reality and that the programmes produced in the latter stages of the Cultural Revolution were impractical and utopian. The Red Guards were characterized as naive and impressionable youth led by 'careerists, adventurers, opportunists, political degenerates, and the hooligan dregs of society' (*Beijing Review*, 5 October 1979: 15, 18, 19). An official resolution on Party history, adopted in 1981, condemned the Cultural Revolution as causing the most severe setback and the heaviest losses suffered by the Party, state and people since the founding of the People's Republic of China (MacFarquhar, 1993: 231).

Fan Hong often emphasizes, and we agree, the importance of Chinese sources, and yet her view of the Cultural Revolution in some aspects differs from some Chinese sources that condemn the Cultural Revolution as a tragedy and an unprecedented disaster for sport. She concludes more positively that

> The Cultural Revolution, in fact, pushed the roots of sports deep into Chinese society ... Sport in the Cultural Revolution developed under very complex and unique social, cultural and political circumstances. It is curious that, unlike the

arts, education, industry and agriculture, on which the revolution had a destructive effect, sport survived and even developed. This fact constitutes a valuable and
interesting phenomenon in the context of Chinese contemporary history. (Hong,
2001: 158–9)

Chinese sport, culture and society were deeply uprooted during the Cultural
Revolution, which created a serious crisis of confidence and disillusionment
among Chinese people – this is perhaps part of the reason why sport developed
so rapidly within the post-Mao reforms. The position taken here is one that is
sympathetic to some of the above interpretations. On the other hand, it is also
suggested that some aspects of the above arguments are problematic. This
chapter allows several points to be made. First, the Cultural Revolution was a
great disaster and tragedy for sport in Chinese history. The majority of Chinese
sports writers agree with the official statements and condemn the Cultural
Revolution as mistakes by Lin Biao and the 'Gang of Four'. The Chinese history
of the Cultural Revolution is still blurred and ambiguous. Most Chinese writers
avoid pointing out that Mao was responsible for the origins of the Cultural
Revolution and has to bear much of the blame for its outcome. The flaw in
Mao's strategy, in other words, was that he waged only half a revolution between
1966 and 1969. He failed to design a viable and enduring alternative political
order to replace the one he sought to overthrow, or to transform the political
resources he had mobilized from destructive into constructive ones. For
example, when the Sports Minister He Long and other sports leaders were
brought down as revisionists, there was no other sports system that could replace
the old one, and in this respect the rapid development of a forceful international
sports system came to a standstill for a period of time.

Secondly, the chaos caused by the Cultural Revolution was also indirectly an
important influence on sports reforms in the post-Mao era. In other words the
Cultural Revolution laid the foundation for the rapid growth of Chinese sports
in the post-Maoist era. Many senior cadres suffered greatly during the Cultural
Revolution, and yet they survived and helped to create the leadership for forms
of economic and political liberalization that included sport. The disillusionment
of many thousands of educated young people and intellectuals during the Red
Guard movement stimulated many radical ideas that were later translated into
concrete sports reforms. The CCP found it difficult to resist pressure for restruc-
turing the political and economic order after the Cultural Revolution. If there
had been no Cultural Revolution, it is unlikely that sports reform would have
gone so far and so fast in the post-Mao era.

Finally the Cultural Revolution was not as complete a disaster as many of the
the official accounts suggest. One reason for this is that many of the children of
intellectuals and other leading social groups under attack escaped doing hard
labour in the countryside by joining sports teams. Thus many people came to
sports who might not have otherwise joined sports teams due to the traditional
class structure in which sports were lower-class. This brought a stream of talent

into the sports world. The reason that the official histories often describe the Cultural Revolution as a disaster is that they were often written by those high officials who had suffered as a result of the event. They suffered either because of the vendetta against the Sports Commission or because they had been affiliated or connected to the YMCA or other bodies associated with Western thought and imperialism. Once this group had been restored to their original posts after the Cultural Revolution they often brought to their posts a renewed zeal and sense of mission to restore or improve the world of sport in order to redeem their suffering. Therefore the Cultural Revolution may indirectly have produced a higher level of motivation among these sports officials than might have ordinarily existed.

Summarizing Remarks

The period between 1949 and 1978 marked a distinctive stage in the development of Chinese sport. It was a stage during which Mao's socialism and the Cultural Revolution were marked by the influence of Mao's interpretation of Marxist-Leninism. Mao's notion of New Democracy provided guidance on what direction physical culture and sports development should take during the early stages of the People's Republic. The New Democracy of physical culture contained at least three spheres of development – the national, the scientific and the mass. National physical culture meant that Chinese sport and physical culture had to break from the old physical culture to become imbued with both nationalism and socialism and begin to develop an incipient form of an advanced sports system, similar to that of the Soviet Union. Scientific physical culture meant that Chinese sport was opposed to all feudal and superstitious ideas, sought the truth, attempted to unite theory and practice and had to contribute to the promotion of Communist political practice in the attack on imperialism and anti-feudalism. Mass physical culture meant that Chinese sport served and belonged to the masses. In reality the New Democratic physical culture, other than in theory, failed in its attempts to produce a sports policy or system on the ground in the New China. As a result, China looked again to learn from Soviet sports experience, but ultimately Mao questioned the Soviet model and embarked upon the Great Leap Forward in 1957. During the Great Leap Forward, sport suffered on account of the tendency to report untruthfully, to be over-ambitious, to exaggerate success and to suffer from overt formalism. On the other hand, the disaster of the famine that in part marked the end of the Great Leap Forward also indirectly influenced the future development of sport. During the pre-Cultural Revolution phase from 1963 to 1966, both elite and mass sports gained support from 'revisionist', 'counter-revolutionary' and 'capitalist roader' camps that held political credibility within the Communist Party.

Mao's restless quest for revolutionary purity in a post-revolutionary age provided the motivation for the Cultural Revolution. From a number of viewpoints the Cultural Revolution was one of the greatest disasters in Chinese history. Sports development was damaged and sports officials suffered both mentally and physically. Sport was supported and restored by Zhou Enlai in the early 1970s when China sought to bring an end to its diplomatic isolation and used sport as a means to break the ice with America in particular. However, the development of sport in China again suffered a setback when the 'Gang of Four' took over the sports system from 1974 to 1976.

In short, the development of sport and physical culture during the Maoist era 1949–1976 was influenced by at least three stages or processes of development: (i) Developing a New China and a New physical culture between about 1949 and 1957; (ii) the emergence of policies behind the Great Leap Forward, the Socialist Education Movement, and an attempt to develop a nationwide system to promote sports between 1957 and 1966; and (iii) the Cultural Revolution during which time sports were officially discontinued in 1966–1969 and 1974–1976, only periodically to be used as a means of promoting diplomatic relations with possible alternative partners in the West. Mao's death marked the end of an era in modern Chinese history. His legacy was an ambivalent one. From 1 October 1949, Mao declared that the Chinese people should stand up and feel patriotically proud of the New China. But the relative failure of Mao's Socialism and the Cultural Revolution meant that China had to find alternative answers and radical change in sport. In the post-Mao era China embarked upon a process of modernization that by the end of the twentieth century had opened the doors for China to embrace a new era of post-colonialism.

Key Readings

Hong, F. (1997), *Foot-binding, Feminism and Freedom: the Liberation of Women's Bodies in Modern China*. London: Frank Cass.

Lu, K. (1963), 'Beijing Young Communist League Committee and Young Communist League Committee of Tsinghua University Call Separate Forums on Redness and Expertness', *Survey of China Mainland Press* 288, 2 January: 2–5.

MacFarquhar, Roderick (1993), *The Politics of China 1949–1989*. Cambridge: Cambridge University Press.

Mao, Zedong (1996), *A Study of Physical Culture*. Beijing: People's Sport Publishing House Press.

Riordan, J. (1993), 'Sport in Capitalist and Socialist Countries: A Western Perspective', in E. Dunning, J. Maquire and R. Pearton (eds), *The Sports Process: A Comparative and Developmental Approach*. Chicago: Human Kinetics: 245–65.

Yan, Jiaqi and Gao, Gao (1989), *Ten Years' History of The Cultural Revolution*, 2 vols (in Chinese). Hong Kong: A Trend (Chaoliu) Publisher.

Journal Articles

Benton, G. (1980), 'China's Opposition', *New Left Review* 122 (1): 59–78.

Benton, G. (1984), 'China's Communism and Democracy', *New Left Review* 148(1): 57–73.

Hong, F. (1999), 'Not All Bad: Communism, Society and Sport in the Great Proletarian Revolution: A Revisionist Perspective', *International Journal of the History of Sport* 16(3): 47–71.

Medvedev, R. (1983), 'The USSR and China: Confrontation or Détente?', *New Left Review* 142(1): 5–29.

Other Readings

Bale, J. and Christenson, M. (eds) (2004), *Post-Olympism? Questioning Sport in the Twenty-First Century*. Oxford: Berg.

Chang, Jung (1993), *Wild Swans: Three Daughters of China*. London: Flamingo.

Li, Zhisui (1994), *The Private Life of Chairman Mao* (in Chinese). Taipei Education: China Times Press.

Liang Lijuan, He Zhenliang and Wu Huan Zhi Lu (2005), *He Zhenliang and the Road to the Olympic Rings*. Beijing: Beijing Foreign Language Press.

Mao, Zedong (1967), *Selected Works of Mao Zedong*, Vol. 1. Oxford: Pergamon.

Mao, Zedong (1967), *Selected Works of Mao Zedong*, Vol. 2. Oxford: Pergamon.

Mao, Zedong (1977), *Selected Works of Mao Zedong*, Vol. 5. Oxford: Pergamon.

CHAPTER 5

Reform, Opening Up and Making Sense of Modern Sport in China

Introduction

Modern China continues to be heavily influenced by international thought but the strength of China's own traditions means it is increasingly developing on its own terms. The issues outlined in this chapter broadly emphasize the extent to which sport in China has developed, opened up and reformed since at least the 1980s, but also that the challenge of China remains the tension between the pursuit of both globalization and democracy. This provides the context for a discussion about sport in Modern China in the late twentieth and early twenty-first centuries. In today's China it is tempting to suggest that pragmatism may have replaced triumphing over other ideologies. The essence of such a view is captured in Deng Xiaoping's cat theory which implies that it does not matter whether the cat is white or black or red – as long as it catches the mice it is a good cat. For many Chinese people it does not matter whether the cat is socialism with Chinese characteristics or capitalism with Confucian colours – as long as it works for China's development it is likely to be viewed as a good-ism.

The structure of China's sports administration has undergone radical reform. As of March 1998 the General Administration of Sport was established under a resolution passed by the commissioners of the National People's Congress (NPC), with the former Physical Culture and Sports Committee of the Central Government being reformed to become the General Administration of Sport. A further non-official organization, the All-China Sports Federation, remains closely aligned to the Ministry of Civil Affairs, and thus the organization and governance of sport in China is monitored primarily by two organizations, one being effectively a legal governance unit and the other being primarily a financial accountant monitoring sports provision. The main duties of the General Administration of Sport are:

(i)   to study and develop policies, plans, and regulations for sport
(ii)   to guide and promote the reformation of the sports system
(iii) to help the nation stay in good health, popularize sports activities,

implement national sports and take on the role of a supervisor in the physical examination of the people

(iv)   to plan and develop athletic competition and hold national competitions in a proper way

(v)   to promote international cooperation in sports, especially cooperation with Hong Kong, Macao, and Taiwan

(vi)   to organize research groups in the field of sports technology

(vii)   to inspect the qualification of the national sports-organizations

(viii)   to undertake the tasks assigned by the Ministry of Civil Affairs. (http://www.sport.gov.cn)

The China of the early twenty-first century has become a vibrant consumer economy where advertising and sponsorship have played a significant and vital role in both attracting new customers and keeping old ones. The rampant fashion in which consumerism has embraced Chinese society has to be seen in the light of the country's immediate past experience of puritan forms of communism. By 2006 China's GDP per capita had already surpassed that of France and Italy and by 2043 it is predicted that China will have overtaken the United States as the world's largest economy. Between 1996 and 2006 China's GDP growth has averaged about 9 per cent per annum and as a result the average real income of the average Chinese citizen has doubled in less than ten years (O'Toole et al., 2006). With the death of Mao, China took a pragmatic turn away from ideological purity to such an extent that conspicuous consumption and modernization have made grand ideologies increasingly problematic for young people in China. The most costly consumer durables a family could own up to the late 1970s had been wristwatches, sewing machines and bicycles. Indeed consumption beyond the limits set by the Party could have been condemned as sign of a corrupt and despicable bourgeois lifestyle. The new economic pragmatism induced a rise in people's living standards but also a pronounced tendency toward an unequal distribution of wealth (Zhao, 1997).

Sport in China has in part embraced capitalism with Chinese characteristics. While Chinese advertising spend represents 0.87 per cent of GDP compared with 1.03 per cent in the United States, the numbers continue to get bigger as the 2008 Beijing Olympic Games fuel further growth in advertising and sponsorship spend. In terms of general sports the Chinese consumer is most interested in those sports in which China dominates with badminton, table tennis and swimming being the top three sports in terms of interest. However, when one looks at the actual time spent consuming sports on television it is noted that badminton is only watched for 2.2 hours per week, basketball 4.1 hours per week and football 4.4 hours per week (O'Toole et al., 2006). The National Basketball Association franchise with CCTV sees the tournament broadcast to more than 300 million Chinese as a result of a partnership deal. The NBA basketball games were sold initially as highlight packages in 1987 before going live in 1994. These NBA basketball games alongside Champions League football, the English Premiership football and the FIFA World Cup all display the absorption of Western brands embedded within capitalism with Chinese characteristics. Since the country has enjoyed such spectacular capitalist style growth, the expectation that the Chinese Communist Party will be the ruler of the world's largest economy within the immediate future may be fulfilled. The current economic, cultural and political conditions have not simply emerged overnight. As a new and modern way of life, consumerism has appeared irresistible to the hitherto materially deprived. Yet the scale and speed of change and consumption has also created new problems to such an extent that the current way of life should not be accepted in either ideological or pragmatic terms as being trouble-free. It is perhaps more insightful at this stage to reflect in some detail upon some of the transformations and tensions present in a post-Maoist era in relation to sport and society.

Sport Opening Up to the Outside World

Sport underwent dramatic changes during the early stages of reform under Deng Xiaoping. At the third plenary of the eleventh Central Committee in December 1978, Deng reversed the course of the Maoist model of revolution and introduced further socialist reforms. Deng claimed that emancipating the mind was a vital political task, that democracy was a major precondition for emancipating the mind and solving old problems (Deng, 1984: 151–65). Both multinational capital and postmodernist culture were allowed to make significant inroads into both the Chinese mode of production and communist ideology. Deng Xiaoping advocated reform policies and socialism that had specific Chinese characteristics. The criticism of Mao and Maoism and the establishment of an alternative rapidly progressed. The CCP continually attacked the mistakes made by the 'Gang of Four'. It also could not deny the fact that Mao Zedong made mistakes during the Cultural Revolution. Deng Xiaoping believed that the political thoughts of Mao Zedong should be a matter of great concern for the CCP and that it was important to both affirm and evaluate the historical role of Mao Zedong. In 'A Resolution on certain questions in the history of our Party since the founding of the People's Republic of China', he noted that

> The appraisal of Comrade Mao Zedong and the exposition of Mao Zedong's thought relate not only to Comrade Mao personally but also to the entire history of our Party and our country ... Mao Zedong's thought was set as the guiding thought for our whole Party at its Seventh National Congress. The Party educated an entire generation in Mao Zedong thought, and that is what enabled us to win the revolutionary war and found the People's Republic of China. The 'Cultural Revolution' was really a gross error ... Now, when we speak of setting things right, we mean that we should undo the damage done by Lin Biao and the Gang of Four, criticize the mistakes Comrade Mao Zedong made in his later years, and put

things back on the right track of Mao Zedong thought. In short, if we fail to include in the resolution a section concerning Mao Zedong thought, which, since it has been proved correct in practice, ought to serve as the guidelines for our future work, we will diminish the practical and historical significance of the revolution and construction we have engaged in and will continue to engage in. It would be a grave historical mistake not to mention Mao Zedong's thought in the resolution or to cease to adhere to it. (Deng, 1984: 285–6)

Deng's speech addressed questions relating to the founding of People's Republic of China in which he insisted upon promoting four cardinal principles during the period of early reform: (i) keeping to a socialist road; (ii) upholding the people's democratic dictatorship; (iii) upholding leadership by the Communist Party, and (iv) upholding Marxism-Leninism and parts of Mao Zedong's thought (Deng, 1984: 339). The core of these cardinal principles was to uphold the Communist Party's leadership. Officially labelled as revolutionary in administrative structure, but not against any person, the bureaucratic reforms had two ostensible and one hidden objective (*Daily Report*, 9 March 1982: 4). The first was to upgrade the quality of the cadre corps by making them revolutionary, better educated, professionally competent and younger in age, the essential Four Transformations, so that they could lead China toward 'modernization'. A further objective was to streamline unruly bureaucracy by reducing the size of cadres, devising a rational division of work, and clearly defining the authority of Deng Xiaoping's reform. This in part was to be achieved by promoting the key political positions held by those cadres to whose personal interests the success of the reforms were tied. He employed a bureaucratic approach toward bureaucratic problems. Sport, like other areas, had to be seen to support and uphold the ideals of the CCP leadership. In order to uphold the CCP leadership in sport, reforms relating to the administration of sport was deemed to be necessary.

Wang Meng was restored to his position as the Minister of the State Physical Culture and Sports Commission in 1977. The State Physical Culture and Sports Commission of China held a national sports meeting in 1978 which clarified the key questions facing sport, namely how to reinforce and reform the CCP leadership in sport; to persist with a combination of a truly popular sports policy; to develop and attract international sports competitions; to approach the top level of sports technique; to develop international diplomatic relations through sport; and to insist on reasonable regulations of a sports system while at the same time establishing a 'red and expert' line of sports teams (State Physical Culture and Sports Commission Policy Research Centre, 1982: 122–31). Wang Meng outlined various measures:

First, we must continually attack the 'Gang of Four' and their absurd statement on former sport leaders as the 'third generation of revisionists'. In order to restore sport leaders, we firmly swept off those disciples of the 'Gang of Four' in the State

Physical Culture and Sports Commission and sports organizations ... Second, we must develop mass sports and socialist competition ... Third, we shall establish a close training system between different levels from junior level upward ... Fourth, we shall reform and improve our sports with proper techniques ... Fifth, we shall restore sports organizations and build up a reasonable regulation of the sports system. (*New Physical Culture* 2, 5 February 1978: 4–6)

Wang's statement provided the initial guidelines for sports reform and reaffirmed a united front on the way forward in terms of sports policy. Sport had its own political function – the essential work of sport was to promote socialist thought and the nation's pride and to develop Olympic sporting events.

China began to pay serious attention to Olympic sports after the 1984 Los Angeles Olympic Games in which China represented the largest communist presence in terms of participants. (Most communist states followed the Soviet-led boycott). China was placed fourth in the 1984 Summer Olympics, a position they held again in the 1992 Barcelona Olympics. They also sent a delegation headed by Wei Zhenlan to learn from the Los Angeles Organizing Committee about how to profit from sport in terms of making it pay for major events such as the Olympic Games. China noted that sport could be a profit-making institution, but also that sport could motivate Chinese nationalism. In particular, the success of Chinese teams aroused Chinese patriotism and nationalism at the 1984 Los Angeles Olympic Games. It was one of the first visible steps for Chinese sport to 'break out of Asia and advance into the world'. The Chinese government approved two key documents in 1984 and 1986 with regard to the reform of sport.

The first document was that the central government of CCP despatch 'A notification about moving further ahead in sports development' to all sport officers on 5 October 1984. A number of crucial points were confirmed. First, Chinese sport had developed well in the 1980s, and the document noted the great achievement of Chinese athletes at the 1984 Los Angeles Olympics. This proved that Chinese sport was approaching world levels of performance and that this had the potential to further promote Chinese national pride and self-confidence. Outside of China it also aroused Chinese patriotism in support of China. Second, while Chinese sport may have progressed there was nonetheless still a gap at the very top level of world sport. To reduce this gap China envisaged promoting a truly popular sports policy. The specific measures of this policy were to: (i) positively develop both rural and urban physical activities; (ii) work hard on promoting people's health; (iii) train junior children in school; (iv) improve training and competition systems and develop scientific training research; and (v) focus upon developing Chinese excellence in sporting events (*Tiyu Bao*, 10 November 1984: 1; *Xinhua Yuebao*, November 1984: 104–5).

The document indicated that the state should establish a sports team of 'redness and expertness' with excellent athletes and a coaching team. The state was to encourage excellence by rewarding athletes with honours and financial inducements. In particular, special achievements in sport would be rewarded. Retired international athletes were to be encouraged to take jobs in higher education as sports lecturers. It was suggested that the budget for sport should be increased. Furthermore, the CCP needed to strengthen sports propaganda by promoting the positive function of sport, thus both popularizing sports knowledge and attracting people to join in physical activities. This literature was also expected to promote the education of patriotism, collectivism, socialism and communism through sports achievement. Finally, at all levels of the Chinese Communist Party's Committee there should be an underlying attempt to provide support for leadership in sport (*Tiyu Bao*, 10 November 1984: 1; *Xinhua Yuebao*, November 1984: 104–5).

The political functions of sports were highlighted in that sport was encouraged actively to build both socialist thinking and a cultured civilization. Athletes, coaches, referees and sports workers were to be educated as socialists with ideas, high moral standards, cultural knowledge and discipline, all of which were to be associated with patriotism, collectivism, socialism and communism. However, there were still problems with some of the reforms. The State Physical Culture and Sports Commission noted that (i) Chinese levels of achievement in sport were still below those of other advanced countries; (ii) although sports development was still influenced by leftist thought there were conservative weaknesses in terms of sport leadership, training and systems of competition; (iii) sports reform did not follow at the same pace as economic reform; and (iv) the sports system needed a greater degree of uniformity.

In order to pursue such sports policies and attain the national target of becoming a super-state of sport, the State Physical Culture and Sports Commission persisted with its reform policy and published a further document in 1986 outlining a draft proposal for reforming the sports system, which was passed on 15 April 1986. This draft policy contained clauses relating to:

(i)   improving the level of sport leadership and confirming the State Physical Culture and Sports Commission's overall role of leadership, coordination and supervision;
(ii)   establishing a scientific training system;
(iii)   improving the system of sport competitions;
(iv)   enhancing and promoting Chinese traditional indigenous sports;
(v)   developing sports scientific research gradually;
(vi)   reforming the sport and physical education system;
(vii)   enhancing political thought on sport;
(viii)   improving the sport prize system;
(ix)   developing flexible open polices in relation to international sport (*Tiyu Bao*, 17 March 1986: 1).

The period between 1978 and 1989 marked a very distinctive stage in the development of sport in China. It was a stage during which China questioned most of the basic elements of Maoism and sought a new form of political authority, economic activity, social organization and cultural expression. Sport in some ways reflected the challenge of China with the inbuilt tension of moving steadily into the global sports system on China's terms, while at the same time wrestling with the expectations of those outside China in terms of sporting ideals and democracy. Society's state and class structures had been undergoing a basic transformation. Sports reform became part of this reform. The CCP's leadership in the reform of the sports system and the promotion of Olympic sports development became a priority for sport in China.

During the first decade of Deng's reform the impulses for structural reform of the polity and the economy tended to ebb and flow. As the movement of 1989 drew the decade to a close, it became clear that economic change had advanced faster than political change. Sports reforms still had the full support of the government. The 1990 Asia Games in Beijing were a major political and social event for China, being a signal to the rest of the world that China was in the market for hosting major international sporting events. The government dominated the television and news coverage and sought to use the Games to boost morale and confidence in the wake of the disaster of 1989. China did well in terms of medals, far better than other countries. The Chinese people were enthusiastic about the Games, in particular the opening and closing ceremonies. Even people who expressed anti-government views seemed to be proud of the Games. Thus, an implication of the Asia Games was that China wished to convince the world of its intention to continue and even expand policies of reform, a message that Chinese leaders took every opportunity to pronounce. As Jiang Zemin claimed, China would move at its own pace, but quickly be seen to 'set up the process of reform and opening up to the outside world' (*China Daily*, 18 October 1990: 1).

Sport, Post-colonialism and Reform in the Late Twentieth Century and Beyond

The notion of post-colonialism can be used in different ways in different contexts. It can reflect contingent historical, cultural and geographical conditions. It can offer ways of thinking across differences to global and transnational operations, such as multinational capitalism and American military aggression that may display itself in many disparate locations. Post-colonialism has also had an inseparable relationship with the expansion of Western capitalism and imperialism. According to some, post-colonialism services the requirements of Western capitalism in its contemporary global and multinational operations just as surely as colonialism served capitalism in an earlier period (McLeod, 2000: 254–5).

The reading of America's relationship with China and China's view of that relationship is worth briefly commenting upon at this point. Whenever sport in Chinese-American relationships is mentioned, inevitably the most celebrated example is that of sport's role in paving the way for the visit of the then President Richard Nixon to the People's Republic of China in 1972. The thawing of the relationship between the then cold-war enemies involved the USA sending a table-tennis team to the PRC followed a year later by a basketball team. The sports were carefully chosen for their diplomatic value. The USA did not possess a highly-ranked table-tennis team, whereas the PRC had consistently produced some of the world's best players. Similarly basketball at the time was a minority sport in China and no loss of dignity would be involved or attached to a Chinese defeat. Since then China has been gradually opening its doors and improving Sino-Western relations through sport. Today, from the outside, China often gives the impression that it is a regime obsessed with the power of America. Many high officials appear convinced that the route America has taken is the way to go, and they have no wish to resist it. Chinese liberals in particular also believe in an 'opening the door' route to democracy and the global system as if all that China has to do is enter the mainstream. Yet there are dangers in accepting this view uncritically in that the hypocrisy of US foreign policy was starkly exposed when the West manoeuvred to ensure that the Olympic Games of 2000 were not held in China but Australia. Many in China disliked the PRC's application to stage the Games, but it was popular with ordinary people angered by Western obstruction, and in particular America's opposition to the 2000 Olympic bid made by China. Both liberals and post-colonial critics of the time argued along the lines of Said's Orientalism in that the colonialist legacies remained a force which indirectly affected China's aspirations to enter the mainstream.

Western capitalists have been setting up sports-related businesses in China since at least the 1980s. It is impossible, nor is it necessary, to give example after example to substantiate the point that is being made. Trans World International (IMG/TWI) in sports televison programming, News Corporation in broadcasting, Nike and Adidas in sporting goods, and some multinational sport sponsors especially from tobacco, beverages and communications, such as Philip Morris, British American Tobacco, Coca-Cola and Ericsson have all been associated with opening up sports markets and sports consumption in China. Soccer at the end of the twentieth century was acknowledged as the number one sport in China (Glendinning, 1999: 20–1). At the time the 14-club premier league was sponsored by Marlboro, an event which could not have happened in the United Kingdom. The Chinese FA cup competition was sponsored by Philips, and the league attracted sponsorships offering perimeter board exclusivity to Budweiser, Clarion, Canon, Ericsson, Ford, Pepsi, Samsung, Fuji Film, General Motors, JVC, Korean Air, Olympus, Santafe and Vinda (a Chinese paper manufacturer). Soccer's dominance is only a relatively recent development, and in team sport it is competing with basketball, in particular, in the minds of Chinese consumers. Basketball was popular throughout the 1990s with NBA basketball games regularly televised and with Michael Jordan being voted the 'Greatest Man in the World' by Chinese students. Recognition of the NBA brand logo among

Chinese teenagers was over 79 per cent (Glendinning, 1999: 20–1).

The Chinese passion for football received a boost when after 44 years China made history by qualifying for the World Cup Finals in 2002. Almost 200 million people in China watched every game of the 2002 World Cup. The scenes of jubilation that followed China's entry echoed those that had earlier greeted the granting of the 2008 Olympic Games to Beijing. More recently it was reported that the 2004 European Football Championships had been greeted with a frenzy, despite the fact that the earliest matches – all being beamed live on state-run TV channels – kicked off at anti-social hours. In 2004 China hosted the Asian Football Cup, the regional equivalent to Euro 2004. The official European Championship website was for the first time made available in the Chinese language. The 'open door' outward-looking policy is reflected in the much-publicized answer of office worker Wang Hao who, when asked about the popularity in China of Western teams answered, 'In China we are always willing to look outward and learn from the best' (Mackenzie, 2004: 23).

In this postcolonial context, the development of global capitalism in China might be viewed as being similar to Ahmad's (1995: 1–20) description of the economic and social situation in some Third World countries. Ahmad points out that 'we should speak not so much of colonialism or post-colonialism but of capitalist modernity, which takes the colonial form in particular places and at particular times'. According to Ahmad, the contemporary global economic situation can be seen as a neo-colonial condition. Multinational capitalist companies are increasingly able to expand their new territories easily in China. Western sports media bypass national borders and transmit Western ideologies and desires for Western cultural products directly to the Chinese people. It is recognized that Western capitalism as a form of neo-colonialism has been successfully engaging with China's economy, culture and society.

The idea of the nation emerged with the growth of Western capitalism and industrialism and was a fundamental component of imperialist expansion. The issue of nationalism as discussed by Fanon is an important marker in the field of post-colonialism. As Fanon's work contends, sport could have played an important role in the construction of a national consciousness in Modern China (Fanon, 1990: 27–9 and 166–99). The PRC, in the decade following the death of Mao Zedong in 1976, experienced a cultural and ideological transformation unprecedented in the history of communist societies. Sport, like the arts, is a political subculture that expresses prevailing ideological trends and, for this reason, the new modernization in China necessitated a new ideological interpretation of sport. Contrary to appearances, the ideological content of the Maoist sport doctrine had, according to some, actually been retained in post-Maoist sport ideology.

What may have changed is the relative degree of emphasis accorded to the four specific ideological elements, which consisted of competition, high-performance sport, sporting ethics and scientific sport (Hoberman, 1987:

156–70). Under these four primary ideological elements, China has sought to 'break out of Asia and advance into the world' and this gives a strong political purpose to Chinese nationalism in the international arena. Accordingly, we may see both the hybridity and the ambivalence of sports development in China. For instance, Chinese leaders intended to appropriate Western sports as a tool to promote Chinese nationalism, patriotism and consumption. At the same time, they also wanted to resist Western culture for fear of enhancing Western ideas or models of democracy. The fine line between old and new and sports compliance within China's reforms is explicit in the following example. After NATO's mistake in bombing the Chinese Embassy in Belgrade on 8 May 1999, one of first actions of the Chinese government was to ban the screening of NBA basketball games on state television as a strong protest at the bombing.

One criticism of post-colonialism is its lack of attention to the problem of class, and Spivak's work *Can the Subaltern Speak?* may be seen as one of the few relative post-colonial discussions on the issues of class by post-colonialists. As Spivak argues on the question of the subaltern in India:

Let us now move to consider the margins (one can just as well say the silent, silenced centre) of the circuit marked out by this epistemic violence, men and women among the illiterate peasantry, the tribals, the lowest strata of the urban sub-proletariat ... On the other side of the question of the international division of labour from socialized capital, inside and outside the circuit of the epistemic violence of imperialist law and education supplementing an earlier economic text, can the subaltern speak? If, in the context of colonial production, the subaltern has no history and cannot speak, the subaltern as female is even more deeply in shadow. (Spivak, 1995: 25–8)

Similarly, the voice of the Chinese subaltern class and women has been disregarded during China's economic boom over the last two decades or more. Mass sports development has been ignored and limited because of a lack of access to sports facilities. Among the reasons given for the lack of sports facilities in China are:

1. the government not paying attention to building sports facilities in public places;
2. the rate of population growth much greater than the rate of increase in building sport facilities;
3. most sports facilities in the sports committee systems often closed to the public;
4. some sports halls used only for competition;
5. school sports facilities not actively used by local residents;
6. a large number of sports facilities swallowed up by factories and enterprises.

Some activities that require a relatively low skill level and few facilities (such as walking, running, traditional Chinese exercises, disco dancing, etc.) remain the most frequent and popular forms of physical activity (Wang and Olson, 1997: 69–85).

Qigong has become one of the most popular mass sports in recent years. It is one of the most ancient of Chinese physical fitness and breathing exercises, which can be traced back to at least the Spring and Autumn period of 770–476 BC. Throughout Chinese history *qigong* has been considered an important means of curing disease, prolonging life and improving the skills of participants in *wushu* (martial arts). The outside world woke up to the case of *qigong* when in Beijing on 25 April 1999 more than 10,000 members of Falun Gong (the way of the Law Wheel or Buddhist Law Cult) staged the largest silent demonstration since the student democracy movement of 1989. The Falun Gong protesters were angry because a number of cult members had been arrested in Tianjin. They also wanted to claim their existence as a legal organization. The leader of Falun Gong, Master Li Hongzhi, said that Falun Gong was based on the belief that human beings can harness their *qi* (vital energy) by meditation and physical exercise. The Falun Gong spokesman also claimed that they had about 70 million members in China and another 30 million or more elsewhere. (This was in contrast to the Chinese Communist Party, which had 60 million.) The state body in charge of *qigong* claimed that Falun Gong could not be officially recognized (*The Economist*, 1 May 1999: 83–4; *Guardian*, 26 April 1999: 13). On 28 April 1999, the government stated, 'This kind of gathering affects public order and is completely wrong'. Punishment, it said, would await those who 'damage social stability under the pretext of practising martial arts'. The Chinese government banned citizens from practising Falun Gong in public in Beijing, with effect from 5:00am on 26 June 1999 (*Central Daily News*, 29 June 1999: 7).

There are several reasons why Chinese citizens practise Falun Gong. First, Falun Gong followers believe *qigong* can fulfil their wish to enjoy good health. Second, the cult advocates truth, goodness and patience, which meet the need of those seeking moral and spiritual life. Finally, Falun Gong followers practise *qigong* collectively, thus allowing them to make friends. If such needs of Chinese citizens can be satisfied by other means, Falun Gong would not have spread so quickly. Falun Gong is practised by government officials, Party members and intellectuals. Li's charisma is only one of the factors that encourage the common people to join the cult. In China, more and more workers have been laid off since the government began to restructure the economy, the health care system is in poor shape and traditional values have arguably declined. It has been suggested that many ordinary people feel empty and crave for support and consolation. With such material and spiritual problems, Falun Gong has found a political and social space and accordingly has spread rapidly (*Ming Pao Daily News*, 23 July 1999: A2, A13–15 and 24 July 1999: A2–A4). Unless these problems are solved, though Falun Gong organizations have been outlawed, similar groups will sooner or later appear. In enforcing strict laws or imposing severe punishment, it is nevertheless impossible to prevent people from having material and spiritual needs. Sport in Modern China contributes to this process. However, the two examples of football and qigong perhaps best illustrate the challenge that is China.

Post-colonialism can also recognize the continuing agency of colonial discourses and relationships of power in the contemporary world. This study has been critical of some existing texts on Chinese sport and pointed out that researches into sport in China have been often been influenced by Western discourse. Said's argument is that Western views of the Orient are not based on what is observed in Oriental lands, but often on Western dreams, fantasies and assumptions that this radically different, contrasting place contains (McLeod, 2000: 41). While this study of sport in China has discussed Chinese sport and post-colonialism, it might be insightful at this point to provide an illustrative example of the equivalent of Orientalism in the Chinese context as it regularly appears in the imaginary psyche of Western sport authorities and media who regularly but mistakenly prioritize drug-taking in sport activities as an explanation for Communist success in those activities.

A study by Darcy C. Plymire (1999: 155–73) concludes that, from the evidence of sports drug tests, there is no single group that is innocent and not a single group that is to blame for the problem. Drug use is a common, although not new, problem in world sport. It is evident that it will not disappear by overtly blaming the Chinese and the other communist nations in terms of legacies, or informed practices. It is possible that Western sports communities are perhaps too quick and unfair to discredit Chinese athletes and coaches. This is an approach that is unbalanced and ideologically-driven given the current international interest in genetically-improved athletes and the inability of the international authorities as a whole to cope with the issue. Yet with specific reference to China, Plymire argues that when the PRC's women set a number of world records in track and field events in 1993, Western journalists immediately insisted that Chinese women could only have succeeded by taking steroids. Plymire (1999: 169) subsequently proceeded to point out the unsubstantiated general assumptions that were consequently attributed to all Chinese women athletes competing within Western and particularly American track and field communities. These were as follows:

1. women are naturally unable to run as fast as Chinese women have done;
2. steroids make Chinese women more like men and so allow them to run unnaturally fast;
3. women from communist countries are more likely to use steroids than women from Western nations;
4. women from communist nations are compelled by state-supported sports 'machines' to take steroids;
5. the Chinese are incapable of developing a knowledge of the human body and its potential that is superior to that produced in the West;
6. the Chinese must be using illicit knowledge gleaned from the former East

German sports 'machine'.

Based on this logic of Western imagination and gaze, the conclusion is clear: Chinese women have borrowed (or stolen) scientific and technical knowledge from the West (represented by steroids) and have used it in illegitimate ways to produce unnatural performances. Plymire's argument vividly exposes ready-made stereotypes of Chinese people that are produced and reproduced by the West in the same way as American images often portray Chinese men as small, weak, cowardly, sensual and deceitful. The characters of many, not all, Chinese people in American films are frequently clumsy, ugly, greasy, loud, stupid, slant-eyed, stereotypical, squawking Chinese bad guys. Many Chinese women athletes, concludes Plymire, would not fit the stereotypical images internalized by American people (Plymire, 1999: 161).

The subject matter of the discussion on sport, the post-colonial issue of global capitalism, class and Orientalism in this section has concerned itself with the development of sport in China in the post-Maoist period and, in particular, China's relationship with the West. As a focus of analysis, Chinese sport is capable of providing a great deal of information about history and social development itself, since one of the central tenets of thought throughout this section is that sport both contributes to and is constitutive of Chinese culture. Sport does not exist in some social or historical vacuum isolated from Chinese history and social development. The development of sport in China toward the end of the twentieth century and into the early twenty-first century in some way can tell us about the challenge that is China. It is perhaps insightful at this point to consider the challenge that is the two Chinas in relation to Chinese national identity and the Olympic Games in a potentially post-colonial world.

National Identities, the Two Chinas and the Olympics

National identity has become one of most important and perhaps overused notions in discussions of sport, culture and society. Sport is frequently viewed as a vehicle for the expression of nationalist sentiment to the extent that politicians are all too willing to harness it for such disparate purposes as nation-building, promoting the nation-state or giving cultural power to separatist movements (Bairner, 2001: xi). In the post-colonial world, sports in the People's Republic of China (PRC) were isolated by Olympic sporting organizations since at least 1949. After an absence of about 32 years the PRC was brought back into the Olympic family and competed at the Los Angeles Olympic Games in August 1984. This was the first time both the PRC and Taiwan had taken part in the same Games in Olympic history. The issues of the two Chinas in international sport has been problematic to many sport organizations since the Chinese Nationalist Party (Kuomintang – KMT) fled to Taiwan in 1949. What is the two-Chinas issue? And how does it affect Chinese sports development in the post-colonial world? In order to answer these questions, it is necessary briefly to describe the history of PRC's relations with Taiwan and international sporting organizations and thereafter provide a post-colonial comment upon this issue.

The two-Chinas issue in sport was a political issue brought about by the aftermath of the Chinese civil war whereby, following defeat, the Chinese nationalists fled to Taiwan in 1949. At the same time, the Chinese Communist Party (CCP) established a new China as the People's Republic of China (PRC) and the KMT reformed in Taiwan under the name of the Republic of China (ROC), a name that had been established by the first leader of the KMT, Dr Sun Yatsen, as early as 1911. The political conflict between the PRC and the ROC brought the two-Chinas issue into the international sporting arena. This issue affected the Olympic movement and subsequently the International Olympic Committee (IOC), since both the PRC and Taiwan claimed to be the sole legitimate representative of China. The two-Chinas issue may be seen as a conflict of national identities that was originally created by the actions of both the CCP and the KMT after 1949.

China's relations with the IOC date back to the early twentieth century when China at the time was under the government of the ROC. China's National Amateur Athletic Federation (CNAAF) was recognized by the IOC as the national Olympic Committee in 1922. Prior to 1949, China under the ROC participated in the Los Angeles Olympic Games of 1932, Berlin in 1936 and the London Olympics in 1948. In 1949, some of the Olympic Committee members fled to Taiwan while the ROC government maintained contact with the IOC and claimed jurisdiction over Olympic affairs in both mainland China and Taiwan. The ROC's claim was challenged by the PRC, since the CNAAF was still based in Nanjing; subsequently, it was reorganized and renamed in October 1949 as the All-China (Amateur) Athletic Federation (AAA) which claimed jurisdiction over all Chinese Olympic activities. These contradictory claims by the PRC and Taiwan produced conflicts between the PRC, Taiwan and the IOC.

The PRC had no communication with the IOC until February 1952, when ACAF sent a message to the IOC expressing its wish to participate in the 1952 Helsinki Olympic Games. The IOC was put in a difficult position, since Taiwan was also prepared to take part in these Games. According to the IOC rule, only one national committee was permitted to represent a country and there were differences of opinion among IOC members as to which Chinese committee should be recognized. Neither the PRC nor Taiwan was willing to negotiate or to form a single team. The IOC adopted a proposal permitting both committees to participate in those events in which they had been recognized by the respective international sport federations. Taiwan was disappointed in the IOC resolution and withdrew from the 1952 Helsinki Olympics to demonstrate its opposition. 1952 was the first time athletes from mainland China participated in the Olympic Games under the authority of the PRC government.

Two years later, in 1954, the PRC under the name of the Olympic Committee of the Chinese Republic was formally recognized as a member of IOC. This name was later changed to the Olympic Committee of Democratic China (*Olympic Review* 66/67, May/June 1973: 172–3). At the same time, Taiwan was recognized under the name of the Chinese Olympic Committee. Consequently the Olympic movement created the situation of having two Chinas. At the 1956 Melbourne Olympics, both the PRC and Taiwan were invited to take part. The PRC withdrew from the Games in protest against Taiwan's participation and continued to demand the expulsion of Taiwan after the Games. Avery Brundage, then the President of the IOC, in a letter of 8 January 1958 to Beijing stated that:

> Everyone knows that there is a separate government in Taiwan, which is recognised internationally, and specifically by the United Nations consisting of the governments of the world. Your government is not recognised by the United Nations. (*Olympic Review* 145, November 1979: 628)

The PRC, disappointed over the representation issue, withdrew its membership in 1958 from the IOC and nine other international sporting organizations in protest against the two-Chinas policy. During the 1960s, there was little contact between the PRC and IOC or other sporting organizations. As a result, Taiwan was able to claim representation on behalf of all China in international sports events. It was not long until October 1971 when the PRC was admitted to the United Nations and the ROC (Taiwan) was expelled. This event helped the PRC's participation in international organizations and its relations with the IOC. The PRC applied to rejoin the IOC in 1975 and was granted admission to the IOC under the Olympic formula in 1979. Since then the PRC has taken an active part in Olympic activities.

Why then did the PRC return to the international sporting arena and how did it overcome the issue of the two-Chinas issue from the late 1970s? As previously alluded to, while China fell into relative chaos during the early stage of the Cultural Revolution, most sports training and competitive systems were dismantled, many sports officials and athletes were attacked, sport academies closed, and sports equipment and facilities were neglected or destroyed. This situation began to change when China rejoined international table-tennis competition at the Scandinavian Open Championship in Sweden on 26 November 1970. This was the first time that Chinese teams had gone abroad for international sports competition since the Cultural Revolution (*The Times*, 27, 28 and 30 November 1970). Later China was invited to join the 31st World Table Tennis Championship in Japan in March–April 1971. Mao agreed with Premier Zhou Enlai's suggestion to send a Chinese table-tennis team to Japan with the famous slogan 'Friendship first, competition second', and Mao went on to say: 'We shall join this competition. We must not be afraid to bear hardship. We must not be nervous and scared' (Li, 1994: 535; Wu 1999: 238). This in reality was the beginning of China's 'Ping Pong Diplomacy'. After 1970, Mao changed his sport policy to one of open engagement with certain partners, in particular the

USA, and consequently a US table-tennis team was invited to play in China in 1971, with this being the first officially sanctioned Sino-American cultural exchange in almost twenty years. As stated earlier, Mao increasingly regarded Soviet hegemony as the greatest threat to China following the border clashes of 1969 between Chinese and Soviet troops on China's north-eastern frontier. Mao considered that a tactical accommodation with the USA would be less of a threat than that of the Soviet Union. Mao's changing attitude was reflected in Premier Zhou Enlai's call for peaceful coexistence and friendly relations between states with different social systems. Accordingly sport became a useful vehicle for making contact with the USA.

The PRC was invited to send an observer delegation to the 1972 Munich Games. The secretary-general of the All-China Sports Federation, Song Zhong, turned down the invitation because of the participation of Taiwan in the Games. China could not tolerate a 'two-Chinas' or a 'one China, one Taiwan' situation (*Beijing Review* 15(35), 1 September 1972: 23). This invitation improved relations between the then Federal Republic of Germany and the PRC and later they established full diplomatic relations in October 1972. In the early part of 1973, The Japanese Olympic Committee, in line with its government's policy, suggested to various international sport federations and national Olympic committees to reinstate China as a member and expel Taiwan (*The Times*, 13 February 1973: 14). In April 1973, Willi Daume, the West German Vice-president of the IOC, went to Beijing to discuss the possibility of China rejoining the Olympic movement (*New York Times*, 22 March 1973: 61). Daume was told that China would not be prepared to rejoin the IOC as long as Taiwan was in the organization. At the same time, however, China made progress in achieving Olympic recognition.

This was an important step toward China's admission in 1973 when the Asian Games Federation voted to admit the PRC and to exclude Taiwan from the Asian Games in Teheran. Thereafter, more federations recognized the PRC. In April 1975, the PRC made a formal application to rejoin the IOC. Its condition of entry was that Taiwan must be expelled from the IOC and that the All-China Sports Federation must be affirmed to be the sole sports organization representing the whole of China. Beijing regarded the existing relationship between the PRC and the IOC as abnormal and unjust after the PRC had become a member of the United Nations (UN) while Taiwan was not (*Beijing Review* 18(23), 6 June 1975: 17). At the 1976 Montreal Olympics, the PRC requested Canada to bar unconditionally the entry of the Taiwanese delegation to Montreal. Instead, the Canadian government required Taiwanese athletes to compete without any reference to the word China or the 'Republic of China'. The IOC considered the Canadian action to be a breach of its promise that was made in 1970 when Montreal was chosen as the venue (Espy, 1979: 152). To avoid further confrontation with the Canadian government, the IOC submitted a plan that Taiwan should be allowed to march as 'Taiwan-ROC' behind a flag bearing the Olympic rings. This solution drew opposition from both the PRC and Taiwan. The PRC indicated that ROC was only an abbreviation of the title Republic of China and to adopt it would be to officially acknowledge the two Chinas. On the other hand, Taiwan insisted on marching and competing under its own flag and name – Republic of China.

China continued to maintain that there was one China not two Chinas or one China, one Taiwan. It refused to accept any situation in which Taiwan could be recognized. To seek a solution to the dilemma, the IOC president, Lord Killanin, tried to arrange a meeting between China, Taiwan and the IOC in 1979. Taiwan refused to enter into direct negotiation with China, and pushed the IOC and PRC to work together for a solution without consulting Taiwan. At the Montevideo meeting of the IOC in April 1979, the plenary session passed a resolution to recognize the Chinese Olympic Committee located in Beijing and to maintain recognition of the Chinese Olympic Committee located in Taipei. The resolution stipulated matters of names, anthems, flags and constitutions of the two committees. In the meeting, Song Zhong claimed that:

> [the] resolution passed ... as it now stands, is unacceptable to us. We hereby reaffirm that there is only one China, that is, the People's Republic of China. And that Taiwan is part of China. The only way to solve the problem of China's representation is to recognise China's Olympic Committee as the national Olympic Committee of the whole of China. As an interim arrangement, the sports organization in Taiwan may remain in the IOC bearing the name of 'China Taiwan Olympic Committee', but it must not use any of the emblems of the 'Republic of China'. We shall only accept solutions compatible with the above-stated conditions. (*Daily Report*, 9 April 1979: K1)

Song's statement indicated that China would not allow Taiwan to use any name associated with the Republic of China or to use the name Chinese Olympic Committee-Taipei which would imply equal state status with China (Chinese Olympic Committee-Beijing). The only solution was that Taiwan must bear the name of China and as part of China. Song called a press conference in Beijing and repeated China's objection to the resolution, saying that it was tantamount to China's acceptance of the idea of two Chinas. Again Song laid down the two necessary conditions: first, that China's Olympic Committee had to be recognized as the sole legitimate Chinese organization in the IOC; and second, that the IOC should forbid the use of the state name, national flag and anthem of the Republic of China.

In June 1979, the IOC executive committee meeting in Puerto Rico confirmed China's Olympic Committee's title as the 'Chinese Olympic Committee'. It also recommended that Taiwan should stay in the IOC as the Chinese Taipei Olympic Committee with a different national anthem and flag. At the IOC executive board meeting in Nagoya, Lord Killanin submitted a resolution to 89 IOC members for a postal vote on 26 October 1979. According to this resolution, the national Olympic committee of the PRC would be named the 'Chinese Olympic

Committee' and it would use the flag and anthem of the PRC. The Olympic committee of Taiwan would be named the Chinese Taipei Olympic Committee and its anthem, flag and emblem would be other than those used and would have to be approved by the executive board of the IOC. China welcomed the result of voting, claiming that the resolution took into consideration the basic fact that there was only one China and Taiwan was a part of China (*Xinhua Yuebao*, December 1979: 111).

Taiwan was disappointed with the IOC decision. Taipei's Olympic Committee and Henry Hsu, an IOC member from Taiwan, filed lawsuits at the Lausanne Civil District Court against the Nagoya resolution and claimed that it violated IOC rules. Taipei's Olympic Committee's claim was rejected by the court and the ruling Judge Pierre Bucher said that it seemed already very obvious that Taipei's Olympic Committee had no right to present a suit against the IOC (*Daily Report*, 17 January 1980: A2). The new IOC President Juan Antonio Samaranch sent a letter dated 4 December 1980 to Hsu that guaranteed that Taipei's Olympic Committee would get the same treatment as any other national committee if Taiwan accepted the conditions of the Nagoya resolution (Chinese Taipei Olympic Committee, 1981: 5–10). Afterward, the Taipei Olympic Committee agreed to change its name to the 'Chinese Taipei Olympic Committee' and to adopt a new flag and emblem. According to the agreement, the Chinese Taipei Olympic Committee was entitled to participate in future Olympic Games and other activities sponsored by the IOC like every national Olympic Committee, with the same status and the same rights (*Olympic Review* 162, April 1981: 211). Temporarily, the question of Chinese representation was settled. To the PRC, there were no two Chinas or one China and one Taiwan. Taiwan was subsumed under China – it was implicit in the names of the two Chinese Olympic committees. The outcome helped to facilitate communication between China and Taiwan through sport and was conducive to the process of incipient reunification. To Taiwan, there was no option but to accept the resolution if it wished to stay in the Olympic movement. To the IOC, the resolution had settled one of the biggest problems over the past twenty years. Thereafter, the IOC formula became the solution for other international sporting organizations as well.

By means of summary and update the following will suffice at this stage. In 1979 China rejoined the IOC after an eleven-year absence following an unsatisfactory resolution of the 'Two Chinas Problem'. Beijing hosted the Asia Games in 1990 but lost the vote to host the 2000 Olympic Games. China subsequently won the bid to host the 2008 Olympic Games. The increasing importance of sport in China reflected the international importance of the Olympic movement. In China, sport has been fought over by many different groups and it is relatively easy to demonstrate sport's role in promoting Chinese nationalism and its importance to the power elite. Under this inflexible ideology of Chinese centrism (Sino-centrism), Taiwan is regarded as part of China. China bans the Taiwanese from using their official national name, flag and anthem in all international competitions. Since 1984, Taiwanese athletes have competed under the name of 'Chinese Taipei' in international arenas, but the Chinese domestic media consistently name Taiwanese sports teams as 'Taipei China'. The sports relationships between China and Taiwan can be critically viewed as a symbol of Chinese internal imperialism and hegemony. Today, the majority of Taiwanese people continue to resist attempts by China to promote unification under the Chinese official nationalist slogan of 'one country, two systems'.

In the 2004 Athens Olympic Games the National Council on Physical Fitness and Sport announced in May 2004 that the Chinese Taipei Olympic Team would consist of eighty-five competitors across twelve events. Coverage of the Olympic Games in Athens was scheduled to be covered by digital broadcast stations throughout Taiwan. It is significant that the IOC granted television-viewing rights to Taiwan Television Enterprise Ltd, China Television Co., Chinese Television Systems and Formosa Television. The Chinese Taipei Olympic Committee praised the IOC for promoting cooperation between the four stations. The mission of the CTOC remains that of promoting the Olympic Movement in Taiwan. The news of the successful Beijing Olympic bid in Taiwan was mixed. In the build-up to the Beijing Olympic bid Yuan Weimin, the President of China's Olympic Committee (COC), declined to rule out the possibility of Taiwan being involved in the co-sponsoring of the Beijing Olympic Games, should the bid be successful, as long as the premise of the One China principle was adhered to. The CTOC argued that co-hosting of the 2008 Games would benefit Taiwan from an economic point of view, but above all would be an opportunity to promote sports exchanges and enhance the process of reconciliation between the two sides of the Taiwan straits. Yuan Weimin asserted that, unlike the Football World Cup and European Championships, which allows for twin bids from different countries, the IOC Olympic Charter only allows the Games to be staged in one city of one country.

Chinese official nationalism involves the imposition of cultural homogeneity from the top through state action. One of the Chinese official actions is to force Taiwanese sports organizations to accept that the PRC is the only central government and that Taiwan is merely a provincial state. Under the continuing threat of PRC, the Taiwanese people are struggling and searching for their own self-definitions, rather than those defined by the Chinese government. The possibility of hybridity through sport has the power to redefine and frame the two-Chinas issue. To a certain degree the debate over the 'two-Chinas problem' has to be shifted to a debate beyond that of two nationalisms or an identity problem. The notion of post-colonialism, it has been suggested here, has the potential power to rethink these concerns in a way that recognizes the complexity of world relations and does not simply reduce sport to a local/global or North/South or First/Second/Third World axis. The danger of the Beijing Olympic Games is that it allows the popularity of sport to whip up spontaneous nationalism in China and this patriotism becomes the logic for state nationalism and a move by the PRC to advance on Taiwan.

Summarizing Remarks

Although tending to imply a historical rupture that signifies the end of the colonial chapter, the term post-colonial means much more. The writing that is emerging in relation to sport and post-colonialism is deliberately revisionist in focus. For writers such as Said this meant the liberal-humanist conceptions of Enlightenment thought. It provides an ideal point of entry for studying sport in China in the twentieth century precisely because it potentially helps China to think through problems of both internal colonialism and external relations with potential imperial forces such as America and Japan. This chapter has highlighted the way in which sports policy under Mao has been subject to 'revisionist' thinking under Deng Xiaoping. The political functions of sport were aimed at contributing to both socialist thinking and cultured civilization. Between 1978 and 1989, China questioned and revised the basic elements of Maoism.

The place of sports in opening up sport in China to other worlds and the place of other sporting worlds in China has also been considered. The development of sporting capitalism in China has also meant rethinking the way in which sport may contribute to breaking out of Asia and advancing into the world on its own terms. The revised modern history of sport in modern China nonetheless necessitates finding a space for Falun Gong and the 'Taipei Gaze'. The development of sport in modern China is best illustrated in the popular development of both football and qigong, which in themselves are less important than the challenge of a modern postcolonial China which needs at least to account for both. The imaginary psyche of Western interpretations of sport in China has also been raised as a further facet of sport and post-colonialism in this chapter. The development of sport in twentieth- and twenty-first-century China is capable of illuminating aspects of both the post-colonial issue of global sporting capitalism in China and the imagination and reality of sport and the two Chinas.

Yet the reforms and progress that mark the making of China Today should not obscure or hide the challenges that exist. In the course of its rapid development China in many ways has created conditions that many capitalists elsewhere would envy. It has embarked upon a robust anti-poverty campaign and successful bid for 2008 Olympic Games. Yet the CCP has also dismantled the state sector, thrown hundreds of millions out of work, given up on collective agriculture, celebrated the art of getting rich, embraced the market with Chinese characteristics, marginalized the principles of free education, healthcare and cheap housing for the workers and created a very unequal society. China's 2005 Human Development Report concluded that inequality was growing fast by every index (Hilton, 2006). Perhaps it is not the most important symbol of social change, but in the context of this study it might be noted that Beijing has long since opened up all the zones formerly declared off-limits to foreign influences that might have threatened the Cultural Revolution. Indeed Tiananmen Square, the site of the June 1989 protests which were suppressed by the People's Liberation Army, has been proposed as a site for beach volleyball at the 2008 Olympic Games.

Key Readings

Bale, John and Cronin, Mike (2003), *Sport and Post-Colonialism*. Oxford: Berg.

Brownell, Susan. (1995), *Training the Body for China: Sport in the Moral Order of the People's Republic*. Chicago: University of Chicago Press.

Dong, Jinxia (2002), *Women, Sport and Society in Modern China: Holding Up More than Half the Sky*. London: Routledge.

Espy, Richard (1979), *The Politics of the Olympic Games*. Berkeley: University of California Press.

O'Toole, J., Sutherden, A., Walshe, P. and Muir, D. (2006), 'Shuttle Cocks and Soccer: The State of Sport in China', *Sport Business* 119, December: 46–9.

Spivak, Gayatri Chakravorty (1995), 'Can the Subaltern Speak?', in B. Ashcroft, G. Griffiths and H. Tiffin (eds), *The Post-Colonial Studies Reader*. London: Routledge, 24–8.

Wang, Hui (2000), 'Fire at the Castle Gate', *New Left Review* 6, November/ December: 69–101.

Journal Articles

Chen, Kuan-Hsing (2001), 'America in East Asia', *New Left Review* 12, November/December: 73–87.

Dong, Jinxia (2001), 'Women, Sport and Society in the Early Years of the New China', *International Journal of the History of Sport* 18(2): 1–35.

Hou, Hsia-Hsien (2004), 'Tensions in Taiwan', *New Left Review* 28, July/August: 19–43.

Plymire, D. C. (1999), 'Too Much, Too Fast, Too Soon: Chinese Women Runners, Accusations of Steroid Use, and the Politics of American Track and Field', *Sociology of Sport Journal* 16: 155–73.

Other Readings

Brownell, S. (2007), 'Sport and Politics Don't Mix: China's Relationship with the IOC during the Cold War', in S. Wagg and D. Andrews (eds), *East Plays West: Politics of the Cold War*. London: Routledge, 261–78.

Fingleton, Eamonn (2004), 'East Asian Alliance', *Prospect*, May: 34–8.

Hill, C. (1992), *Olympic Politics*. Manchester: Manchester University Press.

Lenskyj, H. (2000), *Inside The Olympic Industry: Power, Politics and Activism*. Albany, NY: State University of New York Press.

Mackenzie, Hector (2004), 'Euro 2004 Fever Kicks Off in China', *Sunday Herald*, 20 June: 23.

Mitchell, Kevin (2004) 'Sport Focus: China-The New World Power', *Observer*, 23 May: 12.

Walia, S. (2001), *Edward Said and the Writing of History*. Cambridge: Icon Books.

CHAPTER 6

Capitalist Sport, the Beijing Olympics and Human Rights?

Introduction

Sport and the hosting of major sporting events may not be the key essential criterion of superpower status but with a population of 1.3 billion China could also emerge as a potential powerhouse in world sport. In 2004, representatives of motor sport's governing body, the FIA, were in Shanghai to inspect the track for China's first grand prix that was held in September 2004. At the time, Michael Jordan was pushing his new shoe brand which was selling for £100 per pair in Beijing, Don King was exploring the possibility of taking a world heavyweight title fight to China, and China is already part of the world golf and tennis circuit. The Asian Cup Football Championship was staged in China during July 2004. Both the Shanghai Open and the China Open Golf Tournaments have been established. The arrival of Formula One is perhaps the most surprising development given that the majority of the Chinese population live in rural areas far removed from the glamour of the track. In 2004, however, the demand for tickets at about £250 each was by far outstripping the supply. The traditional sports, table tennis, volleyball, badminton and various martial arts, are still popular despite the global pressures brought about by football and basketball.

The commercial and sporting potential of China will become fully apparent by the time of the 2008 Beijing Olympics. On 13 July 2001, the International Olympic Committee chose Beijing over four other candidate cities, Toronto, Paris, Istanbul and Osaka, as the venue for the 2008 Olympic Games. Beijing had previously lost out to Sydney in the bid to stage the 2000 Olympic Games. The paradox that is the relationship between China, sport and the Olympic Games is complex. At the heart of the debate about whether China should host the 2000 and 2008 Olympic Games was a simple struggle between essentially two points of view. Supporters of the Beijing 2008 Olympic bid argued that staging the Olympics would help to narrow the gap between China and the rest of the world. The media coverage of the event would illustrate that China had come of age as a member of the international community. A sport-obsessed younger generation in a country that contains about a quarter of the world's population would benefit from the legacy of Olympic investment. State media in China estimated that as much as $30 billion could be invested in the reconstruction of Beijing in creating not just a new Olympic district, but in basic public services such as sewers, subway lines and new roads. The Olympic factor saw the value of Beijing-based construction and real estate companies rise significantly on the stock market.

This of course had not been the first time that China had bid to host Olympic Games. At 4.27 p.m. on Friday 24 September 1993 it was announced that Sydney would host the 2000 Olympic Games. The announcement brought to an end the bidding process for the 2000 Sydney Olympic Games, a process that had consisted of four rounds of voting for initially five venues, Istanbul, Berlin, Manchester, Beijing and Sydney. At the end of the first round, Beijing led the other four cities with Sydney in second place and Manchester third. At the end of the second round Beijing had extended its lead over Sydney by seven votes with Manchester remaining in third place. At the end of the third round of voting between the remaining three cities Beijing led Sydney by seventeen votes with Manchester remaining in third place. In the fourth and final round Sydney defeated Beijing by 45 votes to 43 and was awarded the 2000 Olympic Games (Cashman and Hughes, 1999: 43).

Commenting on the media's role in covering the Sydney bidding process Lenskyj (1999: 182) draws attention to the *Herald*'s 1999 article 'How Sydney snatched the 2000 Olympic Games from Beijing', which focused on a plan to discredit the Beijing bid by drawing world attention to China's human-rights record. The involvement of world sporting events with human-rights ideals and issues, argues Roche (2000: 200), is part of the idealization of global governance and global citizenship associated with global sport. The general implication is that the Olympic movement should be involved somehow in the promotion of human-rights issues. The awarding to Beijing of the Olympic Games in 2008 may have been rationalized on the basis of the opportunity to capitalize upon China opening up to the West and the possibility of influencing China's human-rights record as it moves on to the world sporting stage as a major global power. The 2008 Beijing Olympic Bid as far as the critical Western gaze was concerned was a compromise between the political imperative to give the Olympic-host role to China and the ethical imperative to refuse to do so.

The 'China Gaze' upon American coverage of China's efforts to host the Olympiad tends to imply that the hostility and prejudice toward communist ideology means a sustained effort to decry China's political system (*Beijing Review*, 4 August 1997). Any Chinese sporting success tends to be demonized in relation to freedom and democracy through sport and other facets of life in China. Perhaps the Western Christian human-rights concept is directly opposed to an Oriental, Confucianist human-rights approach? The US media generally demonize China by smear campaigns including some or all of the following:

1. China cannot be trusted with its nuclear capacity;
2. China is a threat to its neighbours in Asia and to the USA;

3. Chinese sporting performance can only be explained as unnatural;
4. China is a police state trampling on human rights.

Some claim that such interpretations are imposed upon China and they do not tally with the reality of life in China today.

The Olympic movement often claims, writes Roche (2000), to uphold a traditional, organizational, ideological independence and self-government from the powers of nation-states, but that this in principle should not involve any requirement to be exempt from or unanswerable to the IOC or the UN in relation to human-rights issues. To that extent the premise of global sport implies global citizenship and a universal logic that human rights, including records of human-rights violations through sport in relation to concerns over child labour or child abuse, for example, are universally identifiable, non-negotiable and a consideration in relation to the Olympic bidding process. In this chapter, this issue is explored and in doing so the chapter also questions whether the doctrine of human rights itself may be viewed as Western dogma in which certain beliefs are prioritized over others. The specific problems posed in this chapter also relate to some of the detail relating to the hosting of the 2008 Olympic Games in Beijing. However, the general problems posed in this chapter for sport in general are not particularly new. Are there beliefs common to all humanity, values that are universally recognized, if not observed, and can the Olympics and other international sporting events provide an international framework? Or, on the contrary, are all doctrinal systems mutually impenetrable, condemned either to be ignored or to do battle with each other?

Financing and Marketing of the Beijing Olympic Games

The staging of the Olympic Games has been the focus of a sustained body of research on the political economy of the Olympic Games (Roche, 2000; Forster and Pope, 2004; Preuss, 2004; and Payne, 2005; Jarvie, 2006). To date, very little detail exists on the actual financing and marketing of the Beijing Olympic Games. The IOC awards the Olympic Games only to a City and not to a private institution. When a city is elected, the Host City Contract is signed in a ceremony, as a contract that regulates all financial relations between the IOC and the host city. In the case of Beijing the responsibility for covering any revenue shortfall lies with the Chinese Central and Beijing Municipal Governments. The construction of the infrastructure and sports facilities is covered within this guarantee. According to Preuss (2004: 18) the Olympic Committee for the Olympic Games in Beijing suggested in the bid book a conservative budget of US$1.6 billion, thus leaving the city, region, state or private investment to cover an estimated US$14.3 billion. Within this section the hosting of Beijing Olympics is divided into two parts (i) finances and (ii) marketing, and draws upon only the official sources of data.

Financing of the Beijing Olympic Games

Beijing's economy has been growing at a fast pace over the last decade, reaching an average annual increase of 17.5 per cent in its revenue. There is allegedly a sufficient guarantee for the supply of capital and other resources from the public and private sectors to meet the needs of the Olympic Games. The investment in infrastructure to support the Games is compatible with the long-term economic and social development plan of Beijing and allegedly will not impose any extra financial burden on the city's people. The BOCOG (Beijing Organizing Committee for the Olympic Games) budget, with its associated guarantees, is aimed at ensuring the success of the Games and provides the basis of the opportunities the Games can bring. A financial guarantee of support for Beijing to host the 2008 Olympic Games has been given by the Chinese Central and Beijing Municipal Governments. A copy of this guarantee was jointly signed by the Minister of Finance of China, the Chairman of the State Development and Planning Commission of China, the Director of the Beijing Finance Bureau and the Chairman of the Beijing Development and Planning Commission. The financial guarantee includes:

* funding of any BOCOG revenue shortfalls should they occur;
* pre-financing of all BOCOG expenditures prior to receipt of Games revenue;
* construction of the infrastructure within Beijing to support the Games;
* construction of the venues and facilities required to host the Games.

The Central and Beijing Municipal Governments have pledged that consumer prices and hotel rates in and around Beijing will be effectively managed to ensure that prices are fair and reasonable during the Games period. A guarantee to achieve this level of price control has been jointly signed by the Chairman of the State. For the services provided directly by BOCOG via rate card (such as transportation, radio and telecommunications, and rentals of technical equipment and offices), a final price list will be submitted to the IOC for their approval prior to the hosting of the Games. BOCOG assets at the conclusion of the Games will include the furniture, equipment and temporary fixtures purchased by BOCOG for the conduct of the Games. Assets likely to be included in this category would include items of a practical nature, e.g. sports equipment, computers, and items of a memorabilia nature, e.g. a book of the Games and ceremony assets. The nature of disposal will depend on the procurement strategy agreed for each item. It is anticipated that a significant portion of the items would be disposed of via public tender and/or auction. Opportunities to link procurement strategies with the longer-term needs of Beijing and China will also be examined at this point. The funds received from the sale of any assets will be included as revenue for BOCOG. The sports venues, the Olympic Village, the Media Village and other facilities used to host the Games will be owned by the relevant government authorities or private organizations. These government

authorities and private organizations will be responsible for the ongoing operation and maintenance of the facilities as part of the Beijing legacy.

The current Chinese industrial and commercial tax regime (excluding tariffs
and agricultural tax) comprises seventeen specific taxes. Of these, the following
taxes would apply for the hosting of the Olympic Games in Beijing: business tax,
value-added tax (VAT), consumer tax, corporate income tax, individual income
tax, vehicle and road tax, and stamp duty. BOCOG will be established as an
independent legal entity, legally responsible for civil obligations and liabilities.
Under current Chinese Taxation Law, BOCOG would be a taxpayer. In support
for the Olympic Movement, however, the Chinese Government has promised
that, following approval by the Legislature, BOCOG will be exempt from taxes.
This exemption will include revenues from the sale of broadcasting rights for the
Games, from the Olympic marketing programme, and from sponsorship activities, whether the party that makes payments to BOCOG is resident in China or
elsewhere. In support for the Olympic Movement, the Chinese Government has
promised, upon approval by the Legislature, to exempt the IOC and other
Olympic participants from taxes otherwise required under Chinese Taxation
Law. These would include business tax and withholding tax on income from the
Beijing Olympic Games (e.g. income from the sale of television rights); individual income tax due in China for participating athletes in conjunction with
various monetary prizes; VAT levied on the proceeds from the sale by BOCOG
of sponsored commodities and post-Olympic sale of assets; and reimbursement
to BOCOG of the VAT levied on commodities received as donations or sponsorships or purchases for its own use. While the Chinese Government can grant
tax exemptions within China, residents in foreign countries may be required to
pay withholding or similar taxes in their respective countries for payments to
BOCOG for media rights, the Olympic marketing programme and other sponsorships. The tax exempt status of BOCOG would be favourable for the clarifi-
cation of the conditions of such withholding taxes. In addition BOCOG would
negotiate with the governments of the countries concerned regarding exemptions for these taxes, if necessary.

The forecast budget for the Beijing 2008 Olympic Games was prepared on
the basis of a conservative forecast of receipts and expenditure. The process of
preparing the budget included: consultation with the Governments of China,
the Beijing Municipality and other relevant local areas; consultation with experts
both nationally and internationally for each budget item; detailed review and
analysis of the budgets of previous games, particularly Sydney's; consultation
with the IOC and COC; and a comprehensive review of the budget process by
Arthur Andersen and Bovis Lend Lease who have specialist knowledge relating
to the Sydney Games. The planning and budget for the Games have resulted in
an outcome with little or no risk to the IOC and with significant opportunities
for the IOC, Beijing, China and the world. In particular, the projected budget
results in a surplus and contains responsible contingencies built into each budget
item. The Chinese and Beijing Municipal Governments are committed and have

the financial strength to support BOCOG and all other aspects of the preparation for and hosting of the 2008 Games. The Chinese Central Government, Beijing and other city Governments concerned have guaranteed that the facilities and venues for the Games would be constructed as scheduled, while the Chinese people will offer full support for the Games. The Games would generate significant business opportunities within Beijing and China. In addition, the planning for the Games has been based on: the existing plans and commitments for the construction of major transport, environmental and other infrastructure in Beijing; the extensive use of existing facilities, many of which are being upgraded; the extensive use of the Olympic Green as the centre of the Games; and the construction of facilities which have already been planned for Beijing and which will have a long-term legacy for the city and its people.

What follows is a summary of the forecast receipts, payments and surplus for the 2008 Games with a brief description of each item. The projected revenues from the Olympic lottery, the Olympic coin programme and government subsidies have been endorsed by the competent authorities. Written confirmation has been obtained from the IOC on the split of revenues from TV rights and from the Olympic Partnership (TOP) sponsorship programme. The revenue from television rights of the 2008 Olympic Games allocated to BOCOG is estimated at US$833 million at 2008 prices (according to the IOC fax dated 21 March 2000), which will be US$709 million when converted to 2000 prices. BOCOG is to be allocated a share of approximately US$200 million of the revenue from the TOP programmes, which will be US$130 million when converted to 2000 prices. BOBICO (Beijing 2008 Olympic Games Bidding Committee) has approached a number of multinational and large Chinese corporations on the prospect of sponsorships. It expects to receive US$130 million in sponsorships and services from ten to fifteen multinationals, large corporations and manufacturers of special equipment. The total licensing revenue for the Beijing 2008 Games is estimated to be about US$50 million. To meet the needs of the Games for various equipment, supplies and related services, BOCOG has budgeted US$20 million worth of supplies and services from official suppliers at home and abroad. BOCOG will, in consultation and cooperation with the People's Bank of China, which is China's central bank, ask the governing institution to issue 1.5 million gold and silver Olympic coins. This is expected to generate, for BOCOG, revenue of US$8 million. BOCOG will also, in consultation and cooperation with the State Post Bureau, ask the governing institution to issue Olympic stamps. BOCOG will consult governing departments for the possible issue of commemorative banknotes. BOCOG and the Ministry of Finance are operating an Olympic Games Lottery between 2001 and 2008. The lottery is expected to generate US$180 million in revenue. BOCOG will have an estimated 7 million tickets for sale at home and abroad, which is expected to generate further revenue of US$140 million. Donations from business enterprises, social organizations, and individuals are estimated to be US$20 million. The disposal of assets revenues arising from the disposal of assets owned by BOCOG are estimated to be worth US$80 million. The Central and Beijing Municipal Governments will provide BOCOG with US$100 million in subsidies. Revenues from the licensing and leasing of commercial premises in the Olympic complexes, from the leasing of space, equipment, and facilities of the MPC and the IBC, and from the rentals of accommodation in the Olympic Village before and after the Games are estimated to be worth a further US$46 million.

Marketing of the Beijing Olympic Games

China is not only one of the largest developing countries in the world but also the second-largest investment market. Many multinationals have set up offices and made major investments in the Beijing Olympics through the TOP programme. As China is about to join the WTO, the Chinese market will open up even more to embrace the world, offering further opportunities for domestic and international investors in the Olympic project. This will provide BOCOG with a reliable source of revenue for its Olympic marketing programme. The participation of the 1.25 billion Chinese people in the Games promises great potential for the Olympic marketing programme which will offer many other opportunities on a local and global basis before and after the Games.

The COC Marketing is a joint marketing partnership between BOCOG and COC. BOBICO reached an agreement with the COC on behalf of the candidate city. The COC pledges that in accordance with the requirements of the Manual for Candidate Cities of the 2008 Olympic Games and the Host City Contract, and in the spirit of the IOC Clarifications to Questions 6.1.2 of the Manual of 1 December 2000 concerning the joint marketing programme and the standard agreement, it will develop a joint Olympic marketing programme with BOBICO with regard to the marketing of the 2008 Olympic Games. The principal components of the programme are that:

- the COC guarantees that its sponsorship activities related to Olympic Marketing will cease according to the date defined by the IOC;
- BOCOG and the COC undertake to protect the correct use of the Olympic symbol, emblems, logos, marks and other Olympics-related marks and designations as required by the IOC;
- BOCOG and the COC will begin their implementation of joint marketing plan from 1 January 2003 as required by the IOC;
- the COC will coordinate the marketing plan of its affiliated national associations in order to incorporate their plan in the joint marketing programme with benefit-sharing and ensure that national marketing plan should not be in conflict with the obligations taken by the COC toward the IOC;
- the distributions of the revenue from the joint marketing programme allocated to the COC and the related national associations will be no less than the revenue they expect to generate over the determined period.

It is anticipated that approximately ten international corporations will join the ranks of BOCOG partners, and ten to fifteen large enterprise groups will become BOCOG sponsors.

Apart from the multinational companies included in the IOC's TOP programme, it is anticipated that BOCOG will be able to attract sponsorship from large corporations including the following categories: petroleum and petrochemicals; telecommunications; banking and finance; insurance; machinery and electronics; engineering construction and building materials; metallurgy (nonferrous); textile and light industry (garment materials); civil aviation, rail and air freight services; postal services; energy (water and electricity); transport; foodstuffs; and medical and health care. BOCOG will also work with the IOC to develop special products for the 2008 Olympic Games. BOCOG will also follow the global marketing plan of the International Paralympic Committee in collaboration with the COC and the Chinese Sports Association for the Disabled, and thus a unified Paralympics marketing programme will be implemented. This will facilitate the raising of funds for the hosting of the Paralympics Games through sponsorship, donations, the issuing of licences, organization of lotteries, ticket sales and the issue of commemorative stamps and coins.

A number of marketing strategies in relation to ticket sales have been implemented. Based on the capacity of the competition venues and the competition schedule, it is estimated there will be a total of over 9 million tickets available. It is anticipated that 7 million tickets will be sold. The sale of tickets is to ensure that as many people can participate in the Games as possible. This will be achieved by a number of simple but effective strategies. The overall pricing of tickets will be kept down to an affordable level, giving the widest possible number of people the opportunity to purchase tickets to events. As many events as possible will be allocated reasonable and fair proportion of public seats. A significant number of tickets will be allocated for the disadvantaged and schoolchildren to help ensure that our future generations benefit from the legacy of the Games. The revenue generated from ticket sales is expected to be US$140 million. Average ticket prices have been assumed as follows: Opening and Closing Ceremonies US$260, Primary events US$80 and Secondary events US$15.

It has been agreed with the People's Bank of China that it will work with BOBICO to develop and implement a commemorative coin programme for the Beijing 2008 Olympic Games. Commemorative coins will be issued. These will be distributed in batches each year from 2005 to 2008. There will be twelve different coins produced, of which four will be gold (60,000 of each type) and eight will be silver (200,000 of each type). It is estimated that 1.5 million gold and silver commemorative coins will be sold, bringing a revenue of US$8 million for BOCOG. Furthermore, BOCOG had obtained endorsement from the Ministry of Finance for the conduct of an Olympic Lottery if Beijing was awarded the 2008 Olympic Games. The lottery tickets are sold through the existing networks of China's Sports Lottery. The lottery programme operates from 2001 to 2008 and will produce forecasted revenue of about US$180 million. The relevant authorities of Beijing have pledged to follow the Host City Contract with regard to advertising control. During the required period BOCOG will have complete control over billboard advertising, sky-space advertising and advertising on the public transport system. The IOC's TOP sponsors and the participants of the joint marketing programme will have priority and exclusive rights over the use of these advertising sites. In order to promote the Olympic Movement and safeguard the interests of Olympic sponsors, Beijing authorities have pledged that specific statutes and rules in line with the legislation implemented for the Sydney 2000 Olympic Games will be adopted to prevent ambush marketing during the 2008 Olympic Games. Upon Beijing winning the bid, the Beijing Municipal Government began to enact relevant statutes and regulations in accordance with due legal procedures.

Finally, provision is made within the Olympic Green and at competition sites for a range of sponsor hospitality opportunities. This will be on a tiered basis with Sponsor Hospitality privileges being dependent on the level of sponsorship provided to BOCOG. All Sponsor programmes will be developed on a purely cost-recovery basis. The Sponsor Hospitality programme will include the development of a Sponsor Hospitality Village for use by TOP sponsors. A high-rise, luxury multi-purpose apartment building will be constructed very close to the Main Stadium. This building will offer facilities for entertainment and recreation, business conferences and exhibitions. It is envisaged this building will be suitable to provide Sponsor Hospitality services during the Games period.

Olympic Bidding, Beijing and Human Rights

In many ways the challenge of China and the Beijing Olympics has been how best to maximize the opportunity for commercialization of life in China brought about by the opportunity of a successful Olympic bid, while at the same time ensuring that such commercialization did not destroy China's humanistic spirit. Chinese liberals were worried about the impact of the Olympic Games in camouflaging struggles for social inequality in China. The term 'Chinese liberal' was associated with a critical stance on official marketization that dated back to at least 1993–1994, while the term 'the New Left' was attached to this position after about 1997–1998. The term New Left traditionally was viewed as a throwback to the Cultural Revolution and took on a new meaning critical of the rush to marketization following the 1998 Asian financial crises. The identification of most Chinese intellectuals as liberal or New Left dates from the 1990s, but after 1989 the radicalization of official reform policies created a situation where the term was used to describe a position that involved a mixture of support for and criticism of the government. The liberal or New Left position cautiously welcomed creeping marketization, but disapproved of censorship or violation of human rights. The paradox in many ways reflects the debate that characterized the arguments surrounding China's bid to host the 2008 Olympic Games.

On 25 November 1998 the Municipal Government of Beijing submitted an application to the COC. The bid was approved on 6 January 1999 and, by 6 September 1999, BOBICO had held its first meeting in the Great Hall of the People. The Beijing bid was submitted to the IOC on 17 January 2000. It is perhaps worthwhile at this point to provide a brief background to the bidding process prior to the decision to award Beijing the 2008 Olympic Games. The extent to which BOBICO shaped the Olympic Bid in relation to environmental factors, political campaigns and issues of security and law and order is evident from the following illustrative events within each category:

The Environment

- Beijing's air pollution was thought to be one of the factors why it lost out to Sydney in 2000.
- Since 1998, US$15 billion dollars per year have been invested in transport, communication and environmental improvement.
- In October 2000, the city banned the setting up of barbecue stalls in an attempt to reduce air pollutants.
- In November 2000, the city with the World Bank launched a US$1.25 billion initiative to help Beijing approach WHO clean air standards for cities by 2006, and twenty-two measures to reduce smog were introduced, including the closing of local steel mills by 2002.
- Tianjin, China's third largest city, has launched six major projects aimed at Tianjin (a co-Olympic host city) becoming part of the Beijing-Tianjin Ecological Zone.
- In April 2001, a total of 2,008 trees were planted in a park in Beijing to express support for a 'Green Olympics'.

Political Campaigns

- In October 2000, Chinese President Jiang Zemin wrote to the IOC confirming that China's people were behind the bid.
- In November 2000, Beijing protected its bid from criticism from a British Parliamentary Committee of violating the spirit of the Games.
- In February 2001, Amnesty International's Report on China's Human Rights history was evaluated by two Olympic delegates.
- In March 2001, forty-one members of the US House of Representatives urged the IOC to reject China's bid.
- In May 2001, with more that fifty Tibetan and other anti-China protesters demonstrating outside the IOC headquarters in Lausanne, the Dalai Lama released a statement that China deserved to be an Olympic host.

- In July 2001, Taiwan's Vice-President, Annette Lu, softened Taiwan's hard line on the bid by endorsing the Beijing bid during a speech to Harvard University Alumni.

Order and Security

- In December 2000, protesters sent a petition to the IOC and the governments of China, the US, Britain and Germany, requesting dissidents to be released;
- In January 2001, China detained five people who petitioned the IOC to release democracy organizers.
- In February 2001, Tiananmen Square was closed off during the visit of the IOC Evaluation Committee.
- In June 2001, police, paramilitary armed police and security officers stopped and questioned pedestrians intent on attending the Three Tenors – Luciano Pavarotti, Jose Carreras and Placido Domingo – performance held in the Forbidden City in celebration of World Olympic Day and in support of the Beijing 2008 Olympic Games bid.
- The Olympic bid document claimed that the PRC was a multinational state created jointly by the people of all its nationalities and that China had been free from international terrorism. The framing of the argument implied that, since the celebration of the Olympic Games was in the interests of all religious and ethnic groups, the rise of religious, nationalist and political campaigns was very small.

Following the decision on 13 July 2001 to award the 2008 Olympic Games to Beijing, Chinese President Jiang Zemin in an unannounced appearance made a brief speech, 'Comrades! We express our deep thanks to all our friends around the world and to the IOC for helping to make Beijing successful in its Olympic bid'. He went on, 'I hope the whole nation works hard along with residents of the capital city to stage a successful 2008 Olympic Games. I also welcome our friends around the world to visit Beijing in 2008' (www.cnn.com/2001/WORLD/asiapcf/east/07/13/beijing.win/).

The typical Western press headline that covered the announcement of Beijing's right to hold the 2008 Olympic Games tended to report a qualified victory. The IOC recording of the votes in Moscow was such that the Beijing bid received 56 votes, three more than the required majority and thirty-four votes ahead of second place Toronto. The cnn.com/World headline 'Beijing Games win divides world opinion' explicitly referred to the victory in the face of world-wide concern over China's human-rights record. Amnesty International refused to either welcome or condemn the decision, but urged China to improve its human-rights record.

In New Delhi, the Dalai Lama's Tibetan government in exile was quietly critical of the choice, saying that it would encourage repression in China. As the exiled Tibetan spiritual leader, the Dalai Lama had fled Tibet nine years after Chinese troops marched into Tibet in 1950. In the current debate on Tibet the two opposing sides see almost everything in black and white, despite the opportunity for closer alignment during the late 1970s when Deng Xiaoping indicated a willingness to start a dialogue with the Dalai Lama (Wang, 2002). Yet in relation to the Beijing 2008 Olympic success a spokesperson for the administration remained resolute that Tibet regretted the decision in that it would put the stamp of approval on Beijing's human-rights abuses and would encourage China to escalate repression.

In Paris the French President Jacques Chirac said that he regretted Paris had failed in its bid, but that it would not give up staging a future Games, while the head of the President's foreign-affairs committee paralleled the decision to award the Game to China with the decision to hold the 1936 Olympics in Nazi Germany. François Loncle went on, 'the decision by the IOC goes to justifying a repressive political system that each day flouts freedom and violates human rights – following the example of Nazi Germany in 1936 and the Soviet Union in 1980. Communist China will use (the Games) as a powerful propaganda instrument destined to consolidate its hold on power' (www.cnn.com/2001/ WORLD/asiapcf/east/07/13/beijing.win/). In Germany, Interior Minister Otto Schilly said the decision would help promote democracy in China. In Australia the bid was supported partially due to the potential economic benefits of an Asian Pacific Games. In Taiwan the *United Daily News* mass circulation reported that 'it was like buying an insurance policy that China would not invade Taiwan for at least seven years, but on the other hand Chinese success at the Games could fuel a more powerful nationalist fervour which may lead to a more determined stance on taking Taiwan back after 2008.

The decision to award the Games to China had several internal political consequences. The challenge of China as mentioned previously has been to accept China into the global market place, while at the same time enabling China to come to its own decisions about internal democracy. The hosting of the Olympic Games will encourage international engagement and open up contact with other countries. With tens of thousands of foreign visitors expected, supporters argue that the Olympics will force China to open up more to the rest of the world and generate heightened scrutiny of the government's behaviour. The pro-Olympic argument rests upon the belief that the Olympics will accelerate social liberalization. China has succeeded in its bid against the backcloth of unrest, social dislocation and apparent corruption and yet the Olympic backdrop, it was thought initially, would strengthen the hand of then President Jiang Zemin, due to step down from power in 2002, because he would be seen as the person who brought Beijing the Olympics.

In effect we have a position where people have no political freedom but, because of the Olympics and liberal reform, the possibility of an expansion of personal freedoms may exist. Amnesty International hoped that the Olympic spirit of fair play and respect for universal fundamental ethical principles would extend to the people of China long before 2008. For instance, it was hoped that an increasing number of scholars and Falun Gong supporters would be released in a similar fashion to that of dissident Wei Jingsheng who was freed after fourteen years of jail prior to the 2000 Beijing Olympic bid. Wei Jingsheng, who supported the 2000 Games, was re-arrested after the bid failed, and is now exiled in the USA. He has subsequently argued that the success of 2008 will only encourage China to violate human rights further.

Just over a week after the IOC decision to award China the Olympic Games, then Vice-Premier Li Lanqing made a direct link between Beijing's success and the regime's crackdown on Falun Gong. The remarks have been interpreted by critics as equally being relevant to the claim of international support for suppressing Tibetans or democracy between China and Taiwan. Li Lanqing stated, 'we have won a great victory against Falun Gong and we have won the right to host the 2008 Olympic Games. This shows that the international community has acknowledged the fact that China is marked by social stability and progress, its economy is prospering and its people living a peaceful and comfortable life' (*Australian*, 23 July 2001: 4). The Associated Press reported on 8 July that the Lithuanian Government had responded to Chinese instructions that demonstrators with Tibetan flags were to be taken away during a visit by President Jang Zemin. In reality, the 2008 Beijing Olympic Games will likely be presided over by a New Chinese leadership of current President Hu Jintao and Prime Minister Wen Jianbao, but the challenge of China remains the same. At the same time, it is also evident that China's international aspirations are such that, while the Beijing Organizing Committee is not wooing international marketing agencies to sell the Games, it is not actively discouraging them either. Football and basketball still have the potential capacity in China to drive the commercialization of the sports sector.

Sport and Human Rights: Imperialist Credo or Common Resource?

The collection of human rights specified in international human-rights law draws on a long tradition of rights from philosophy, history and normative political theory and includes at least three sets of rights, (i) civil and political rights, (ii) economic, social and cultural rights, and (iii) solidarity rights. Human rights have a pre-eminent place in current political, social, legal and moral thinking, and to such an extent that one might think of them as totalitarian in their force. The absolutist view on human rights, although not rights, tends to view human rights not as a social or individual choice but rather a particular set of rights that are meant to constrain individual or social choice in relation to some form of universality. Some have argued that they express the moral fundamentalism of Western civilization. The relativist view asserts that fundamentalist or absolutist views should not be imposed or prescribed for subsequent generations.

Toleration is encouraged, morality is viewed as being entirely relative and, where conflict does arise, resolutions are sought through creating continuing processes of toleration. Eastern forms of fundamentalism have often brought into question Western moral relativism as if it were imperialist dogma.

Sport has generally not figured in debates about human rights, but where the broader notion of rights is concerned sport has been mentioned in some or all of the following ways:

1. the right of children to sport and play;
2. the right or not to participate in sports such as fox-hunting and other blood sports;
3. the protection of sporting cultural rights as in the case of minority sports cultures;
4. the right to meaningful leisure and quality free time;
5. the right for young high-performance athletes to be protected from the demands of high-performance sport or sports labour;
6. the right of athletes to be free from the fear of sexual exploitation or racial harassment;
7. the articulation of articles 2, 3, 4,6, 8 and 10 of the European Human Rights Act as it applies to sport.

The issue of human hights, however, has clouded the development of Olympic sport in China, and yet perhaps the real problem here is whether there are beliefs common to all humanity and values that are universally recognized – if not observed – in different parts of the world. How are we to resolve peacefully not just the issue of sport and human rights to enable sport and physical culture to be available to all as a human right? To that end, the first step might be to consider the issue that human rights in sport is currently a further credo or form of Western imperialism even in some post-colonial contexts. To see human rights as a corpus of dogma allows us to question the values at work within global sport or a globalized world rather differently. The twin pitfalls that must be avoided remain those of absolutist or relativist attitudes toward rights, mentioned earlier.

Chinese Government white papers are critical of absolutist approaches in the sense that they argue, for example,

> The issue of human rights has become one of great significance and common concern in the world community. The series of declarations and conventions adopted by the United Nations have won support and respect from many countries. The Chinese Government has also highly appraised the Universal Declaration of Human Rights, considering it the first international human rights document that has laid the foundation for the practice of human rights in the world arena. However, the evolution of human rights is circumscribed by the historical, social, economic and cultural conditions of various nations, and involves a process of historical development. Owing to tremendous differences in historical

background, social system, cultural tradition and economic development, countries differ in their understanding and practice of human rights. From their different situations, they have taken different attitudes toward the relevant UN conventions. Despite its international aspect, the issue of human rights falls by and large within the sovereignty of each country. Therefore, a country's human rights situation should not be judged in total disregard of its history and national conditions, nor can it be evaluated according to a preconceived model or the conditions of another country or region. Such is the practical attitude, the attitude of seeking truth from facts. (International Office of the State Council of the PRC, 2000: 52–53)

Absolutist approaches to human rights and sport run the danger of being viewed as a set of sacred commandments revealed to other societies by the Northern or Western sporting hemispheres. Such rights might include absolutist approaches to differences between the sexes in sport, or differences between minority groups in sport or the special status given to group a, b, c or d with the verdict being that this is the way it has to be. Absolutist approaches to sport and human rights run the danger of becoming forms of messianic fundamentalism often propagated by Western interpretation of human rights across the rest of the world. The relativist view is equally fundamental if it considers that human rights suit only the West, and freedom, equality and democracy in sport is something that is only really driven from the West. For instance, such views would see the part played by sport in the downfall of apartheid in South Africa as emanating from the West rather than from within South Africa itself. The fundamentalism of the relativist view on human rights and sport locks people into the notion that Western sport endowed with democratic freedoms and human rights by comparison with those of other places are the drivers of their own fate. In the international arena relativism of this kind downgrades sport in other communities or the post-colonial world in favour of an imperial or relative fundamental way of doing things.

Both the absolutist and relative approaches to human rights and sport present 'other' countries, and particularly the poorest countries of the South, with a simple alternative: either transform yourself by denying who you are and play the game our way or give up any idea of full representation for your particular indigenous sports in the Olympics. The escape from such a vicious circle lies perhaps not in the notion of global or closed sport, but in international and open sport in which the notion of sport and human rights are *both* viewed as a common resource. There is no need for a Western monopoly of the interpretation of human rights in sport or human rights per se. To be common, a resource must be open to general appropriation and therefore just as the IOC might have raised the issues over time of human rights in relation to countries such as China, it might equally question levels of violence and civil unrest in many parts of the Western world as a basis for bidding for the Olympic Games. Perhaps more importantly, when one hears of capitalism with Chinese characteristics, African values or East Asian spirit, the spaces of the Northern and Western hemispheres must be more open to exposing Western conceptions of sport, human rights or any other form of fundamentalism that poses a threat.

The social dimension of international sport is destined to remain an empty slogan as long as there is no institutional means for the people of 'other' communities to propose to the North their own interpretation of sport or human rights. By the same token, political democracy in China will not come about from a legally impartial market, secured by constitutional amendments, but from the strength of social movements internal to China to interact with other movements, public discussion and institutional innovations. This point is central in that it reinforces the argument that China can say no, just as Taiwan can say no and Tibet can say no – but say no to what? American universalism? Western authority? The International Olympic Movement? Globalization? China has long since rejected the notion that all the issues now raised by critical intellectuals come from America or Europe. The democracy that social movements in China were looking for was not simply a legal universal framework, but also sprang from economic justice and social equality – it was a comprehensive social value. As mentioned at the outset, the problems here are not particularly new, but as a question or problem it is perhaps posed today as a matter of particular urgency given the current state of world relations. The answers involve moving beyond viewing human rights, or Western Sport or Olympism as dogma to contributing to a common resource. However, the condition for such a move might involve the countries of the West or even the North ceasing to impose their own ideas on the rest of the world and starting to learn from other cultures, in a common enterprise of self-examination. Such an examination would probably lead to the North having to admit its historical violation of the principles it claims as a creed. Asia and 'other' worlds offer alternatives that might yet lead to a celebration of post-colonial sporting hybridity.

Furthermore, while sport at times reproduces the politics of contested national and other identities, it should not be at the expense of an acceptance of the possibility of internationality or focus upon common humanity. Living sporting identities are in constant flux, producing an ever-changing, international balance of similarities and differences that may contribute to what it is that makes life worth living, and what connects us with the rest of the changing world. If we are to come to terms with the contemporary crisis of sporting identities then we need to transcend the nationalist or global-local simplicities and celebrate difference without demonizing it. Increasing similarity of sporting tastes, choices and aspirations can exist without implying homogeneity. As such, the notion of international sport and new forms of internationality must remain part of the vocabulary of global and regional sporting debates not just because it is a more reality-congruent way of explaining the governance of sport today, but because it tempers the all-consuming notion of globalization and provides grounds for explaining the 'other' worlds of sport outside the transnational corporation or the West.

Summarizing Remarks

Human Rights, it might be argued, form part of a techno-scientific enterprise of the West. They serve both to legitimate it and to canonize it as dogmatic or doctrinal. The rich catalogue of atrocities committed in the twentieth century shows how indispensable human-rights-protection policies are. But if human rights are to continue to fulfil this salutary function, they perhaps need to be reinterpreted in keeping with the development of other worlds. This presupposes appropriate enrichment of the idea and scope of human rights by non-Western peoples. Only then, it has been argued in this chapter, will human rights in sport and other areas cease to be a credo imposed on the rest of humanity and become a common dogmatic resource available to all.

In an insightful review of human rights in sport, Kidd and Donnelly (2000) are at pains to point out that governments in the first world (their terms), like those of the USA and Canada, often use the appeal to human rights as a tactic of international propaganda. The threat and the promise of liberal freedoms being fought for with authoritarian regimes such as Iraq and North Korea are pressed, while at the same time they ignore the denial of the same freedoms in areas such as Indonesia and Guatemala and the rights of their own citizens. They remind us that the USA remains one of the few nations not to sign the International Convention on the Rights of the Child (1989) or endorse the 1980 UNESCO International Charter of Physical Education and Sport (Kidd and Donnelly, 2000: 135).

Statements about human rights in sport and elsewhere tend to be normative and prescriptive. Critics reject the idea of universality or allege that particular accounts are merely ideological and culture-specific and that in any case the rights may be violated for reasons of state or public emergency. Human-rights claims challenge state sovereignty and power, but on the other hand states may enhance their international legitimacy and thereby external security by displaying a respect for human rights. Yet to view human rights as a corpus of dogma or imperialism allows us to approach the question of values in an international if not globalized world in a different way. If sport is global – and that is open to question – then a commitment to global sport might entail a commitment to global social rights. We have argued that, if new forms of internationality in sport are to be supported in relation to human rights in sport, a condition is that the more powerful international sporting organizations cease to impose their own ideas and interpretation on the rest of the world and start to learn from *other* cultures, in a common enterprise of self-examination.

Perhaps the emergence of a more socially committed approach to both the Olympics and International sport has to start from actively acknowledging the huge differences of opportunities, wealth, democracy, sporting tastes, and models of professional sport that divide the world. The deep challenge facing global sport is to outline the mechanisms by which sport can be actively seen to contribute to social and economic welfare on an international scale. At the international level the more powerful sporting nations would seem to have the power to enforce many of the rules and decisions affecting world sport, and yet there are perhaps unprecedented opportunities at the beginning of the twenty-first century in that sport is free from the cold-war politics of the twentieth century. Perhaps the most obvious and disturbing concern is the extent to which the core institutions of sport are trusted and sensitive to ways of addressing the interests of the majority in the non-Western world. The chief causes of inequality in global sport remain twofold: the transformation of global sport by financial capital and the displacement of democratic political power in sport by unaccountable market power.

Key Readings

Beijing Olympic 2008 Bid (2004) www.websitesaboutchina.com/main/2008_olym/part1/olympic_8.htm accessed 26 July 2004.

Cashman, R. and Hughes, A. (1999), *Staging The Olympics: The Event and its Impact.* Sydney: University of New South Wales Press.

Close, P., Askew, D. and Xu, X. (2007), *The Beijing Olympiad: The Political Economy of a Sporting Mega Event.* London: Routledge.

Dong, Jinxia (2005), 'Women, Nationalism and the Beijing Olympics: Preparing for Glory', *International Journal of the History of Sport* 22(4): 530–44.

Hong, F., Ping, W. and Huan, X. (2005), 'Beijing Ambitions: An Analysis of the Chinese Elite Sports System and its Olympic Strategy for the 2008 Olympic Games', *International Journal of the History of Sport* 22(4): 510–29.

Preuss, Holger (2004), *The Economics of Staging the Olympics: A Comparison of the Games 1972–2008.* Northampton: Edward Elgar.

Roche, M. (2000), *Mega-Events Modernity: Olympics and Expos in the Growth of Global Culture.* London: Routledge.

Journal Articles

Chen, Kuan-Hsing (2001), 'America in East Asia: The Club 51 Syndrome', *New Left Review* 12, November/December: 73–87.

Donnelly, P. (1997), 'Child Labour, Sport Labour: Applying Child Labour Laws to Sport', *International Review for the Sociology of Sport* 32(4): 389–406.

Kidd, B. and Donnelly, P. (2000), 'Human Rights in Sport', *International Review for the Sociology of Sport* 35(2): 131–48.

Reddy, S. (2007), 'Death in China', *New Left Review* 45, May/June: 49–65.

Supiot, A. (2003), 'The Labyrinth of Human Rights', *New Left Review* 21, May/June: 118–36.

Wasserstrom, J. (1999), 'Student Protests in Fin De Siècle China', *New Left Review* 237(1): 52–76.

Wright, Erik-Olin (2006), 'Compass Points: Towards a Social Alternative', *New Left Review* 41, September/October: 93–124.

Other Readings

Bale, J. and Cronin, M. (2003), *Sport and Postcolonialism*. Oxford: Berg.

Doise, W. (2002), *Human Rights as Social Representations*. London: Routledge.

Eichberg, H. (2004), *The People of Democracy: Understanding Self-Determination on the Basis of Body Movement*. Arhus: Klim.

Gorman, J. (2003), *Rights and Reason*. Chesham: Acumen.

Sport in China (2004), www.china.org.cn/english/sports/100251.htm accessed 26 July 2004.

Wang, Hui (2006) 'Depoliticized Politics: From East to West', *New Left Review* 41, September/October: 29–43.

Conclusion: Sport, Social Change and the Public Intellectual

The historical and sociological study of sport and physical culture in China matters for a number of reasons: it (i) helps to avoid a parochial or insular understanding of sport and physical culture; (ii) stops research retreating into the present; (iii) provides the tools by which to evaluate change, whether it be social or otherwise, continuity and meaning; (iv) helps, like sociology, to destroy sporting myths; (v) warns against uncritical acceptance of sporting heritage, traditions and identities; and (vi) helps to illuminate past themes, events and changes in their own terms as mattered at the time, and therefore sport in the past is explained on its own terms. All human beings, institutions and collectivities need a past, and to that end sport and physical culture in China is no different. All historical and/or sociological studies of sport are part of a larger and more complex world, and therefore the historical-sociological study of sport designed for only a particular section or part of that world cannot on its own be good history or sociology, because it needs to engage with other sporting worlds. The historical and sociological study of sport tends to remain dominated by the study of Western sport, despite notable and valuable advances in such areas as anthropology and geography. Identity sports history, sociology, geography or anthropology, although it may be comforting to particular groups, left on its own can be dangerous if it leads or contributes to forms of fundamentalism.

It is hoped that *Sport, Revolution and the Beijing Olympics* helps with all of the above. It may be easy at the beginning of the twenty-first century to be pessimistic about the future prospects of a socialism of social empowerment, but it is important to remember also that around the world many different proposals or paths to alternative societies are being experimented with. We do not know what the limits of such partial and piecemeal experimentation and innovation are within capitalism, but what is certain is that we have not reached these limits yet, and the study of sport and physical culture in China provides ample evidence of the promise and possibilities of sport and physical culture in China.

When the first summit of the world's leading nations met in 1975 it was an informal get-together involving the United States, Britain, France, Germany, Japan and Italy who met to discuss the recession caused by an Arab embargo on oil exports. The G6 summit became the G7 in 1976 when the then US President Ford invited Canada to balance out the Europeans, and then in 1988 the G7 became the G8 with the inclusion of Russia. In June 2004, ahead of the meeting of a leading group of eight nations in Savannah, Georgia, one of the key recommendations of a special report on China was that China should be invited to join the group. The authors pointed out that with China becoming one of the major trading nations of the world, its foreign-exchange reserves being second only to Japan and its plans to reform its financial markets, justified and more importantly necessitated its membership at the top table (O'Neil and Hormats, 2004). One month earlier, in May the then British Prime Minister Tony Blair had met with President Wen Jiabao to discuss issues of democracy and human rights in relation to Hong Kong and Tibet. Britain was concerned that the National People's Congress had effectively ruled out democratic elections in Hong Kong until 2007–2008. The visit to London by the Chinese President meant that he was met by the Queen and the Foreign Office, but also was confronted by protesters from the Falun Gong Movement and the Free Tibet Campaign. The protesters at the time viewed Wen Jiabao as a part of the new generation of Chinese leaders and were reported to be remaining optimistic about his leadership and the issue of China's 54-year occupation of Tibet.

These two accounts in many ways reflect the challenge that is China in the twenty-first century. In China privatization is occurring before democratization, with China moving toward a closer relationship with globalization on its own terms – in other words, what has been referred to in this study as creeping toward capitalism with Chinese characteristics. Social, economic and cultural changes have been afoot in China following the perceived failure of Mao's egalitarian socialism in which an understanding of China's own approach to consumerism, Confucianism and communism is only part of the guidebook to making sense of China today. There has been a close East Asian Alliance between China and Japan which may eventually wish to challenge any perceived US-led world order. There is dialogue with Tibet, Hong Kong has been handed over and Beijing has been awarded the 2008 Olympic Games. The awarding of the Olympic Games in many ways encapsulates the challenge that is China in that the promise and possibilities are framed not in terms of the strengths and weaknesses of communism and capitalism but in the tantalizing notion of reconciliation, internationality and wealth, limited by divergent views and solutions to issues such as democracy, corruption and rural poverty – problems that in themselves are widespread internationally and involve places and spaces that are far beyond the boundaries or borders of, for example, China, America or Africa.

Sport, Revolution and the Beijing Olympics has attempted to provide an understanding and insight into the challenge that is China by examining the role of sport and physical culture during periods of revolution, evolution, socialism and communism, culminating in the 2008 bid to host the Olympic Games in Beijing. It provides a critical account of the transformative value of sport between about 1860 and the early part of the twenty-first century. It has attempted to complement and add to our knowledge of sport in an 'other' non-Western community, but also add to what little we know about the part played by sport, exercise and physical culture in China's history and social-political development.

Implicit within this study has been the conviction that a historical and sociologically based study of sport in China can provide insights into a number of secondary problem areas. This has involved providing substantive evidence in order to answer the following questions: (i) What impact has imperialism had upon the development of sport and physical culture in China? (ii) How did early communism and nationalism influence sporting development and opportunities in China? (iii) What was involved in the development of the New Physical Culture under Mao Zedong and what impact did the Cultural Revolution and the Great Leap Forward have on sport? (iv) How has sport been implicated in attempts to reconcile political relations between the two Chinas and other countries? (v) Why would the hosting of the Olympic Games be important to China? and (vi) What is the relationship between Sport, the Olympics and Human Rights?

Much of the existing information provided by researchers and students interested in sport in society has sought to destroy many taken-for-granted myths about sport, to appraise critically and evaluate the actions of the powerful in sport as well as the impact upon the less powerful, and to inform and champion the promise of sport in terms of social change and social inequality. This can happen at different levels, including that of the nation. It is only a relatively recent factor that sport's contribution to human rights campaigns has become less residual. It has also been said that sociology is the power of the powerless, and yet there is no guarantee that – having acquired sociological or historical understanding – one can dissolve or disempower the resistance put up by the tough realities of life in different parts of the world. The power of understanding is no match for the pressures of coercion allied with resigned and submissive common sense; however, if it were not for this understanding the chance of further freedoms being won through and in sport would be slimmer still. Such concerns are as much to do with sport in the West as they are about sport in other parts of the world.

By enabling us to know about other centuries and other cultures, an understanding of the social and historical development of sport provides one of the best antidotes against both a temporal sporting parochialism that assumes that the only time is now and a geographical parochialism that assumes that the only place is here. This holds true for the study of sport in China as it does for other places. There is not only here and now, there is also there and then. One of the best defences against retreating into the present is sports historiography, in part because it helps us understand how other sporting worlds have developed. The impact of historical interventions and ideas upon the study of sport has been one of the richest and most enduring. As with other areas it has had to answer postmodern debates about facts, objectivity and truth, post-colonial debates about the non-Western worlds, colonialism and other histories and representations of sport, while at the same time adding plausibility and complexity to what we know about sport in the past and present.

Yet a simple charting of sport in society is unsatisfactory in the sense that it fails to consider what was referred to at the beginning of this book as the transformative capacity of sport and physical culture. While global neo-liberalism is an intellectually complex body of knowledge involving diverse strands of argument, its politics is pristinely simple in that politics ceases to have any meaning beyond terms prescribed by the market. To accept such logic would be to deny or reduce to a matter of insignificance the many opportunities for social change and social reform that are presented by and through contemporary sport both within China and beyond. To say that such opportunities exist would be as utopian as thinking that older variants of capitalism remain the way of the twenty-first century – the latter way of thinking is of course not accurate. New parameters of global politics exist just as capitalism with Chinese characteristics continues to forge an increasing interdependence with global sport. The politics of sport and physical culture in China have been thought out and fought, policies have been forged and implemented, while political ideas have waxed and waned. Opportunities for social change through sport and physical culture in China remain to such an extent that they potentially provide resources of hope for many people.

We should not overemphasize the capacity of sport to collapse social barriers. At the same time it is crucial to acknowledge the capacity of sport to facilitate social change within sport. The ways in which sport may contribute to other alternatives should not be overemphasized either, but neither should they be ignored. The strength of sports capacity to produce change perhaps lies in its popularity in different parts of the world, its capacity to symbolize graphically and poignantly social and political success and failure. The old and new politics of sport and physical culture in China have been commented upon in this book and illustrated further with discussion of some of the manners in which sport has attempted to produce and struggle for alternative ways of change, reform and intervention. Such alternatives both influence and are influenced by different visions of a world that continues to struggle with inequality, turmoil and lack of clarity about the nature of both capitalism and democracy in China.

We should not think that contemporary researchers, teachers and thinkers about sport don't care about the type of world that we live in now or will inhabit in future. However, the early twenty-first century needs the input of the public intellectual. All too often disparaging remarks are made about academics and intellectuals as if they have no place in the public or worldly debate about sport, never mind other concerns such as the gap between rich and poor, human rights, democracy, going to war or moves to promote internationality and reconciliation. Yet such concerns must be balanced against the positive transformative capacity of sport to help bring about real change.

The late writer and public intellectual Susan Sontag (2002) talking about the novel commented that any novel worth reading was an education of the heart in that it enlarged your sense of human possibilities and of what human nature had the capacity to do. She was a fervent believer in the capacity of art to delight, to inform and transform the world in which we live. Such arguments are readily accepted about the arts, but they need also to make sense in relation to other areas of social life such as sport and the possible capacity of sport to fulfil its potential and to enlarge one's sense of human possibilities, to delight, to inform and ultimately help to transform the worlds in which we live. There is no single agent, group or movement that can carry the hopes of humanity, but there are many points of engagement through sport that offer good causes for optimism that things can get better.

Let us return to one the key points made in the introduction to this book. Writers such as Said are explicit about the public role of the intellectual, which is 'to uncover the contest, to challenge and defeat both an imposed silence and normalized quiet or unseen power' (Said, 2001) wherever and whenever possible. Said laid out a powerful case for regarding intellectuals as those who are never more themselves than when – moved by metaphysical passions and disinterested principles of justice and truth – they denounce corruption, defend the weak and defy imperfect or oppressive authority. They speak the truth to power and refuse to be shackled by the constraints of disciplinarity that tends to weaken and depoliticize the intellectual strengths of academic writing. The role of the public intellectual in sport is fundamentally different from the role of the academic in sport. Public intellectuals are not only different from many academics, although academia might be a stepping stone along the road to becoming a public intellectual. Academics – not always, but usually – plough a narrow disciplinary or interdisciplinary path, whereas public intellectuals roam ambitiously from one theme to another. Academics are interested in ideas, research and analysis whereas public intellectuals, also interested in ideas, research and analysis, are concerned as well with the intersection between ideas and public debate or ideas and helping ordinary people.

Several final points we feel need to be made with specific reference to *Sport, Revolution and the Beijing Olympics*. The first of these relates to the contemporary challenge of sport in China and how contemporary sporting success will provide a platform for sporting opportunity within China. Conventional logic has long dictated that with a population in excess of Western Europe's, China should or could become a sustained major sporting power. At the beginning of the twenty-first century China hosted the 2004 Asian Football Cup and, with a potential sports pool of talent to be drawn from a population estimated to be in the region of 1.3 billion people, perhaps more needs to be asked of the opportunities that exist for the majority of people in China to benefit from sport, physical culture and the legacy of the 2008 Olympic Games. Do all citizens within the People's Republic of China have the right to sport, exercise and physical culture on a regular basis? History also tells us that proclaiming the principle of equality does not suffice to make reality of it. Mere declarations of formal equality have frequently served to strip the weak of traditional protections. So how will the real assets produced from professional sport or Olympism be used to open up further sporting possibilities for a rural population, with increased recognition for women, and will a peaceful political platform secured through Olympic recognition be used to further a reconciliation of the differences between China and other communities and within China itself?

The second point relates to the study of sport, culture and society. In the same way as globalization has been blind to the uneven and differentiated models of state formation emerging in the twenty-first century, then the same point might be made about our current knowledge of sport in the world today. It is impossible at this stage to draw up a balance sheet of the combined effects of sport and other social forces with their many contradictions, their exceptions and their unevenness. By the same token it is also impossible to provide a fixed map of the changing patterns of sport in the world today, but it is essential that any contemporary understanding of sport, culture and society must come from actively listening to and engaging with other sporting communities, places and voices such as those coming out of China. Perhaps the overall value of this lies in its method as a safeguard against inward-looking parochialism and as the conscience of cosmopolitan or global sport, lest it forget 'other' traditions of sport, the poor or the use of cheap labour in sporting production, or the potential humanitarian power of sport in 'other' parts of the world as well as the West. Perhaps it is impossible for humanity to arrive at an understanding of the values that unite it, but if the countries of the North cease to automatically impose their own ideas on the rest of the sporting world and start to take due cognizance of other sporting cultures in a *common exercise* of critical self-examination, then perhaps the aspiration of global sport may become more just and less charitable.

A further point is concern that the social and historical context that is China today remains Chinese, not Western. Looking to the future, despite the checks and balances brought about by international acceptance symbolized by a potential seat at the top economic table, an invitation to be part of the World Trade Organization and the symbolism of being an Olympic host, the path or specific route to democracy with Chinese characteristics remains unclear. If democratization comes it is doubtful if it will be brought through a Mandela-style political reconciliation between the state and the people. It is also doubtful if a fair redistribution of state assets as happened in the Czech Republic will occur peacefully. The marriage of democratization and privatization in the break-up of the former Soviet Union was also unjust in that President Yeltsin allowed the assets to fall into the hands of a few private oligarchs who removed the money from the country and invested in the play-things of the Western world such as football clubs. If China's future involves the selling-off of state-owned assets, and if privatization is carried out in the dark under authoritarian rule, it will inevitably be a robbery of ordinary people, and yet the door to change remains very much open at the beginning of the twenty-first century in both the world of sport and broader social and political concerns.

History tells us that sport in China has been influenced by processes of imperialism, communism and post-colonialism. It remains one of the possible vehicles by which successive governments pursue a complex ideology of patriotism, collectivism, socialism and capitalism with Chinese characteristics. Perhaps, both imperialism and post-colonialism may not explain the total development of sport in the Chinese social context; however, they have opened up new ways of thinking about sport both in and between non-Western and Western worlds. This study has hoped to contribute to opening up new ways of thinking about the relationships between sport, physical culture and the Olympics in China. It not only attends to cultural, historical, social, political and geographical difference, but also thinks between and across such differences. Indeed, these comparative modes of thought remain a valuable means of critique. They need not lead to generality and universalism. A relativist view of the development of sport in China would uphold the notion that different countries have different values and that it is difficult if not problematic to say that one way of life is better than another. This can be said without denying the fact that sport in the world today needs to be more just, accountable and transparent, and less charitable.

The emergence of a more socially committed approach to global or international sport has to start from actively acknowledging the huge differences of opportunities, wealth, democracy, sporting tastes, and models of professional sport that divide the world. The deep challenge facing global sport is to outline the mechanisms by which sport can be actively seen to contribute to social and economic welfare on an international scale. At the international level the more powerful sporting nations would seem to have the power to enforce many of the rules and decisions affecting world sport, and yet there are perhaps unprecedented opportunities at the beginning of the twenty-first century for change. Perhaps the most obvious and disturbing concern is the extent to which the core institutions of sport are trusted and sensitive to ways of addressing the interests of the majority in the non-Western world. The chief causes of inequality in global sport remain twofold – the transformation of global sport by financial capital, and the displacement of democratic political power in sport by unaccountable market power. In all of this any study of sport and physical culture in China is instructive precisely because it acknowledges not just that other sporting worlds are powerful but that sport and capitalism is not primarily about just economic wealth and market share but also social concerns.

Finally, there is undoubtedly a considerable but perhaps premature cynicism about the demise of national mainstream politics, the prospects of a more just and less charitable social order in which important social and political problems are not reduced to matters of efficiency or profit. Yet for the public intellectual interested in sport there are a number of fault lines running through the different worlds of sport that have sustained agendas for change and have illustrated that any number of entry and exit points may be chosen as a basis for substantiating and encouraging the transformative capacity of sport. Writers such as Sontag and Said and others remind us of the impressive array of opportunities offered by the lecture platform, the pamphlet, the radio, the interview, the internet, the research newsletter, the guest lecture, the letter to the newspaper open to us and others.

It is not as if there were a lack of areas for concern. Almost universally phrases such as 'globalization', 'global sport', 'free-market', 'privatization' and 'public/private funding for sport' are in the public realm as given, and yet all of these need to be properly explained and tend to be accepted tacitly as if they were the preordained only way to do things. What are the alternatives and how does one create genuine climates in which the controversial aspects surrounding the world of sport are encouraged, openly valued as a contribution to public debate in the very best traditions of freedom of speech, in a healthy functioning sporting world that is perhaps more just, accountable, transparent, open, democratic? To ignore the capacity of sport to assist with social change is not an option for the public intellectual interested and steeped in an understanding of what sport can do.

The great walls of discourse – China and the West, us and them – that exist about China are not immune to disproof and need to be continually broken down. Not only are there new ways and possibilities of thinking about China but, more importantly, there are currently new openings in a long march toward social, economic and political democracy in China; as such, it may be more fruitful to grasp the complexity not only of the social consequences of the Beijing Olympiad but also the international consequences of capitalism with Chinese characteristics. For the public intellectual keen to examine the social impact of the Beijing Olympics, the opportunity exists to comment upon the impact – both internal and external – of the Olympic Games, not so much in terms of the unofficial medal table but on the peoples of Beijing, China, Taiwan, as well as on the athletes, the volunteers, children and the disabled. Perhaps the duty of public-sport intellectuals looking at the Beijing 2008 Olympic Games is to uncover as much of what is *not* said as of what is *officially* said, to uncover the real contest, which may be to acknowledge the transformative capacity of sport while at the same time evaluating whether sport, China or indeed the world is a more just place, a more trusting place, a more humane place, a more safe and secure place to be as a result of sport, revolution and the legacy of the Beijing Olympics.

Key Readings

Giroux, Henry (2006), *The Giroux Reader*. Boulder, CO: Paradigm Publishers.
Jarvie, Grant (2006), *Sport, Culture and Society: Can Sport Change the World?* London: Routledge.
Li, Lillian, Dray-Novey, Alison and Kong, Haili (2007), *Beijing: From Imperial Capital to Olympic City*. New York: Palgrave-Macmillan.
Said, Edward (2001), 'The Writer as the Public Intellectual', *The Nation*, October, p. 31.

Journal Articles

Qin, Hui (2003), 'The Stolypins of China', *New Left Review* 20, March/April: 83–113.

Turner, B. (2006), 'Public Intellectuals, Globalization and the Sociology Calling', *British Journal of Sociology* 57(3): 345–51.

Wright, Erik-Olin (2006), 'Compass Points: Towards a Social Alternative', *New Left Review* 41, September/October: 93–124.

Zhang, X. (1999), 'Postmodernism and Post-Socialist Society: Cultural Politics in China After the "New Era"', *New Left Review* 237(1): 77–105.

Zhao, B. (1997), 'Consumerism, Confucianism, and Communism: Making Sense of China Today', *New Left Review* 222, March/April: 43–59.

Other Readings

Byrnes, Sholto (2005), 'New Statesman Essay', *New Statesman*, 3 October: 32–6.

Gourley, B. (2002), 'In Defence of the Intellectual', Robbins Lecture. Stirling: Stirling University Publications.

McRobbie, Angela (2005), 'Under the Skin of the Woman in Black', *The Times Higher Education Supplement*, 21 January: 14–17.

Reeves, R. (2003), 'There is a Character Missing from the Cast of Political Life: The Public Intellectual', *New Statesman*, 7 July: 23–6.

Bibliography

Newspapers, Magazines and Reports

Archive of the State General Sports Administration of China
Australian, The
Beijing Review
Central Daily News (Taipei, Taiwan)
China Daily (Taipei, Taiwan)
China Mission Year Book
China Year Book
China Youth Daily
Contemporary China, Vol. 3, 1958/59 (Hong Kong)
Current Background
Daily Report
Eastern Times (Shanghai)
Economist, The
Eleventh National Congress of the Communist Party of China – documents, 1977
Extracts from China Mainland Magazines
Guardian, The
Hongqi
L'impartial (Tianjin)
Liberation Army News
Liberation Daily
Min Li Pao
Ming Pao Daily News (Hong Kong)
New China Daily
New Physical Culture
New York Times, The
New Youth
North China Herald
Olympic Review
People's Daily
Physical Culture Weekly (*Tiyu Chou Pao*)
Physical Training
San Pao

Shanghai
Shun Pao (Shanghai)
Soo Pao
South China Morning Post (Hong Kong)
Sport Business
Survey of China Mainland Press
Tianjin Young Men
Times, The (London)
Tiyu Bao (China Sports Daily)
Xinhua Yuebao (New China Monthly)

Books and Articles

Abram, Philip (1982), *Historical Sociology*. New York: Cornell University Press.
Ahmad, Aijaz (1992), *In Theory: Classes, Nations, Literatures*. Oxford: Oxford University Press.
Ahmad, Aijaz (1995), 'The Politics of Literary Postcoloniality', *Race and Class* 36(3): 1–20.
Aidoo, Ama Ata (1991), 'That Capacious Topic: Gender Politics', in Phil Mariani (ed.), *Critical Fictions*. Seattle, WA: Bay Press: 151–4.
Ashcroft, P., Griffiths, T. and Tiffin, D. (eds), *The Post-Colonial Studies Reader*. London: Routledge.
Bairner, Alan (2001), *Sport, Nationalism, and Globalization: European and North American Perspectives*. Albany, NY: State University of New York Press.
Bale, John (2002), 'Human Geography and the Study of Sport', in J. Coakley and E. Dunning (eds), *Handbook of Sports Studies*. London: Sage: 171–86.
Bale, John (2003), *Sports Geography*. London: Routledge.
Bale, John and Cronin, Mike (2003), *Sport and Postcolonialism*. Oxford: Berg.
Bale, John and Christenson, M. (eds) (2004), *Post-Olympism? Questioning Sport in the Twenty-First Century*. Oxford: Berg.
Bale, John and Maguire, Joseph (1994), *The Global Sports Arena: Athlete Talent Migration in an Interdependent World*. London: Frank Cass.
Bale, John, Eichberg, Henning and Philo, Chris (1998), *Body Cultures: Essays on Sport, Space and Identity*. Albany, NY: State University of New York Press.
Barrington Moore, Jr. (1967), *Social Origins of Dictatorship and Democracy: Lord and Peasant in the Making of the Modern World*. Boston, MA: Beacon Press.
Bary, Wm Theodore, Chan, Wing-tsit and Tan, Chester (1964), *Source of Chinese Tradition*, Vol. II. New York: Columbia University Press.
Becker, Jasper (1999), *Hungry Ghosts: China's Secret Famine*. London: John Murray.
Becker, Marc (1986), *China: Politics, Economics and Society*. London: Frances Pinter.

Benton, G. (1980) 'China's Opposition', *New Left Review* 122(1): 59–78.
Benton, G. (1984) 'China's Communism and Democracy' *New Left Review* 148(1): 57–73.
Bhabha, Homi K. (1990), *Nation and Narration*. London: Routledge.
Bhabha, Homi K. (1994), *The Location of Culture*. London: Routledge.
Bickers, Robert (1999), *Britain in China: Community, Culture and Colonialism 1900–1949*. Manchester: Manchester University Press.
Biggerstaffe, Knight (1972), *The Earliest Modern Government Schools in China*. New York: Kennikat Press.
Blanchard, Kendall (1995), *The Anthropology of Sport: An Introduction*. Westport, CT: Greenwood.
Blanchard, Kendall (2002), 'The Anthropology of Sport', in J. Coakley and E. Dunning (eds), *Handbook of Sports Studies*. London: Sage: 144–56.
Bleaney, M. F. (1976), *Under-Consumption Theories*. London: Lawrence & Wishart.
Blecher, Marc (1986), *China: Politics, Economics and Society*. London: Frances Pinter.
Blecher, Marc (1997), *China Against the Tides*. London: Pinter.
Bottomore, Tom (1983), *A Dictionary of Marxist Thought*. Oxford: Blackwell.
Brockman, Fletcher S. (1935) *I Discover the Orient*. New York: Harper & Brothers.
Brownell, Susan (1991) 'Sport in Britain and China, 1850–1920: An Explanatory Overview', *International Journal of the History of Sport* 8(2): 284–90.
Brownell, Susan (1995) *Training the Body for China: Sport in the Moral Order of the People's Republic*. Chicago: University of Chicago Press.
Brownell, Susan (1996), 'China Bashing at the Olympic Games: Why the Cold War Continues in Sports Journalism', at http://ieas.berkeley.edu/shornenstein/1996.10.html.
Brownell, Susan (1998), 'Thinking Dangerously: The Person and His Ideas', in J. Bale et al. (eds), *Body Cultures: Essays on Sport, Space and Identity*. London: Routledge: 22 47.
Brownell, Susan (1999), 'The Body and the Beautiful in Chinese Nationalism: Sportswomen and Fashion Models in the Reform Era', *China Information* 13(2/3): 36–58.
Brownell, Susan (2000), 'Why Should an Anthropologist Study in China', in Noel Dyck (ed.), *Games, Sports and Culture*. Oxford: Berg: 43–63.
Brownell, Susan (2001), 'Making Dream Bodies in Beijing: Athletes, Fashion Models and Urban Mystique in China', in Nancy Chen, Suzanne Clark and Lyn Jeffrey (eds), *China Urban*. Durham, NC: Duke University Press, 123–42.
Brownell, Susan (2004), 'China and Olympism', in J. Bale and M. Christenson (eds), *Post-Olympism? Questioning Sport in the Twenty-First Century*. Oxford: Berg: 51–64.

Brownell, Susan (2005), 'Challenged America: China and America – Women and Sport, Past Present and Future', *International Journal of the History of Sport* 22(6): 1173–93.

Brownell, Susan (2007), 'Sport and Politics Don't Mix: China's Relationship with the IOC during the Cold War', in S. Wagg and D. Andrews (eds), *East Plays West: Politics of the Cold War*. London: Routledge: 261–78.

Brownell, S. and Wasserstrom, J. (2002), *Chinese Femininities and Chinese Masculinities*. Berkeley: University of California Press.

Burnett, John (2000), *Riot, Revelry and Rowt: Sport in Lowland Scotland before 1860*. East Lothian: Tuckwell Press.

Byrnes, Sholto (2005), 'New Statesman Essay', *New Statesman*, 3 October: 32–6.

Callinicos, Alex (1994), *Marxism and The New Imperialism*. London: Bookmarks.

Carrington, Charles (1955), *Rudyard Kipling: His Life and Work*. London: Macmillan.

Cashman, R. and Hughes, A. (1999), *Staging The Olympics: The Event and its Impact*. Sydney: University of New South Wales Press.

Chan, Yuan-Chi (1931), *Tsui Chiu San Shih Wu Nien Chih Chung Kuo Chiao Yu* (The Last 35 Years of Chinese Education). Shanghai: Commercial Press.

Chang, Jung (1993), *Wild Swans: Three Daughters of China*. London: Flamingo.

Chen, Jerome (1979), *China and the West: Society and Culture 1815–1937*. London: Hutchinson.

Chen, Kuan-Hsing (2001), 'America in East Asia: The Club 51 Syndrome', *New Left Review* 12, November/December: 73–87.

Chen, Nancy, Clark, Suzanne and Lyn Jeffrey (eds) (1997), *China Urban*. Durham, NC: Duke University Press.

Chen, Rong (1999), 'The Characteristics of the Development of Sports Ideology in New China', *Journal of Sport History and Culture*, no. 1, 23 January: 4–8.

Chesneaux, Jean, Bastid, Marianne and Bergère, Marie-Claire (1996), *China: From the Opium Years to the 1911 Revolution*. Sussex: Harvester Wheatsheaf.

Chien, T. S. (1970), *The Government and Politics of China 1912–1949*. Stanford, CA: Stanford University Press.

Chinese Taipei Olympic Committee (1981), *The Olympic Ideology: A Report of ROC National Olympic Academic IV*. Taipei: Taiwan.

Chiou, Z., Zhang, X. and Song, Q. (1996), *China Can Say No* (in Chinese). Hong Kong: Mingpao Press.

Chow, Rey (1993), *Writing Diaspora: Tactics of Intervention in Contemporary Cultural Studies*. Bloomington, IN: Indiana University Press.

Chow, Rey (1997),'Can One Say No to China?' *New Literary History* 28(1), Winter: 147–51.

Chow, Tse-tsung (1960), *The May Fourth Movement: Intellectual Revolution in Modern China*. Cambridge, MA: Harvard University Press.

Chudinov, I. D. (1959) *Osnovnye postanovleniya i instruktsii po voprosam fizich-eskoi kul'tury i sportu, 1917–1957*, Moscow.

Close, P., Askew, D. and Xu, X. (2007), *The Beijing Olympiad: The Political Economy of a Sporting Mega Event*. London: Routledge.

Coakley, J. and Dunning, E. (eds), *Handbook of Sports Studies*. London: Sage: 171–86.

Collins English Dictionary, 5th edn (1973). Glasgow: HarperCollins.

Coronil, Fernand (1992),'Can Postcoloniality be Decolonized? Imperial Banality and Post-colonial Power', *Public Culture* 5(1): 89–108.

Crew, C. (1940), *Foreign Devils in the Flowery Kingdom*. London: Harper and Ross.

Cronin, Mike and Mayall, David (1998), *Sporting Nationalisms: Identity, Ethnicity, Immigration and Assimilation*. London: Frank Cass.

Cui, Lequan (1998), *Tiyu Shihua: A Brief History of Chinese Physical Culture*. Beijing: China Encyclopaedia Press.

Deng, Xiaoping (1984), *Selected Works of Deng Xiaoping*. Beijing: Foreign Languages Press.

Dillon, Michael (1998), *China: A Cultural and Historical Dictionary*. Surrey: Curzon.

Dirlik, Arif (1994), 'The Postcolonial Aura: Third World Criticism in the Age of Global Capitalism', *Critical Inquiry* 20, Winter: 328–56.

Doise, W. (2002), *Human Rights as Social Representations*. London: Routledge.

Dong, Jinxia (2001), 'Women, Sport and Society in the Early Years of the New China', *International Journal of the History of Sport* 18(2): 1–35.

Dong, Jinxia (2002), *Women, Sport and Society in Modern China: Holding Up More than Half the Sky*. London: Routledge.

Dong, Jinxia (2005), 'Women, Nationalism and the Beijing Olympics: Preparing for Glory', *International Journal of the History of Sport* 22(4): 530–44.

Donnelly, P. (1997), 'Child Labour, Sport Labour: Applying Child Labour Laws to Sport', *International Review for the Sociology of Sport* 32(4): 389–406.

Dreyer, June (2003), *China's Political System: Modernization and Tradition*. Upper Saddle River, NJ: Prentice Hall.

Dunning, Eric and Sheard, Kenneth (1979), *Barbarians, Gentlemen and Players*. Oxford: Martin Robertson & Co.

Dunning, E., Maguire, J. A. and Pearton, R. E. (1993), *The Sports Process: A Comparative and Developmental Approach*. Chicago: Human Kinetics Press

During, Simon (1987), 'Postmodernism or Post-Colonialism Today', *Textual Practice* 1(1): 32–47.

Durkheim, Emile (1964), *The Rule of Sociological Method*. New York: Free Press.

Dyck, Noel (ed.), (2000), *Games, Sports and Culture*. Oxford: Berg: 43–63.

Ebrey, Patricia Buckley (1993), *Chinese Civilization: A Sourcebook*. Oxford: Collier Macmillan.

Eichberg, Henning (1973), *Der Weg des Sports in die industrielle Zivilisation*. Baden-Baden: Nomos.

Eichberg, Henning (1989), 'Body Culture as Paradigm: the Danish Sociology of Sport', *International Review for the Sociology of Sport* 24(1): 45–61.

Eichberg, Henning (1993), 'Der Dialogische Körper: Uber einen dritten Weg der Körperanthropologischen Aufmerksamkeit' (The Dialogical Body: On a Third Kind of Attentiveness in the Anthropology of the Body), in Knut Dietrich and Henning Eichberg (eds), *Körpersprache: Uber Identität und Konflikt* (Body Language: On Identity and Conflict). Butzbach: Afra: 257–308.

Eichberg, Henning (2004), *The People of Democracy: Understanding Self-Determination on the Basis of Body Movement*. Arhus: Klim.

Elias, Norbert (1956), 'Problem of Involvement and Detachment', *British Journal of Sociology* 7: 165–84.

Elias, Norbert (1978), *What is Sociology?* Oxford: Basil Blackwell.

Elias, Norbert (1983), *The Court Society*. Oxford: Basil Blackwell.

Elias, Norbert (1987), *Involvement and Detachment*. Oxford: Basil Blackwell.

Espy, Richard (1979), *The Politics of the Olympic Games*. Berkeley: University of California Press.

Exner, Max J. (1911), 'Physical Training in China', *Physical Training* 8(6), April: 19.

Fairbank, John King (1978), *The Cambridge History of China*, Vol. 10: *Late China, 1800–1911*, Part 1, Cambridge: Cambridge University Press.

Fanon, Franz (1965), *A Dying Colonialism*. New York: Grove.

Fanon, Franz (1967), *Toward the African Revolution*. New York: Grove.

Fanon, Franz (1986), *Black Skin, White Masks*. London: Pluto.

Fanon, Franz (1990), *The Wretched of the Earth*. London: Penguin.

Feuerwerker, Albert (1958), *China's Early Industrialization: Sheng Hsuan-huai (1844–1916)*. Cambridge: Cambridge University Press.

Fingleton, Eamonn (2004), 'East Asian Alliance', *Prospect*, May: 34–8.

Forster, J. and Pope, N. (2004), *The Political Economy of Global Sports Organizations*. London: Routledge.

Foucault, Michel (1972), *The Archaeology of Knowledge*. London: Tavistock.

Foucault, Michel (1978), *Discipline and Punish*. London: Tavistock.

Giroux, Henry (2006), *The Giroux Reader*. Boulder: Paradigm Publishers.

Glendinning, M. (1999), 'China Set for Twenty-First Century Success', *Sport Business*, January: 20–1.

Gorman, J. (2003), *Rights and Reason*. Chesham: Acumen.

Gourley, B. (2002), 'In Defence of the Intellectual', Robbins Lecture. Stirling: Stirling University Publications.

Gray, Jack (1990), *Rebellions and Revolutions: China From the 1800s to the 1980s*. Oxford: Oxford University Press.

Gray, John (2003), 'Why Boycott Zimbabwe, but Not China?', *New Statesman*, 6 January: 4–6.

Gruneau, Richard (1988), *Popular Culture and Political Practices*. Toronto: Garamond.

Gruneau, Richard (1999), *Class, Sports and Social Development*. Amherst: University of Massachusetts Press.

Gu, Shiquan (1986), 'The Development of Sports in Lenin Primary School, Junior Groups and Young Pioneers During the Chinese Soviet Republic Period', Beijing, *Journal of Sport History and Culture* 6: 28–30 (in Chinese).

Gu, Shiquan (1989), *Modern Chinese History of Sports*. Beijing: Beijing University of Physical Education (in Chinese).

Gu, Shiquan (1990), 'Introduction to Ancient and Modern Chinese Physical Culture', in H. Knuttgen, Q. Ma and Z. Wu (eds), *Sport in China*. Chicago: Human Kinetics: 3–24.

Gu, Shiquan (1997), *Chinese History of Sports* (in Chinese). Beijing: Beijing University of Physical Education.

Guttmann, Allen (1978), *From Ritual to Record*. New York: Columbia University Press.

Guttmann, Allen (1994), *Games and Empires: Modern Sports and Cultural Imperialism*. New York: Columbia University Press.

Han, Shuifa (1998), *Max Weber* (in Chinese). Taipei: Dongda Books.

He, Qinglian (2000), 'China's Listing Social Structure', *New Left Review* 5, September/October: 69–99.

Hegel, G. W. Friedrich. (1956), The *Philosophy of History*. London: Constable.

Hill, C. (1992), *Olympic Politics*. Manchester: Manchester University Press.

Hill, Jeff (2002), *Sport, Leisure and Culture in Twentieth Century Britain*. London: Palgrave.

Hilton, Isobel (2006), 'Karl: China Needs You', *New Statesman*, 20 February, 28–31.

Hoberman, John M. (1984), *Sport and Political Ideology*. London: Heinemann.

Hoberman, John M. (1987), 'Sport and Social Change: The Transformation of Maoist Sport', *Sociology of Sport Journal* (4): 156–70.

Hobsbawm, Eric (1987), *The Age of Empire 1875–1914*. London: Weidenfeld & Nicolson.

Hobsbawm, Eric (1997), *On History*. London: Weidenfeld & Nicholson.

Hoh, Gunsun (1926), *Physical Education in China*. Shanghai: Commercial Press.

Holt, Richard (1989), *Sport and the British*. Oxford: Clarendon.

Hong, F. (1997), *Footbinding, Feminism and Freedom: the Liberation of Women's Bodies in Modern China*. London: Frank Cass.

Hong, F. (1999), 'Not All Bad: Communism, Society and Sport in the Great Proletarian Revolution: A Revisionist Perspective', *International Journal of the History of Sport* 16(3): 47–71.

Hong, F. (2000), 'Blue Shirts, Nationalists and Nationalism: Fascism in 1930s China', in J. Mangan (ed.), *Superman, Supreme: Fascist Body as Political Icon/Global Fascism*. London: Frank Cass.

Hong, F. (2001), 'Two Roads to China: The Inadequate and the Adequate', *International Journal of the History of Sport* 18(2), June: 148–67.

Hong, F. and Mangan, J. A. (2001), 'A Martyr for Modernity: Qui Jin, Feminist, Warrior and Revolutionary', *International Journal of the History of Sport* 18(1): 27–55.

Hong, F., Ping, W. and Huan, X. (2005), 'Beijing Ambitions: An Analysis of the Chinese Elite Sports System and its Olympic Strategy for the 2008 Olympic Games', *International Journal of the History of Sport* 22(4): 510–29.

Hook, Brian (1982), *The Cambridge Encyclopedia of China*. Cambridge: Cambridge University Press.

Hsia-Hsien, Hou (2004), 'Tensions in Taiwan', *New Left Review* 28, July/August: 19–43.

Hsu, I-hsiung (1996), *Physical Education Thoughts in Modern China*. Taipei: Chi Ying Co. Ltd.

Hsu, I-hsiung and Hsu, Yuan-ming (1999), *Physical Education in Modern Chinese School – the Development of Goals* (in Chinese). Taipei: Shi Da Shu Yuan: National Taiwan Normal University Press.

Hu, Shi Ming and Seifman, Eli (1976), *Toward A New World Outlook: A Documentary of Education in the People's Republic of China, 1949–1976*. New York: AMS Press.

Hume, M. (2002), 'The Anti-Imperialism of Fools', *New Statesman*, 17 June: 29–34.

Hurst, G. Cameron (1998), *Armed Martial Arts of Japan: Swordsmanship and Archery*. New Haven, CT and London: Yale University Press.

Hutchings, Graham (2001), *Modern China: A Companion to a Rising Power*. London: Penguin.

Hwang, T. and Jarvie, G. (2001), 'Sport, Nationalism and the Early Chinese Republic, 1912–1927', *Sports Historian* 21(2): 1–19.

JanMohamed, Abdul R. (1985), 'The Economy of Manichean Allegory: The Function of Radical Difference in Colonialist Literature', *Critical Inquiry* 12(1): 59–87. Also in Bill Ashcroft, Gareth Griffiths and Helen Tiffin (eds) (1995), *The Post-Colonial Studies Reader*. London, Routledge: 18–23.

Jarvie, Grant (1991), *Highland Games: The Making of the Myth*. Edinburgh, Edinburgh University Press.

Jarvie, Grant (1992), 'Sport, Gaelic Nationalism and Scottish Politics 1879–1920', Paper for International ISHPES Seminar 'Sport and Cultural Minorities', Turku, Finland, 8–13 June.

Jarvie, Grant (2006), *Sport, Culture and Society: Can Sport Change the World?* London: Routledge.

Jarvie, Grant and Maguire, Joseph (1994), *Sport and Leisure in Social Thought*. London: Routledge.

Jin, Zhong (1999), *Fifty Years of Communist China 1949–1999*. Hong Kong: Open Magazine Press.

Johnson, C. (1962), *Peasant Nationalism and Communist Power*. Stanford, CA: Stanford University Press.

Kidd, Bruce (1996), *The Struggle for Canadian Sport*. Toronto: University of Toronto Press.

Kidd, Bruce and Donnelly, P. (2000), 'Human Rights in Sport', *International Review for the Sociology of Sport* 35(2): 131–48.

King Anthony (2002), *The End of the Terraces: The Transition of English Football in the 1990s*. London: Routledge.

Kinnock, G. (2003), 'It's All About Justice', *Fabian Global Forum* at www.fabianglobalforum.net/forum/article027.htm.

Kipling, Rudyard (1966 [1901]), *Kim*. London: Macmillan.

Kirby, E. Stuart (1960), *Contemporary China: Economic and Social Studies Documents, Chronology, Bibliography*. Hong Kong: Hong Kong University.

Knuttgen, Howard G., Ma, Qiwei and Wu, Zhongyuan (1990), *Sport in China*. Chicago: Human Kinetics.

Kolatch, Jonathan (1972), *Sports, Politics and Ideology in China*. New York: Jonathan David.

Lawrance, G. and Rowe, D. (1986), *Power Play*. Sydney: Halel & Iremonger.

Lee, Chungli (1999), *Jindai Zhongguo Shehui Wenhua Bianqianlu*, Vol. 1 (Social and Cultural Changes in Modern China). Chekiang: Chekiang People's Publishing House Press.

Lee, Hong Yung (1993), 'Political and Administrative Reform of 1982–86: The Changing Party Leadership and State Bureaucracy', in Michael Ying-Mao Kau and Susan H. Marsh (eds), *China in the Era of Deng Xiaoping: A Decade of Reform*. New York: East Gate, 36–54.

Lenin, V. I. (1963) *Polnoye sobranie sochinenii* (Collected Works, Vols 3 and 4). Moscow: Foreign Languages Publishing House.

Lenskyy, H. (2000), *Inside The Olympic Industry: Power, Politics and Activism*. Albany, NY: State University of New York Press.

Li, Lillian, Dray-Novey, Alison and Kong Haili (2007), *Beijing: From Imperial Capital to Olympic City*. New York. Palgrave-Macmillan.

Li, Zhisui (1994), *The Private Life of Chairman Mao* (in Chinese). Taipei: China Times Press.

Liang Lijuan, He Zhenliang and Wu Huan Zhi Lu (2005), *He Zhenliang and the Road to the Olympic Rings*. Beijing: Beijing Foreign Language Press.

Liu, Ai-feng (1964), 'Do School Physical Culture Well and Develop Students' Physique', *Extracts from China Mainland Magazines*, No. 434, 14 September: 34–6.

Liu, Serena (2006), 'Towards an Analytical Theory of Social Change: The Case of China', *British Journal of Sociology* 57(3): 503–20.

Loomba, Ania (1998), *Colonialism/ Postcolonialism*. London: Routledge.

Lu, K. (1963), 'Beijing Young Communist League Committee and Young Communist League Committee of Tsinghua University Call Separate Forums on Redness and Expertness', *Survey of China Mainland Press* 288, 2 January: 2–5.

Lutz, Jessie Gregory (1971), *China and the Christian Colleges 1850–1950*. London: Cornell University Press.

Ma, Hsu-lun (1951), 'Minister of Education Ma Hsu-lun Reports on Education Accomplishments During the Past Year', *Survey of China Mainland Press* 142, 25 July: 5–12.

MacFarquhar, Roderick (1972), *China Under Mao: Politics Takes Command*. Cambridge, MA: Massachusetts Institute of Technology Press.

MacFarquhar, Roderick (1993) *The Politics of China 1949–1989*. Cambridge: Cambridge University Press.

Mackenzie, Hector (2004), 'Euro 2004 Fever Kicks Off in China', *Sunday Herald*, 20 June: 23.

Maguire, Joseph (1999), *Global Sport: Identities, Societies and Civilization*. Cambridge: Polity.

Mangan, J. A. (1981), *Athleticism in the Victorian and Edwardian Public School: the Emergence and Consolidation of an Educational Ideology*. Cambridge, Cambridge University Press.

Mangan, J. A. (1984), 'Christ and the Imperial Games Fields', *British Journal of Sports History* 1(2): 184–201.

Mangan, J. A. (1992), *The Cultural Bond: Sport, Empire and Society*. London: Frank Cass.

Mangan, J. A. (1998), *The Games Ethic and Imperialism: Aspects of the Diffusion of an Ideal*. London: Frank Cass.

Mangan, J.A. (ed.) (2000), *Superman, Supreme: Fascist Body as Political Icon/Global Fascism*. London: Frank Cass.

Mao, Zedong (1967), *Selected Works of Mao Zedong*, Vols 1, 2. Oxford: Pergamon.

Mao, Zedong (1977), *Selected Works of Mao Zedong*, Vol. 5. Oxford: Pergamon.

Mao, Zedong (1996), *A Study of Physical Culture*. Beijing: People's Sport Publishing House Press.

Marshall, Gordon (1994), *Oxford Dictionary of Sociology*. Oxford: Oxford University Press.

Marx, Karl (1965), *Capitalism: A Critical Analysis of Capitalist Production*. Moscow: Progress Publisher.

Marx, K. and Engels, F. (1969), *Selected Works*, Vol. 2. Moscow: Progress Publishers.

Mason, A. (1990), 'Football on the Maidan: Cultural Imperialism in Calcutta', *International Journal of the History of Sport* 7(1): 85–96.

McLeod, John (2000), *Beginning Postcolonialism*. Manchester: Manchester University Press.

McRobbie, Angela (2005), 'Under the Skin of the Woman in Black', *The Times Higher Education Supplement*, 21 January: 14–17.

Mechikoff, Robert A. and Estes, Steven G. (1998), *A History and Philosophy of Sport and Physical Education: From Ancient Civilizations to the Modern World*. New York: McGraw-Hill.

Medvedev, R. (1983), 'The USSR and China: Confrontation or Détente?', *New Left Review* 142 (1): 5–29.

Metcalfe, Alan (1991), 'The Anatomy of Power in Amateur Sport in Ontario, 1918–1936', *Canadian Journal of the History of Sport* 22(2): 47–67.

Mills, C. Wright (1970), *The Sociological Imagination.* Harmondsworth: Penguin.

Milton, David, Milton, Nancy and Schurmann, Franz (1977), *People's China: Social_Experimentation, Politics, Entry on to the World Scene 1966–1972.* Harmondsworth: Penguin.

Mitchell, Kevin (2004), 'Sport Focus: China – The New World Power', *Observer*, 23 May: 12.

Miyazaki, Ichisada (1976), *China's Examination Hell: the Civil Service Examinations_of Imperial China.* New York: Weatherhill.

National Research Institute of Martial Arts (1996), *A History of the Chinese Martial_Arts* (in Chinese). Beijing: People's Sport Publishing House Press.

Nichols, B. (2001), 'Olympics Could Help US-China Diplomacy', *USA Today*, 15 July: 5.

O'Neil, J. and Hormats, R. (2004), *Special Report on China.* New York: Goldman Sachs.

O'Toole, J., Sutherden, A., Walshe, P. and Muir, D. (2006), 'Shuttle Cocks and Soccer: The State of Sport in China', *Sport Business* 119, December: 46–9.

Parratt, C. (1998), 'About Turns: Reflecting on Sport History in the 1990s', *Sport History Review*, 29(1): 4–17.

Parry, Benita (1987), 'Current Problems in the Study of Colonial Discourse', *Oxford Literary Review* 9(1/2): 27–58.

Percival, W. S. (1989), *The Land of the Dragon.* London: Hurst & Blackett.

Payne, M. (2005) *Olympic Turn Around.* Basingstoke: Palgrave Macmillan.

Pfister, Gertrud (1999), *Sport im Lebenszusammenhaug von Frauen.* Cologne: Verlag Karl Hofman Schorndorf.

Plymire, D. C. (1999), 'Too Much, Too Fast, Too Soon: Chinese Women Runners, Accusations of Steroid Use, and the Politics of American Track and Field', *Sociology of Sport Journal* 16: 155–73.

Preuss, Holger (2004), *The Economics of Staging the Olympics: A Comparison of the Games 1972–2008.* Northampton: Edward Elgar.

Purcell, Victor (1936), *Problems of Chinese Education.* London: Kegan Paul.

Qin, Hui (2003), 'The Stolypins of China', *New Left Review* 20, March/April: 83–113.

Radhakrishnan, R. (1994), 'Postmodernism and the Rest of the World', *Organisation* 1(2), October: 305–40.

Reddy, S. (2007), ' Death in China', *New Left Review* 45, May/June: 49–65.

Reeves, R. (2003), 'There is a Character Missing from the Cast of Political Life: The Public Intellectual', *New Statesman*, 7 July: 23–6.

Riordan, James (1977), *Sport in Soviet Society: Development of Sport and Physical Education in Russia and the USSR.* Cambridge: Cambridge University Press.

Riordan, James (1991), *Sport, Politics and Communism.* Manchester: Manchester University Press.

Riordan, J. (1993), 'Sport in Capitalist and Socialist Countries: A Western Perpective', in E. Dunning, J. Maguire and R. Pearton (eds), *The Sports Process: A Comparative and Developmental Approach*. Chicago: Human Kinetics Press: 245–65.

Riordan, James and Jones, Robin (1999), *Sport and Physical Education in China*. London: E & FN Spon.

Roberts, Kevin (2004), 'Opportunity Knocks', *Sport Business International* 91: 43.

Robinson, Thomas W. (1971), *The Cultural Revolution in China*. Berkeley: University of California University Press.

Roche, M. (2000), *Mega-Events Modernity: Olympics and Expos in the Growth of Global Culture*. London: Routledge.

Said, Edward (1993), *Culture and Imperialism*. London: Vintage.

Said, Edward (1995 [1978]), *Orientalism*. London: Penguin.

Said, Edward (2001a), 'The Case for the Intellectual', *The Age*, May: 5–12.

Said, Edward (2001b), 'The Writer as the Public Intellectual', *The Nation*, October: 31.

Sarup, Madan (1998), *Identity, Culture and The Post-modern World*. Edinburgh: Edinburgh University Press.

Schumpeter, J. A. (1976 [1951]), *Capitalism, Socialism, and Democracy*. London: Allen & Unwin.

Schwarcz, Vera (1986), *The Chinese Enlightenment: Intellectuals and Legacy of the May Fourth Movement of 1919*. Berkeley: University of California Press.

Shakya, Tsering (2002), 'Blood in the Snows', *New Left Review* 15, May/June: 39–60.

Shanghai Library (1998), *Laoshanhai Fengqinglu (IV)* (The Collections of Old Shanghai Scenery). Shanghai: Shanghai Culture Press.

Sharman, L. (1968), *Sun Yat-sen – His Life and its Meaning*. Stanford, CA: Stanford University Press.

Shilling, Chris (1993), *The Body and Social Theory*. London: Sage.

Shohat, Ella (1996), 'Notes on the Post-Colonial', in Padmini Mongia (ed.), *Contemporary Postcolonial Theory*. London: Arnold: 321–34.

Smith, Richard (1997), 'Creative Destruction: Capitalist Development and China's Environment', *New Left Review*, March/April: 1–31.

Sontag, S. (2002), *Where the Stress Falls*. London: Jonathan Cape.

Speak, Cyrus H. (1932), *Nationalism and Education in Modern China*. New York: Columbia University Press.

Speak, Mike (1999), 'Recreation and Sport in Ancient China: Primitive Society to AD 960', in James Riordan and Robin Jones (eds), *Sport and Physical Education in China*. London: E & FN Spon, 20–44.

Spence, Jonathan D. (1990), *The Search for Modern China*. New York: Norton.

Spivak, Gayatri Chakravorty (1988), *In Other Worlds*. London: Routledge.

Spivak, Gayatri Chakravorty (1990), 'The Post-Colonial Critic', in Sarah Harasym (ed.), *The Post-Colonial Critic*. London: Routledge: 67–74.

Spivak, Gayatri Chakravorty (1995) 'Can the Subaltern Speak?', in B. Ashcroft, G. Griffiths and H. Tiffin (eds), *The Post-Colonial Studies Reader*. London: Routledge: 24–8.

State Physical Culture and Sports Commission Policy Research Centre (1982), 'Contents of 1978 National Sport Work Conference', in *Sports Documents Selections 1949–1981*. Beijing: People's Sport Publishing House Press: 122–31.

Stoddart, B. (1986), 'Sport, Cultural Imperialism and Colonial Response in the British Empire: A Framework for Analysis', in Proceedings of the Fourth Annual Conference of the British Society of Sports History (1): 8–19.

Stoddart, B. (1998), 'Other Cultures', in B. Stoddart and K. Sandiford (eds), *The Imperial Game*, Manchester: Manchester University Press: 135–49.

Stoddart, B. and Sandiford, A. (1998), *The Imperial Game*. Manchester: Manchester University Press.

Su, Wenming (1983), *A Nation at School*. Beijing: Beijing Review Publications.

Sun, Yat-sen (1927), *San Min Chu I* (The Three Principles of Sun Yat-sen). Shanghai: China Committee of the Institute of Pacific Relations.

Supiot, Alain (2003), 'The Labyrinth of Human Rights', *New Left Review* 21, May/June: 118–36.

Swan, Alfred H. (1913), Physical Education Director Shanghai YMCA. Annual Report for the Year Ending 30 September 1913.

Swan, Alfred H. (1916), 'Physical Education in a City Association', *China's Young Men* 11(10), 15 June: 537–46.

Sweezy, Paul M. (1970), *The Theory of Capitalist Development*. New York: Monthly Review Press.

Tamura, Eileen (1997), *China: Understanding its Past*. Honolulu: University of Hawaii.

Tan, Fang and Zhao, Wumian (1996), *Highlights of Da-zi-bao: During the Cultural_Revolution* (in Chinese). New York: Mirror Books.

Tang, Leang-Li (1935), *Reconstruction in China*. Shanghai: China United Press.

Tang, Ssu-tung (1958), *Jen-hsueh* (in Chinese). Beijing: Chunghwa Books.

Teiwes, Frederick C. (1987), 'Establishment and consolidation of the new regime', in Roderick MacFarquhar and John K. Fairbank (eds), *The Cambridge History of China*, Vol. 14, *The People's Republic*, Part 1: *The Emergence of Revolutionary China_1949–1965*. Cambridge: Cambridge University Press: 51–143.

Teng, Ssu-Yu and Fairbank, John K. (1971), *Chinese Response to the West, a Documentary Survey 1839–1923*. Cambridge, MA: Harvard University Press.

Tomlinson, Alan (1981), *Leisure and Social Control*. Brighton: Chelsea School.

Tsai, Jing-jie (1996), 'Physical Education Thought of YMCA 1895–1928', in Hsu, Yi-hsiung (ed.), *Physical Education Thoughts in Modern China* (in Chinese). Taipei: Chi Ying Culture Co. Ltd: 123–98.

Tung, Tsun-tsai (1958), 'Two Major Reform Measures on General Education', *Extracts from China Mainland Magazines*, No. 141, 8 September: 14–22.

Turner, B. (1996), *The Body and Society: Explorations in Social Theory*, 2nd edn. London: Sage.

Turner, B. (2006), 'Public Intellectuals, Globalization and the Sociology Calling', *British Journal of Sociology* 57(3): 345–51.

Vamplew, Wray (1988), *Professional Sport in Britain, 1875–1914: Pay Up and Play the Game*. Cambridge: Cambridge University Press.

Walia, S. (2001), *Edward Said and the Writing of History*, Cambridge: Icon Books.

Wang, Hsueh-Cheng (1967), *Ti Yu Kai Lun* (A Summary of Physical Culture). Taipei: Taiwan Shang Wu Yin Shu Kuan Press.

Wang, Hui (2000), 'Fire at the Castle Gate', *New Left Review* 6, November/December: 69–101.

Wang, Hui (2006), 'Depoliticized Politics: From East to West', *New Left Review* 41, September/October: 29–43.

Wang, L. (2002), 'Reflections on Tibet', *New Left Review* 14, March/April: 79–111.

Wang, Ning. (1997), 'Postmodernism Theory and the "Decolonization" of Chinese Culture', in *Review of International English* 28: 4, October: 33–47.

Wang, Y. C. (1966), *Chinese Intellectuals and the West 1872–1949*. Chapel Hill, NC: University of North Carolina Press.

Wang, Zeshan (1990), 'Traditional and Popular Sports', in Knuttgen, Ma and Wu (eds), *Sport in China*. Chicago: Human Kinetics: 89–105.

Wang, Zhen and Olson, E. G. (1997), 'Present Status, Potential and Strategies of Physical Activity in China', *International Review for the Sociology of Sport* 32(2): 69–85.

Warren, B. (1980), *Imperialism: Pioneer of Capitalism*. London: New Left Books.

Wasserstrom, J. (1999), 'Student Protests in Fin De Siècle China', *New Left Review* 237(1): 52–76.

Weber, Max (1951), *The Religion of China: Confucianism and Taoism*, trans. Hans H. Gerth. New York: Free Press.

Williams, Raymond (1958), *Culture and Society*. Harmondsworth: Penguin.

Williams, Raymond (1961), *The Long Revolution*. Harmondsworth: Penguin.

Williams, Raymond (1977), *Marxism and Literature*. Oxford: Oxford University Press.

Williams, Raymond (1981), *Key Words*. London: Fontana.

Wright, Erik-Olin (2006), 'Compass Points: Towards a Social Alternative', *New Left Review* 41, September/October: 93–124.

Wu, Chih-Kang (1956), 'The Influence of the YMCA on the Development of Physical Education in China'. Ann Arbor, MI, University of Michigan unpublished PhD thesis.

Wu, Shaozu (1999), *Sports History of the People's Republic of China 1949–1999*. Beijing: China Books Publisher.

Wu, Wen-Chung (1962), *Ti Yu Shih* (A History of Physical Culture) (in Chinese). Taipei: Kuo Li Pien Yi Kuan.

Wu, Wen-Chung (1981), *A History of the Development of Physical Culture in China* (in Chinese). Taipei: San Ming Books Press.

Xie, Shaobo (1997), 'Rethinking the Problem of Postcolonialism', *New Literary History* 28: 7–19.

Xu, Guoqi (2008), *Olympic Dreams: China and Sport 1895–2008*. Cambridge MA: Harvard University Press.

Yan, Jiaqi and Gao, Gao (1989), *Ten Years' History of the Cultural Revolution*, 2 vols (in Chinese). Hong Kong: A Trend (Chaoliu) Publisher.

Yeh, Shuping and Zheng, Zuan (1998), *Old Fashions of Shanghai*. Beijing: People's Arts Press.

Yeh, Wen-hsin (1990), *The Alienated Academy: Culture and Politics in Republican China, 1919–1937*. Council on East Asian Studies: Harvard University.

Yen, Fu (1969 [1895]), *Yuan Qiang* (On Strength) (in Chinese), in Seng, Yun-long (ed.), *The Collections of Historical Materials in Modern China*, Vol. 42. Taipei: Wen Hai Publisher, 24–66.

Yu, Jixing (1997), *Old Postcard – Building* (in Chinese). Shanghai: Shanghai Pictorial Publishing House.

Yu, Yun Tai (1985), *A History of Chinese Martial Arts* (in Chinese). Beijing: People's Physical Education Publisher.

Zetkin, C. (1955), *Vospominaniya o Vladimire Il'yiche Lenin*, Part 2. Moscow: Gospolitizdat.

Zhang, X. (1999), 'Postmodernism and Post-Socialist Society: Cultural Politics in China After the "New Era"', *New Left Review* 237(1): 77–105.

Zhao, B. (1997), 'Consumerism, Confucianism, Communism: Making Sense of China Today', *New Left Review* 222, March/April: 43–59.

Zhao, Yiheng (1998), 'Post-Isms and Chinese New Conservatism', in Wang Hui and Yu Kwok-Leung (eds), *Post-ism in the Nineties* (in Chinese). Hong Kong: Chinese University of Hong Kong Press: 137–56.

Index

Date Due